DARK MOUNTAIN

DARK MOUNTAIN

ISSUE I · SUMMER 2010

I went looking for the wild one, the howler, the vatic tramp.
The one for whom the wounded hills are body burns, whose
blood is stained with the old love-wine of poet and Earth –
warrior poet, slinging battle flak out at the static
shattering polite conversations everywhere.

I looked in the anthologies, listening for echoes,
traced for signs in the quarterlies, magazines, best ofs.
I learned it's been a good year for poetry. Grants and awards
keep coming in. Contests and prizes are proliferating,
the wise grey consensus counsels a return to the classics.

Meanwhile, poor scientist holds extinction
in a palm full of numbers
with nothing but data
to howl with.

Rob Lewis

Published by the Dark Mountain Project 2010

www.dark-mountain.net

ISBN 978-0-9564960-0-3

Logo and cover design by Steven Ounanian

Set in Linotype Granjon
Typesetting by Christian Brett at Bracketpress

Printed in Great Britain by the MPG Books Group, Bodmin and King's Lynn

DARK MOUNTAIN

ISSUE I · SUMMER 2010

Contents

conversations

images

others

It's the end of the world as we know it (and we feel fine)

Writing a manifesto is like speaking through a megaphone. Your voice sounds different; you find yourself coming out with slogans that might be out of place in ordinary conversation. The language you use, the way that you use it – everything is amplified. It needs to be, or you don't get heard.

When we published *Uncivilisation: the Dark Mountain Manifesto* in the summer of 2009, we had no way of knowing whether anyone would hear us. We had a hunch that people would get it; that it was time for these things to be said and that there would be people willing to listen. We had spent two years kicking around the ideas it contained, talking them over in the corners of pubs, scribbling notes and lists of names, introducing each other to writers we hadn't heard of, shooting emails back and forth – and as the text came into shape, each month's headlines seemed to reinforce its urgency. All the same, when the ink hit the page and the first copies were on their way to the first readers, there was inevitably a moment of doubt; like waiting for the first guests to arrive when you throw a party, and wondering if anyone will show up at all.

We needn't have worried. For a slim, self-published pamphlet, *Uncivilisation* travelled a long way. Its message – that it's time to stop pretending our current way of living can be made 'sustainable'; that 'saving the planet' has become a bad joke; that we are entering an age of massive disruption, and our task is to live through it as best we can; that how good or bad a job we make of this is as much down to the stories we tell ourselves, our ways of seeing the world, as it is to the technologies or international treaties on which the environmental movement has pinned its hopes – all of this seemed to resonate. It seemed like a message whose time had come.

In the months that followed, the Dark Mountain Manifesto, to our surprise, was reviewed in publications ranging from the *New Statesman*, the *Morning Star* and the *Independent* in the UK, to the *Australian Financial*

Review. Orders came in from around the globe, we were invited to speak on US talk radio shows and to collaborate on art projects. But what overwhelmed us most of all were the messages, thousands of them, from people who found their own thoughts and feelings reflected in our words: writers, artists, gardeners, campaigners, artisans, students, farmers, journalists, teachers, scientists, poets ... Again and again in these messages, what came through most powerfully was a sense of *relief.* Many people had been feeling this way for a long time, it seemed, but they had not put it into words, or they had not found a place to gather with others who felt the same and wanted to explore what came next. There was an overwhelming sense of excitement; of the hope that comes from letting go, from no longer having to pretend.

Of course, not everyone felt this way. Critics of the project soon emerged: we were called 'crazy collapsitarians', 'Romantic dreamers', 'utopians' and 'nihilists'. Much of this criticism revolved around a series of misinterpretations. There were those who, with some justice, expected a manifesto to end in proposals for action or strictures about the new kind of writing we had talked about. For those expecting a party line, we were embarrassingly vague. Activists and campaigners asked us: if this is the future you see, what are you going to *do* about it? We replied that the first thing we were going to do was to stop worrying about how to 'change the world': the world is changing so fast now that the best we can do is to become more observant, more agile, better able to move with it and to understand what is happening. Our manifesto represented, as all manifestoes do, the raising of a flag. But we hadn't raised it in order to lead a march on the capital; we had raised it so that we could find each other in the coming chaos.

Then there were those who thought they heard us as calling for the overthrow of industrial civilisation or dreaming of the utopia that would rise from its ruins. Professor John Gray, in the pages of the *New Statesman,* decided that the Dark Mountain Project was based on a longing for a 'cleansing catastrophe' to purge the poison of civilisation from our veins. 'In their own catastrophist fashion,' he wrote, 'the authors have swallowed the progressive fairy tale that animates the civilisation they reject.'

John Gray probably sees apocalyptic utopians lurking under his bed at night, but his misreading of the manifesto was not an uncommon one, confusing an attempt to face the realities of our likely future with a desire to welcome, or to revel in, apocalypse. This is ironic, because this project has never been a quest for apocalyptic narratives, but rather an attempt to get beyond them.

There are two kinds of future which we in the industrialised world are good at imagining. One represents business-as-usual – the life we have grown up with projected into the future, usually with some technological and political improvements. The other is the apocalyptic anti-future. There is nothing radical today about apocalyptic visions: they are the stuff of mainstream popular culture, the nightmares we love to relive at the cinema, post-religious fantasies charged with the lingering energy of our Christian heritage. It is not hard to imagine the end of the world, because we have seen it in every zombie flick: the supermarket shelves empty, the cars out of petrol, the television snowing blankly.

One of the most talked-about novels of the last couple of years has been Cormac McCarthy's *The Road*: a horrific vision of a dead world populated by roving cannibal gangs. It is a brilliantly-written, terrifying and dispiriting tale, but it is not an original one, and it serves in a curious way to validate a central deception of our culture: the claim that life without the components of our current way of living is simply unliveable. That the future will give us either unbroken progress or apocalypse, and there are no spaces between.

The spaces between, however, are the spaces in which our real future is likely to be played out. They represent a gap in our cultural imagination; a gap in which the Dark Mountain Project has pitched its camp. *Uncivilisation* addressed what we believe to be the inevitable crumbling of our current way of our life. This is not the same thing as a 'cleansing catastrophe' or some kind of apocalyptic event. It is not *The Road* or *The Day After Tomorrow*; it is the world we are already living in.

Industrial society, after only two centuries, is reaching the limits of its capabilities. From climate change to the emptying of the oceans, from mass extinction to the continued razing of the forests, we are pushing at the boundaries of the possible and eating away at the heart of the natural world. To imagine that this great engine of *taking*, which strip-mines the world's riches to manufacture excess for two or three billion people, could do the same for nine or ten billion of us, at the same time as we face a convergence of emergencies ranging from climate change to the peaking of our fossil fuel supplies, is pure fantasy. Windfarms or no windfarms, the world we have known is coming to an end. To those who accuse us of wanting to overthrow this civilisation, we might respond: why would we bother? It doesn't need overthrowing: the historical force of gravity is already acting on it. When something is falling, the best move is often to get out of the way.

We are facing the end of the world as we know it; but this is not the same thing as the end of the world full stop. The decline or stuttering collapse of a civilisation, a way of life, is not the same thing as an apocalypse. It is simply a reality of history. The Dark Mountain Project, in other words, is not concerned with fantasising about catastrophe. It is concerned with being honest about reality; something which most of us, as human beings, find painfully hard.

When you accept this vision of the future – and it seems that a growing number of people do – then questions inevitably arise: what do we do with our lives? How does this change our choices, and the assumptions on which those choices are made? What kinds of action still make sense? And, deeper still, there is the question which underpinned the manifesto: what stories do we tell ourselves? Because a civilisation is built on stories: when its self-belief falters and its myths are no longer believed in, its end is probably inevitable. All around us, as well as the signs of our ecological and economic decline, are signs that we – modern industrial civilisation, the liberal democracies, the market economies, the rich – have stopped believing in our own stories. Without meaning or purpose, even cornucopia is not enough to live for.

Uncivilisation laid out a challenge to its readers and to us: find the new stories. Question the old ones, unravel the threads that hold our narratives together, re-weave them in a new form. We believe that finding new stories, and new storytellers, to accompany us on what will be a hard journey is a vital task. What you hold in your hands is our first attempt to pull those stories together. We're excited by what we have uncovered.

This is the voice of the megaphone: the call to cut through the old tales which bind our understanding and to rediscover those which can ground us in the realities of the only world we ever had. If the manifesto represented the start of an expedition into the unknown, this volume represents the establishment of a base camp in the foothills of some dark and uncharted range.

Within these covers you will find stories of all kinds; stories in words and in pictures, in essay and in verse, in fiction and graphic narrative. You will find some of the best and most challenging writers and artists at work today, engaged in the process of navigating the unknown by the dim light of the stars. You will find, we hope, the beginnings of a new direction.

Paul Kingsnorth and Dougald Hine, editors
Ulverston and London February 2010

Kim Holleman, *The Layers*

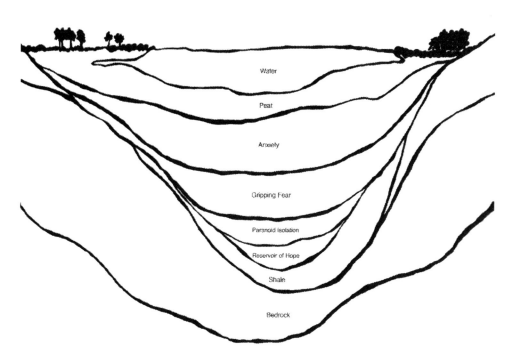

JOHN MICHAEL GREER

The falling years:
an Inhumanist vision

I

Robinson Jeffers' name is hardly one to conjure with these days. The odd anthology of American poetry occasionally quotes his less troubling nature poems, and a few tourist shops in Carmel and Monterey have made a minor industry out of him, the way other towns lionise dead rock musicians or football stars. Outside of these limited circles, it's not often one hears of him.

Not until 2001 did a solid collection of his major poetic works appear – try to think of another major twentieth-century poet who was nearly forty years dead when this first happened – and *The Selected Poetry of Robinson Jeffers* set only the quietest ripples in motion. Gone are the days when Jeffers was so controversial that his own publishers put a note in one book of his poems distancing themselves from his views. Those who play at rebelliousness in contemporary letters might take note: make a show of iconoclasm in acceptable ways and you can count on a lasting reputation; stray into actual iconoclasm, rejecting the fashions of the avant-garde along with those of the mainstream, and the world of culture will forget you just as soon as it can.

A few details will put this extraordinary figure in his proper setting.[1] Born in 1887, he belonged to the same generation of American poets as T.S. Eliot and Ezra Pound. Like them, he saw the facile modernist faith in progress refute itself in the cultural sterility of the Gilded Age and the crowning catastrophe of the First World War, and went in search of stronger foundations for his poetry. Eliot found his Archimedean point in a willed acceptance of Christianity; Pound, less successfully, tried to cobble together a tradition of his own from a rag-heap of sources embracing everything from Provençal minstrelsy to fascist economics. Both turned to Europe for a sense of depth they could not find on American soil.

Jeffers took a more daring approach. In the years just before the First World

6

War, when Eliot and Pound were rising stars in a poetic galaxy rotating around the twin hubs of London and Paris, Jeffers moved to a sparsely settled stretch of the California coastline near Carmel, where he built a house and, later, a stone tower with his own hands.[2] His quest for foundations could not be satisfied at any merely human depth, and finally came to rest in nature itself.

He called his theory of poetry 'inhumanism,' and sketched it in uncompromising terms: 'It is based on a recognition of the astonishing beauty of things and their living wholeness, and on a rational acceptance of the fact that mankind is neither central nor important in the universe; our vices and blazing crimes are as insignificant as our happiness. […] Turn outward from each other, so far as need and kindness permit, to the vast life and inexhaustible beauty beyond humanity. This is not a slight matter, but an essential condition of freedom, and of moral and vital sanity.'[3]

Put another way, the core of inhumanism is the principled rejection of anthropocentrism, and the pursuit of what might as well be called an ecocentric standpoint: one in which nature takes centre stage, not as a receptacle for human activities, emotions, or narratives, but as itself, on its own inhuman terms. It's an appallingly difficult project, difficult enough that Jeffers himself couldn't always sustain it; critics have pointed out the places in Jeffers' verse where poetry gives way to lecture, or descends into an inverted sentimentality that wallows in images of suffering and despair. When Jeffers achieved the task he set himself, though, the results are stunning: for a moment, at least, the claims humanity loves to make on behalf of its own importance fall silent before a universe that was busy with its own affairs for billions of years before us and won't take the time to notice our absence when we are gone.

Jeffers is thus among the few figures in literature to grasp the core feature of the universe revealed by Darwin and his successors, the perspective that the late Stephen Jay Gould called 'deep time' – the sense of human existence as an eyeblink in the long history of the planet. His answer to the spread of suburban sprawl over his beloved Carmel Point is typical:

> It has all time. It knows the people are a tide
> That swells and in time will ebb, and all
> Their works dissolve. Meanwhile the image of the pristine beauty
> Lives in the very grain of the granite,
> Safe as the endless ocean that climbs our cliff. – As for us:
> We must uncenter our minds from ourselves;

> *We must unhumanize our views a little, and become confident*
> *As the rock and ocean that we were made from.*[4]

As poetics, this is hard enough. As a programme for any more pragmatic engagement with the world, it poses a staggering challenge. Jeffers didn't shy away from the places where poetics and politics intersect; Shelley gave him a sense of the poets' role as the world's unacknowledged legislators,[5] and he addressed the political arena directly in such poems as 'Shine, Perishing Republic' and 'The Day is a Poem'. Still, his politics – like his poetics – found few listeners. Most of the few critics who discussed his work at all, slid past the complex political vision that frames much of Jeffers' work with a few comments about 'isolationism', and maybe a nod to Spengler and Vico. Jeffers' prophetic ear was exact, but no one else was listening:

> *There is no returning now.*
> *Two bloody summers from now (I suppose) we shall have to take up the*
>   *corrupting burden and curse of victory.*
> *We shall have to hold half the earth; we shall be sick with self-disgust,*
> *And hated by friend and foe, and hold half the earth – or let it go, and*
>   *go down with it.*[6]

Still, Jeffers knew as well as anyone that poets' legislation needs time to have its effect. The rising spiral of environmental crises shaping today's headlines marks, I have come to believe, the point where Jeffers' vision becomes an historical fact, and his inhumanism a centre of gravity toward which any meaningful response to the predicament of industrial society must move. In saying that, I'm not claiming that responses to our crisis *ought* to move toward inhumanism; I'm saying that they *will* do so, even if those who think they are defending the environment have to be dragged kicking and screaming along that route.

I say that with some confidence because most of the journey has already happened. The anthropocentrism that runs through the environmental movement, even, or rather especially, among those who most bitterly condemn humanity and all its works, seems to me to mark a final, frantic attempt to cling to the illusion of a human-centred cosmos. As today's environmental narratives join the ruins of earlier lines of defence in history's compost heap, it's not easy to imagine any place where anthropocentrism can stake a further claim against the massed inevitabilities of nature. At that point Jeffers' inhumanism offers a glimpse at the foundations on which human thought will have to rebuild itself.

II

The environmental movement as a social phenomenon still awaits its historian, though there have been capable histories of the ecological ideas that have inspired it.[7] A first approximation, though, shows three overlapping periods of environmental activism, each with its own distinct narratives and purposes.

The first was the period of *recreational environmentalism*, and ran from the late nineteenth-century through to the 1960s. Environmental rhetoric in this period focused so tautly on the value of nature as a recreational resource, that its opponents, without too much inaccuracy, could accuse conservationists of simply wanting the Government to subsidise their vacation spots. Though it's easy to dismiss the period in retrospect, its great achievement – the invention of the national park concept and its deployment over much of the industrial world – marks a historical watershed of some importance. For the first time since the felling of the old Pagan groves, the Western world recognised the point of setting aside space for nature on its own terms.

The second phase, from the early 1960s through to the 1980s, was the period of *sentimental environmentalism*. The spark for the transition was Rachel Carson's epochal *Silent Spring*, which brought extinction out of scientific journals and into the public sphere. The results shared far too much with the rest of the popular culture of the time to accomplish much – the baby seals whose Holly Hobby faces made them the mascot of the movement, for example, received far more attention than many more substantive issues – but the underlying shift in awareness is worth noting. For a significant number of people, feelings of loyalty and love once fixed firmly within the human sphere widened to embrace nonhuman nature.

The third phase followed promptly. The first stirrings of *apocalyptic environmentalism* appeared while the age of sentimental environmentalism was barely underway, and once it worked its way out of the fringes it quickly borrowed the same durable tropes about the end of the world that proved their appeal in other contexts. The last two decades have accordingly seen all the usual changes rung on the theme of an imminent Judgement Day, with Gaia pressed into the role more usually filled by an avenging Jehovah.

Surf the web or visit a bookstore and the resulting sermons may be found without too much effort. Alongside claims that a future of ecological horror –

sinners in the hands of an angry biosphere! – can be averted if we renounce our wicked ways and get right with Gaia, you can find claims that it's already too late and the wrath of an offended planet will turn sinful humanity into so much compost, upon which the righteous remnant will presumably plant the organic gardens of the New Green Jerusalem. Gospels backstopping these sermons with a giddy range of dubious historical mythologies have flooded the market at nearly the same pace.

It's crucial to recognise the hits as well as the misses of apocalyptic environmentalism. Many of the issues that underlie claims of imminent Ecogeddon are quite real, though some have been exaggerated to the point of absurdity. Where these narratives fail is in forcing the ecological crisis into anthropocentric narratives that falsify far more than they explain.

The function of apocalyptic myth, after all, is to console the unimportant by feeding them fantasies of their own cosmic significance. It's thus no accident that, for example, the seedtimes of apocalyptic ideas in Judaism have been epochs when Jews were a powerless minority whose beliefs and hopes were of no concern to anyone but themselves, just as the apocalyptic strain in today's Christianity clusters in the regions and classes of the industrial world that were most heavily marginalised during the era of so-called 'globalisation'. The environmental apocalyptic narrative is partly a reaction to the impact of deep time on our collective sense of self-importance: faced with a planetary history in which geological forces and mass extinctions hold the important roles, we've tried to claim the role of a geological force and a cause of mass extinctions.

That probably couldn't have been avoided. Like the phases before it, apocalyptic environmentalism inevitably got tripped up by the anthropocentricity it tried to escape. Recreational environmentalism reached for the insight that we owe nature space of its own, and fell back to thinking of nature as a resource for outdoor holidays. Sentimental environmentalism reached for the more challenging insight that we owe nature the same bonds of love and loyalty more usually applied to family, community, and nation, and fell back to thinking of nature as a resource for emotional indulgence.

Apocalyptic environmentalism, in turn, reached for the most challenging insight of all: the recognition that we owe nature our existence, and could follow the dodo and the passenger pigeon into extinction if we mess up our relations with the rest of the world badly enough. Like its predecessors, its reach exceeded its grasp and it fell back to thinking of nature as a resource for narratives that celebrate the supposed uniqueness of humanity just as obsessively as ever. Portraying humanity as the uniquely destructive ravager of nature, after all, is just as anthropocentric as portraying it as the uniquely creative conqueror of nature. The resemblance between the concepts is not accidental; like a spoiled child who misbehaves to get the attention good behaviour won't bring, we're willing to see ourselves in any role, even the villain's, as long as we get to occupy centre stage.

III

Still, talking about the anthropocentric obsessions of today's ecological thought in general terms is less helpful than catching sight of those obsessions in their native habitat, in the collective conversation that shapes our world. Nothing is as easy as denouncing an abstract representation of a habit of thought on which one's thinking continues to be based. Think of the way that 'dualism' was all but burnt in effigy a few years back by a flurry of liberal religious writers who insisted that all religions without exception are either dualist or nondualist, and dualism is absolutely evil while nondualism is absolutely good![8]

No doubt we'll shortly see a critique of anthropocentrism along the same lines: arguing, perhaps, that the habit of anthropocentric delusion is what sets our species apart from the rest of nature and marks us out for some uniquely tragic destiny or other. Thus it's important to get past the label and examine specific ways that anthropocentrism distorts the response of today's environmental movement to the incoming tide of ecological crisis.

Compare the recent and continuing furore over anthropogenic climate change to the more muted response to the rapid depletion of the world's remaining petroleum reserves, and one such distortion stands out clearly. Both these problems are unquestionably real;[9] both were predicted decades ago, both could quite readily force modern industrial civilisation to its knees, and both are already having measurable impacts around the world.

Yet the response to the two differs in instructive ways. Anthropogenic climate change has become a cause célèbre, splashed across the mainstream media, researched by thousands of scientists funded by lavish government grants, and earnestly discussed by heads of state at summit meetings. Nothing is actually being done to stop it, to be sure, and most likely nothing will be done; not even the climate campaigners who urge drastic action in the loudest voices and most extreme terms have shown much willingness to accept the drastic changes in their own lives that would cut carbon dioxide emissions soon enough to matter. Still, the narrative of climate change has found plenty of eager listeners around the world.

None of this has happened with peak oil. The evidence backing the claim that the world has already passed the peak of petroleum production and faces a future of declining energy and economic contraction is every bit as solid as the evidence for anthropogenic climate change;[10] the arguments opposing it are just as meretricious; its potential for economic and human costs is as great, solutions are as difficult to reach, and it can feed apocalyptic fantasies almost as extreme as those that have gathered around climate change. Still, no summit meetings are being called by heads of state to discuss the end of the age of oil; there has been no barrage of mainstream media attention concerning it, and precious few government grants. Climate change is mediagenic; peak oil is not.

A core difference between the two crises explains why. Climate change, as a cultural narrative, is a story about human power. We have become so almighty through technological progress, the climate change narrative argues, that we threaten the Earth itself. The only limits that can prevent catastrophe are those we place on ourselves, since nothing else can stop us; and even our own efforts might not be enough to stand in our way. It's nearly a parody of the old atheist gibe: to prove our own omnipotence, we've made a crisis so big that not even we can lift it out of our way.

Peak oil as a cultural narrative, on the other hand, is not a celebration of human power but a warning about human limits. At the core of the peak oil story is the recognition that the power we claimed was never really ours. We never conquered nature; we merely stole some of the Earth's carbon and burnt our way through it in three short centuries. All the feverish dreams and accomplishments of that era were simply the results of wasting a vast amount of cheap fuel. Now that the easy pickings are running out, and we have to think about getting by without half a billion years of stored and concentrated solar energy to burn, our fantasies of power are proving unexpectedly fragile, and the future ahead of us involves more humility and less grandiosity than we want to think about.

One rich irony here is that the limits imposed by peak oil are, among other things, limits on our power to destroy the world via climate change. The IPCC projections of climate change assume that the world's nations can increase their coal, oil, and natural gas consumption straight through to 2100. Doubtless they would do so if they could, but the fact remains that they can't. Conventional petroleum production peaked in 2005 and has been declining since then; unconventional petroleum production, even if it recovers from the slump following the crash of 2008, will tip into decline well before 2015; natural gas is on schedule to reach its peak by 2030, and coal by 2040.[11] As those peaks pass, fossil fuel consumption will decline, not because we want it to decline, but because our ability to extract fuels from the ground runs into geological limits. This awkward reality has not found its way into the climate change debate; nor will it, until the anthropocentric foundations of that debate are seen for what they are.

The same point can be made even more forcefully of the greater irony that surrounds the climate change debate: the fact that the shifts in global temperature painted in doomsday terms in today's media are modest, in scale and speed, compared to those Earth has experienced many times before. A mere 11,000 years ago, at the end of the last ice age, global temperatures jolted up 8°C in under a decade[12] – a heatwave more severe than the wildest scenarios in circulation these days. Nor was this anything novel; the Earth's long history is full of such events.

Since the beginning of the Pliocene epoch some 10 million years ago, Earth's climate has been in a phase of severe cooling, and for four-fifths or so of the time that life has existed on this planet global temperatures have been far warmer than the IPCC's worst case scenarios imagine. When the Earth's climate is normal, on this inhumanly broad scale, most of its land surface is covered by jungle, and ice caps and glaciers do not exist. A reversion to that normal temperature would obliterate our industrial civilisation with the inevitability of a boot descending on an eggshell, and could well push our species over the edge into extinction, but the usual adjustments would soon bring the biosphere into balance, as they have after the other climate changes of the planetary past. The fact that we will not be around to see this, if it comes to that, concerns no one but ourselves.

These ironies, furthermore, have direct practical implications. While anthropogenic global warming is a real and serious problem, its consequences are subject to natural limits that current thinking, fixated on images of human triumphalism, is poorly equipped to grasp. Meanwhile, another real and serious problem – the depletion of the nonrenewable energy resources that prop up today's industrial economy and keep seven billion people alive – gets next to no attention, because it conflicts with those same triumphalist obsessions. It's no exaggeration to say that the modern world might solve the global warming crisis and then collapse anyway, because it only dealt with those of its problems that proved congenial to its self-image.

I V

Sometimes, when sleep keeps its distance in the small hours of the night, I wonder if the grand purpose for which humanity came into being was simply that Earth needed a species good at digging to pull a few billion tons of stored carbon out of the ground and nudge up its thermostat a bit. During daylight hours, I don't actually believe this; if the Earth has conscious purposes we will almost certainly never know, and if by some chance we do find out, our chances of understanding those purposes are right up there with the chance that a dust mite in Mozart's wig could have understood his music or his marital problems.

It's easy to dismiss reflections such as these as a display of misanthropy. Still, it shows no contempt for an individual to recognise that he or she isn't more important than anyone else in the world. Personal maturity begins, after all, with letting go the infantile self-regard that puts the ego and its cravings at the centre of the cosmos. It's arguably time to apply that same insight to humanity as a whole. As Jeffers wrote:

> It seems to me wasteful that almost the whole of human energy is expended inward, on itself, on loving, hating, governing, cajoling, amusing, its own members. It is like a newborn babe, conscious almost exclusively of its own processes and where its food comes from. As the child grows up, its attention must be drawn from itself to the more important world around it. [13]

The environmental crises of the present bid fair to make that shift in attention inevitable, no matter how hard we fight to keep ourselves at the centre of our own imagined universe; and in the process most of the presuppositions of human thought will have to change. Crucially, we will be forced to come to terms with the fact that no special providence guarantees our species the fulfilment of its hopes, or even its survival. Sooner or later humanity, like every other species, will become extinct, and it's a safe bet that the history that unfolds between the present moment and that hopefully distant time will be just as sparing of Utopian dreams fulfilled as has human history so far.

This doesn't deny us the possibility of improving our lives, our societies, and our relationships with the cosmos that surrounds us; it does mean that those improvements, like everything else in the real world, will take place against a background of hard natural limits that will inevitably restrict what can be attained.

One consequence is that the faith in perpetual progress that forms the unacknowledged state religion of the modern world faces a shattering disillusionment. Progress, as we have known it, amounts to little more than the race to find ever more extravagant ways to burn cheap, abundant fossil fuels. Those fuels are no longer as cheap or abundant as they once were; in the not too distant future they will be scarce and expensive, and not all that much further down the curve of history they will be so scarce, and so expensive, that burning them to power what remains of an industrial society will no longer be a viable option.[14]

Nor can we simply count on, as too many people are counting on, the hope that some other energy source equally cheap, convenient, and concentrated will come along just as we need it. The fossil fuels we burn so blithely today are the product of hundreds of millions of years of complex ecological and geological processes. At the dawn of our now-receding Age of Excess, they represented the single largest concentration of readily accessible chemical energy in the known solar system. Insisting that an industrial civilisation dependent on this vast surplus can thrive on the sparser and less concentrated energy flows the Earth receives from the Sun day by day – which is what most current advocates of 'sustainability' propose – flies in the face of ecological and thermodynamic reality; it's as though someone who won a huge lottery payoff, and spent it all in a few short years, insisted he could keep up the same extravagant lifestyle with the income from a job flipping burgers for minimum wage.

Instead of fantasising about the kind of future we want humanity to have, in other words, or confusing our daydreams with our destiny, we need to start thinking hard about what kind of future humanity can afford, and taking a hard look at social habits that require levels of energy and resource inputs we won't be able to maintain for much longer. A rethinking of this kind is not optional; if we refuse it, nature will do the job for us. Ecology teaches us that every species either evolves ways to limit the burden it places on nature or suffers from limits imposed on it by outside factors, and we are no more exempt from that law than we are from the law of gravity.

At this moment in history, only a massive worldwide effort of more than wartime intensity might have even a modest chance of managing a controlled descent from industrial civilisation's extravagance to some more durable form of society. The window of opportunity for so staggering a project is narrow, if it has not already closed, and the political will that would be needed to carry it out is nowhere in sight. Thus the same sort of uncontrolled descent that ended the history of so many earlier civilisations has become the most likely future for ours. Certainly this was Jeffers' view:

> *These are the falling years,*
> *They will go deep,*
> *Never weep, never weep.*
> *With clear eyes explore the pit.*
> *Watch the great fall*
> *With religious awe.* [15]

Still, it's precisely in the troubled years ahead of us, as our civilisation stumbles down the long broken slope toward a future that will make a mockery of our fantasies of progress and cosmic importance, that Jeffers' perspective offers its most important gifts. It's the man or woman who comes to terms with the inevitability of his or her own death that best knows how to grapple with life. In the same way, Jeffers' inhumanist perspective can be a crucial source of strength now, and even more so in time to come. When we realise that human history is nothing unique – from nature's perspective, we're simply one more species that overshot the carrying capacity of its environment and is about to pay the routine price – we can get past the habit of wallowing in a self-blame that is first cousin to self-praise, face up to the hard choices ahead, and make them with some sense of perspective and, at least potentially, some possibility of grace. Humanity cannot and need not bear the burden of being the measure of all things, Jeffers is telling us, for a saner and stronger measure is all around us:

> *Integrity is wholeness, the greatest beauty is*
> *Organic wholeness, the wholeness of life and things, the divine*
>   *beauty of the universe. Love that, not man*
> *Apart from that.* [16]

Notes

1. I have used Melba Berry Bennett's *The Stone Mason of Tor House,* Ward Ritchie, 1966 and Arthur B. Coffin's *Robinson Jeffers: Poet of Inhumanism,* University of Wisconsin Press, 1971 for this brief sketch.

2. It's a curiosity of poetic history that Jeffers and Yeats, one of the few modern poets Jeffers praised, both built themselves stone towers in the years following the First World War.

3. From 'Preface to The Double Ax and Other Poems,' in *Hunt,* ed., op. cit., p719 and 721.

4. From 'Carmel Point,' in *Hunt,* ed., op. cit., p676.

5. Percy Bysshe Shelley, *A Defence of Poetry*; see also Coffin, op. cit., p18.

6. From 'Historical Choice', in *Hunt,* ed., op. cit., p580; this poem was written in 1943.

7. See particularly Donald Worster's *Nature's Economy,* Cambridge University Press, 1994.

8. Matthew Fox's *The Coming of the Cosmic Christ,* Harper & Row, 1988 is a particularly embarrassing example; pp134–5 includes a handy table of polar oppositions, in which one side is 'dualist' and thus evil, and the other 'nondualist' and thus good.

9. There seems little point here in revisiting the overwhelming evidence backing both humanity's role in climate change and the progressive and severe depletion of accessible oil reserves. Those who already recognise the severity of both problems will need no convincing, while those who disagree with either aren't likely to listen to another review of the facts.

10. For a good general survey, see Richard Heinberg's *The Party's Over: Oil, War, and the Fate of Industrial Societies,* New Society, 2003.

11. See Richard Heinberg, *Peak Everything,* New Society, 2008 for a detailed discussion of these resource peaks and their consequences.

12. This figure, along with supporting research, is cited in Richard B. Alley, *The Two Mile Time Machine,* Princeton University Press, 2000.

13. Letter from Jeffers to Rudolph Gilbert, in Gilbert's *Shine, Perishing Republic: Robinson Jeffers and the Tragic Sense in Modern Poetry,* Haskell House, 1965, frontispiece.

14. I have discussed these points in much more detail in my book *The Long Descent,* New Society, 2008.

15. From 'For Una,' in *Hunt,* ed., op. cit., pp565–567.

16. From 'The Answer,' in *Hunt,* ed., op. cit., p522.

Hostage

Strip naked in the centre of town in broad daylight. Declare that from now on you will own nothing and will trust in everything holy that it will all work out. When your dad – rich, influential, mortified – finally unlocks the basement a few weeks later and lets you out, start again, giving away all your swanky stuff in the name of love.

Neighbours, family, friends, strangers all think you're nuts. But you are happy – gleeful, even. Stripped down to feeling a dying man's hot, dry breath and the mountains' cool, moist breath, hungry unless the merciful feed you, and how many of those do you meet?

You were on to something. We might still have a chance.

It took just a few years for six thousand people to join you, longing to give up everything to live as you did, your call spreading at the maximum thirteenth-century land speed of a guy on a horse on a rutted road. Salvation was an understandably sharp hook back then, but even those numbed by luxury or power had to have wondered who all these people were, these penitents, flooding in to see you. Their unruly tide surged against the rising islands of finely appointed villas and the brocaded brokers inside. Soon tens of thousands of believers swore peace, refused to bear arms, refused to take oaths of fealty. How could the nobles of Assisi raise an army against the bellicose nobles of Perugia, or Perugia against the insulting nobles of Siena, if their grunts and footsoldiers balked in order to favour their souls? Who could force them once the pope protected these legions of simplicity seekers with a papal bull? Who could have imagined that the steep stone stairway of feudalism would start to erode under the shuffle of dusty, sandaled feet?

Eight hundred years later, here we are. Many of us believe in your god and some of us don't. It doesn't matter. It is common knowledge that you are loved by Catholics, Protestants, Jews, atheists, Buddhists, agnostics, Muslims. Yes, you are more popular than Jesus. Just an average October Tuesday, and we can still taste the morning's first espresso, but tour buses, cars and motorbikes pack the car park. Taxis and city buses unload arrivals from the train station at

Santa Maria degli Angeli and thread back through the city walls. We are mustering. Cameras, bags, maps at the ready. Tour guides hoist their coloured pennants, gather their troops, brief them in English, Italian, German, Korean, Japanese, Spanish, Portuguese, Swedish, Chinese. We begin our march up the hill.

Eleven thousand of us will come today and eleven thousand tomorrow, and five million every year. We will swarm your cathedral; we will all circuit your steep, narrow streets; we will all reach that piazza in the centre of town. You could ask us. Better yet, you could insist, in this same square where you made such a show of relinquishing. We would put down our gelati and panini and cappuccini and listen, quiet as the birds. You could begin by telling us why we're really here.

We might think we've come to view Giotto's honeyed frescoes; to imbibe some 'mystical' experience hawked in a tourist brochure; to say the prescribed prayers of the Assisi Pardon and be granted a free pass from purgatory (Jesus and Mary appeared, offered you a favour, and that's what you chose on our behalf. Could you ask again?) Or we're here to put a face on faith (we have nothing verifiable of Jesus', but these are your shabby sandals, your letters, the rags you held to your oozing hands). Or we are here to pay homage to a man who would not sit at the holy table unless he could set places for birds, wind, water, wolves and herbs; or to spend an afternoon in this town built from pink stones and then check it off our lists. Five million of us a year, even though there are more Giottos in Florence and Bologna, we can be pardoned in Rome, and Umbria holds other hill towns that will blush and serve us truffles.

You were a warrior once – surely your fellow soldiers joined up for different reasons. Weren't some adventurers, runaways, lovers of hot blood and battle, idealists, avengers, careerists of the heaved sword, all forged into something new and invincible once someone with conviction pointed to the target and gave the spur?

Five million of us, and here is the extent of our instruction: you must all stay together, you must wait until four to shop, you must be back at the hotel at seven, announce the tour guides. You *have* to pick up some of those cute Francis refrigerator magnets for the grandkids, insists the American matron to another. You must stop a moment and let the Franciscan spirit surround you, says the tony British voice on the digital basilica tour, as each of us is surrounded by others instructed to stop a moment and let the Franciscan spirit surround them.

We are wandering, and there is no sign of where to go. You know you could take us there.

Which is why I have shoved you headfirst into this coffee mug of pebbles (the four inch plastic you, available everywhere in town). To get your attention – your intercession, if we need to be formal about it. Nothing personal, just the formula. If I were selling a house, I'd bury St. Joseph the carpenter on his head; if I were looking for a husband, St. Anthony of Padua, the finder, would be my upended hostage. You are the patron saint of ecology, the last pope said. I can't pray anymore, but this people's witchcraft of the religion I once shared with you makes as much sense. So as long as I'm here, with your bones just up the street, your sweat no doubt baked into the pores of some brick nearby, you and your non-biodegradable congregation of tiny plastic birds will remain upside-down on the sink of this disturbingly deluxe tiled bath of my monastery guest room.

Not that I think you're uncomfortable. Italy is full of rocks where you lay your head and slept. Days and weeks on end you prayed in stony clefts and fissures. Your medieval geology, or was it your personal one, told you those rocks split open during the biblical earthquake that marked the crucifixion. To you they rang with a saving sound.

An earthquake is always the death of something and the birth of something else. Ten years ago here, the force that birthed these hills pushed again, hard. Roofs, roads collapsed. In the basilica, birds hearing your frozen sermon crumbled and alighted on the ground, an oak beam returning to earth brought with him a soft brown monk. We know now that earthquakes come from a power below and not one above, and that their echoes ring through a chasm of deep time you thought reserved for heaven or hell. What you heard reverberating in your stony hermitages was a holy sound, yes, but not of some unnecessary redemption. You heard our creation. It was the labour that delivered us into the holy family of Mother Earth, Brother Sun, Sister Water, Brother Fire, the marrow-deep bonds you sang about. It was the love song of the trilobite as she gave herself up for the limestone that cradled the aquifer that fed the Umbrian chestnuts that surrendered their fruit to the grinding stone to feed your blood.

What are the stones chanting now, down there in your mug? Can you hear the sigh of Sister Water passing through? She is still useful, and humble, and precious, but she is far from pure. Ask the stones to sing to you of glaciers they have ridden, of icecaps you couldn't have known in your time, of continents and creatures unfathomable to you, and of the measurements and thresholds we've devised to mark how we silence them forever.

Reach back and remember your rage – written in the old sources, not available in gift shops – how you ripped into your monks when they succumbed to comfort. How you threw sick brothers out of a too-posh house; how you ordered a library in Bologna burned – monks can't own anything, not even books, you ranted. How you cursed the monk who loved the books, refused his brother monks' pleas for mercy and sent a burning drop of sulphur to bore through his skull.

If you can work miracles – and some here believe ruined crucifixes talked to you, and I'll believe anything if it works – come out from under your stifling cloak of mildness and try again. Preach to us of poverty, because if we were poor we wouldn't be here. Stare down your failure and ours – that insistence on heaven at the expense of earth. You're the only one who can, at least here. You went alone out into the winter woods and embraced the feared she-wolf of Gubbio because you knew she killed from hunger. So do we. Dare us to strip off our wrinkle-resistant travel separates in this same piazza, cast us to our knees, not to pray but to feel our flesh and bones hard against the terrifying stone and wet, saving dirt. 'All which you used to avoid will bring you great sweetness and joy,' you said. We will chant it. Then send us home to keep stripping away, to reveal our naked, joyful animal bodies.

Now that our vision must adjust to the frescoes' seismic cracks, it could well be that the birds were preaching back.

LOUIS JENKINS

Wrong Turn

You missed your turn two miles back because
you weren't paying attention: daydreaming.
So now you have decided to turn here, on the
wrong road, just because you are too lazy to
turn around. You have decided to turn here
just because of some vague notion. You have
decided to turn here just because you aren't
smart enough not to. You have decided to turn
here ... just because. Listen, help is available.
There are people who have experience with this
kind of thing, people who have been through
this. There are hotlines. There are brochures.
There are programs, support groups. There is
financial aid. Listen. The angels gather around
you like gnats, strumming their guitars, singing
songs of salvation, singing songs of freedom
and diversity. But you aren't listening. Here you
are on the genuine road less traveled. The road
never snowplowed. Nothing to do but follow the
ruts. Here the snow is too deep to turn around.
You are going to have to follow this road to
whatever nowhere it leads to.

Loss Soup

FIGURE 1a: the dining hall. Located, it seems, in an abandoned subway tunnel, panelled incongruously in teak, mahogany and other unsustainable hardwoods. Insufficiently lit by dim, recessed lights that give the room an atmosphere of twilight. Walls dustily cluttered with half-completed objects, broken bits of statuary that appear familiar at first glance, and at second glance unrecognisable. Things that make you say to yourself, 'I'll have a closer look at that later,' but, of course, you never do.

FIGURE 1b: the dining table. It stretches the full length of the hall, and appears to be constructed from railway sleepers, or planks from some old galleon. It must weigh many tonnes. Glancing beneath, you see it is supported by a forest of legs of many different shapes and sizes, cannibalised from tables, chairs, pedestals, crutches, walking sticks. Laid out upon the bare expanse of wood are two rows of dusty glasses, two rows of earthenware bowls, and some wooden spoons.

FIGURE 1c: the diners. At first you assume there are scores of them, but later adjust your estimate to just a few dozen. Calculating numbers is surprisingly tricky, due to the insufficiency of light and the peculiar amorphousness of facial features. Various races are represented here, and there's an equal ratio of women to men, but around this table they all appear generic. It's not helped by the fact they keep changing position without you noticing them move. You turn away from the man to your left, a Slavic gentleman with impressive moustaches, and when you turn back it's an old Asian lady with spectacles like the lenses from antique telescopes. But it's hard to be sure. Your concentration keeps slipping. Perhaps this is still the same person, with a different facial expression.

FIGURE 2: the egg-timer (a). It stands at the furthest end of the table, about the height of a grandfather clock, a truly impressive object. A baroque monstrosity of piped and fluted metal, like something from the palace of the Tsars. The dirty, golden sand hisses audibly from the top chamber to the bottom, and an ingenious pivoting mechanism allows the whole thing to be rotated when the bottom chamber is full. This task, you imagine, will be performed by the diners sitting on either side, who are watching the sand's flow closely. But the top chamber isn't empty yet.

FIGURE 3a: the soup tureen. It is wheeled in on a serving trolley, and lifted onto the table by three waiters. Its arrival elicits little excitement from the assembled diners, though you, a first-timer, are awed by its size. 'Could fit a whole lot of soup in there,' you scribble on the first page of your notebook. But the tureen, as far as you see, has yet to be filled.

FIGURE 3b: the ladle. It's a big one.

FIGURE 4: the observer. This is you. You still can't quite believe you've been chosen to attend the fabled annual Dinner of Loss, but here you sit, notebook on table, wooden spoon in hand. A poorly accredited freelance journalist with a vague interest in 'disappearing things' – you've written articles on language extinction, vanishing glaciers, memory loss – you received the invitation three days ago, and cancelled all previous engagements. You've come across mention of the Dinner of Loss in the course of your researches, of course, but were doubtful if the rumours were true. As far as you know, one lucky observer is invited to attend every year, but you can't imagine how the organisers came to choose you.

You came here in an ordinary taxi, though half expecting to be blindfolded and spun around for disorientation. You entered through an ordinary door, following the instructions. You descended several flights of stairs, walked down a mothball-smelling corridor, entered the long dining hall, and found your place-name waiting.

You've been here about 45 minutes. The dinner is due to begin.

FIGURE 5: the gong. It gongs. A silence settles around the table.

FIGURE 6: the first intonations. Delivered by one diner after another, passing around the table in turn, at a steady metronomic pace, in an anticlockwise direction. Running, as far as you can note, as follows:
'The auroch. The Barbary lion. The Japanese wolf. The giant short-faced bear.

The upland moa. The American bison. The broad-faced potoroo. The American lion. The elephant bird. The Caucasian wisent. The cave bear. The Nendo tube-nosed fruit bat. The Darling Downs hopping mouse. The dwarf elephant. The Syrian wild ass. The St Lucy giant rice rat … '

You scribble as fast as your biro can go, but the separately spoken intonations dissolve into a quiet cacophony of names, murmuring like a disturbed sea, with little rhyme or rhythm. They don't appear to follow any order, whether categorical or chronological. Your writing degrades into improvised shorthand you're not even sure you'll be able to read.

'The ground sloth. The pig-footed bandicoot. The Balearic shrew. The Ilin Island cloudrunner. The Arabian gazelle. The Schomburgk's deer. The sea mink. The Javan tiger. The tarpan. The great auk. The Alaotra grebe. The Bermuda night heron. The laughing owl. The bluebuck. The quagga. The western black rhinosaurus. The Sturdee's pipistrelle. The turquoise-throated puffleg … '

At last the intonations stop. Page after page of your notebook is covered in increasingly frenetic scrawls. You think perhaps an hour has passed, but since they removed your watch at the door you have no way of knowing. The only indicator of time is the giant egg-timer down the table, the snakey sand still hissing inside, though the top chamber still isn't empty. Your writing hand throbs painfully, and you're glad of the few minutes' interregnum in which each diner finds their glass has been filled with wine at some point during the proceedings. Following the lead of the other diners, you raise your glass into the air, casting wobbling wine-shadows over the wood.

'Lost animals,' a voice concludes quietly. And as the glasses chime together, the trio of waiters re-enters the hall bearing a steaming vat.

FIGURE 7: loss soup (a). The waiters approach the soup tureen. You rise from your chair to get a better look, thrilled to be witness to the fabled soup itself, and a slight tut-tut of disapproval issues from the diners beside you. You disregard this. You're a journalist. You can't help but elicit disapproval at times. You lean across the table, on tiptoes, to get closer to the action.

Actually, there isn't much to see. The waiters remove the tureen's heavy lid and upend the steaming vat. You strain to get a good look at the soup as it sloppily cascades into the tureen, but all you can make out is a viscous gruel, thickened occasionally with matter you can't from this distance identify, a greasy sludge of no definable colour. Although the vat is of no small proportions, you guess the soup that has been poured must cover only an inch or two at the base of the vast tureen. When the gush comes to an end, the waiters shake the last drops out, replace the cumbersome china lid, bow to no-one in particular, and retire.

FIGURE 8: the second intonations. Before you are even resettled in your seat, the next round has begun.

'Geeze. Nagumi. Kw'adza. Eyak. Esselen. Island Chumash. Hittite. Eel River Athabaskan. Lycian. Kalkatungic. Moabite. Coptic. Oti. Karipuna. Totoro. Ancient Nubian. Yahuna. Wasu. Old Prussian. Old Tatar. Modern Gutnish. Skepi Creole Dutch…'

You begin to feel a little light-headed. Your biro loses track. You are forced to resort to abbreviations you despair of ever deciphering. But still, you must attempt to keep pace with the murmuring litany of names, must try to record as many as you can, for they are fast disappearing.

The air itself seems to draw them in. They have no body, no substance. The sounds are like vapour, amorphous, removed from reality.

'Akkala Sámi. Old Church Slavonic. Bo. Kseireins. Scythian. Cuman. Pictish. Karnic. Etruscan. Wagaya-Warluwaric. Edomite. Tangut. Ammonite. Minaean. Phoenician. Ugaritic. Basque-Icelandic pidgin…'

'Lost languages,' the soft voice says, dropping at last a tangible sound – if there can exist a thing – into a silence you hadn't been made aware of. Glasses clink. You have missed the toast. You are still trying to scribble the last names before the sounds go out of your head. But it's no good, you can't remember.

FIGURE 9: loss soup (b). Again, the waiters bring the vat, and you get to your feet to see the gruel slide like an oil slick into the tureen, billowing up clouds of steam. It gives a thin, faintly saline smell. The lid is replaced. The table settles down. The sand inside the egg-timer whispers to itself in the corner.

FIGURE 10: the third intonations.

'The Fijian weinmannia. The Skottsberg's wikstroemia. The Prony Bay xanthostemon. The Maui ruta tree. The root-spine palm. The Franklin tree. The Cuban erythroxylum. The fuzzyflower cyrtandra. The Szaferi birch. The Cuban holly. The Hastings County neomacounia. The Yunnan malva. The toromiro. The Mason River myrtle…'

'Lost plants and trees,' says the voice, and you have the sensation of a door softly closed, a latch slipping down inside. Again, you weren't aware the litany had ended. Your biro moves across the table, overshooting its mark. It occurs to you that much time has gone. You were lost in the murmuration, and when you skip back over the pages you find that your notebook is almost full. Hurriedly you fumble in your journalist's pouch in search of a replacement. Glasses clink mildly around the table. You have missed the toast again. The waiters bring the vat.

FIGURE 11: loss soup (c). The giant tureen still echoes emptily as the soup crashes into the china depths. It looks as if an ocean could slide in there. The oily smell rises unpleasantly, saturating the air around. The smell makes you uncomfortable. It's better to breathe through your mouth.

FIGURE 12: the fourth intonations.
'The arctops. The sycosarus. The gorgonops. The broomisaurus. The eoarctops. The cephalicustriodus. The dinogorgon. The leontocephalus. The inostrancevia. The pravoslaveria. The viatkogorgon. The aelurognathus tigriceps.'
'Gorgonopsians,' says the voice. You don't even know what this word means. You check the egg-timer timidly, shaking the cramp from your pen-clawed hand, but the sand is still flowing down, a never-ending stream.

FIGURE 13: loss soup (d). Another greyish slurry emits from the vat, frothing as it hits the china walls. You notice some of the diners' mouths are shielded with scented handkerchiefs. The stink is becoming immense.

FIGURE 14: the fifth intonations.
'The Gallina. The Karankawa. The Anasazi. The Caribs. The Thraco-Cimmerians. The Lusatians. The Khazars. The Kipchaks. The Sassanids. The Great Zimbabweans. The Olmecs. The Hittites. The Etruscans. The Babylonians. The Picts. The Fir Chera. The Gauls. The Philistines. The Tasmanian Aborigines. The Copts. The Yeehats. The Sumerians. The Cathaginians. The Calusa. The Taino. The Ojibwa. The Mohicans. The Cahokia. The Aquitani. The Vindelici. The Belgae. The Brigantes. The Maya. The Dal gCais. The Ui Liathain. The Thracians. The Hibernians. The Kushans. The Macedons. The Amalekites. The Hereros. The Zapatecs. The Atakapas. The Zunghars. The Harappans. The Mughals. The Magadhas. The Moabites. The Pandyans. The Nazcans. The Timurids. The Seljuks. The Huari. The Chachapoya...'
You find yourself filled with a sense of despair. There appears no meaning behind these names. There is nothing to clutch onto here, they scarcely seem worth the breath they're spoken with. You halt your hopeless scribbling –

already you have skipped dozens, scores, perhaps hundreds have not been committed to paper, you will never recall them now – and scan instead the line of faces seated around the dining table, pointlessly and passionlessly intoning. They have no features, no identifying markings. They have reverted to a monotype. Ethnically, sexually and culturally dilute. It's as if every race in the world has been boiled down to its component paste and stirred together into a beige-coloured blandness.

In increasing journalistic desperation, you search for something, anything. Some clue as to who these people are, or more importantly, why they care. But do they care? Why are they here? You try to remember what you have heard in the past about the Dinner of Loss, but find even this has slipped away. What is this roll call supposed to be for? What are you meant to be observing?

You close your notebook, and then your eyes. You'd like to close your nose as well, but the reek of the soup is all-pervading, it's already inside your skin.

FIGURE 15a: the egg-timer (b). The silence is more general than before, and it takes you a while to understand why. The sand. The sand has finally stopped hissing. You open your eyes, and see that the diners have turned their heads to the far end of the hall, where, sure enough, the top chamber stands empty, and the bottom chamber is full.

FIGURE 15b: the egg-timer (c). More servants appear, and commence an operation that involves a set of tiny keys, which they use to loosen the brackets that hold it together. You realise the entire egg-timer unscrews, to divide the top from the bottom chamber. The empty top chamber is leant against the wall, while it takes six men to carry the bottom, staggering towards the dining table with the great sand-filled glass bell.

Somehow they lift it onto the table, and then clamber up on the table themselves, dragging it over to the soup tureen. Amid much grunting and strenuous groans, the sand is poured into the soup, every last grain shaken out of the chamber. Then the concoction is thoroughly stirred with the oversized ladle.

The pungency of the odour mounts. The diners are gagging politely. You pull your sweater over your face and try not to breathe it in.

Finally the servants do the rounds, ladling soup into each wooden bowl.

'Ladies and gentleman, loss soup,' says the voice, with infinite sadness.

FIGURE 16: loss soup (e). You stare in some horror at what lies before you. It reeks of bilges, dishwater. An oily film slides on its surface, and when you poke it with the spoon you disturb partially suspended bands of sallow browns and greys. Occasionally a translucent lump of matter rises to the surface, slowly revolves, and then sinks back into the anonymous slop. The sand forms a silt at the bottom of the bowl, something like Turkish coffee.

You cannot remember what you expected, but surely it was something better than this. Perhaps you imagined them swimming down there – shades of the Kipchaks, the wisents, the grebes, the canopies of long-extinct trees, intimations of dead Aboriginal tongues, the auroch and the Neanderthal, Homo floresiensis, the glaciers, megafauna – but you find yourself confronted instead with a sewer-stinking broth. There's not even any wine left to wash the stuff down. Is this perhaps some awful joke?

You look around. The diners are eating, ferrying the soup from their bowls to their mouths with mute determination. The liquid dribbles from their loose lips, splashing back into the bowls. Apart from the pitter-patter of soup drops, the only sound around the table is the steady champing of teeth against sand. Throat muscles clench and gulp. They are actually swallowing the stuff.

Somehow, as unlikely as it seems, you find yourself incredibly hungry. You feel as if you haven't eaten for weeks. You've lost track of how long you've been in this place. Your stomach aches with emptiness, a hunger of bottomless proportions. Steeling your nerves, you take a spoonful and bring it towards your mouth. But something tells you that would only make it worse. You just can't do it. An enormous sadness grips you. Your spoon tips and the soup splashes onto the open page of your notebook, soaking through the paper and blotting the words.

You put the notebook back in its pouch and weakly rise to your feet.

'I'd like … I'd like to add my own,' you say, holding up your empty glass. Hollow eyes swivel, but no-one speaks. 'My contribution … Such as it is. I lost my father. I mean, we don't speak. We don't know who each other are anymore. And long before that, I lost a toy that wouldn't have meant much to anyone, but for me it was the only thing that seemed at all important. I left it under a tree in some woods. I used to think about it getting rained on. And … and I lost many friends. One in particular. I guess he decided he didn't see the value in our friendship anymore. I lost contact with all my old girlfriends, and even the ones I stayed in touch with, I've lost them forever too. And I lost a love that needn't have been lost. I could have kept it alive but I chose not to. And … I've forgotten certain smells and ideas. What the light was like at this or that moment, things I thought I could never forget … Someone's face, someone else's name … Who I was before … '

The words trail off. You've lost yourself now. Something tugs dully at the back of your mind, and for a moment you almost know what it is, but then it disappears like everything else, and you sit back in your seat.

The diners stare at you gloomily. Their jaws continue working up and down. The only sound is the sound of champing sand.

Finally you bring the soup to your lips. It doesn't taste of anything at all.

A D R I E N N E   O D A S S O

Vision

Let us begin by saying that the theatre burned,
and I was in it. We reached out to many
in terror, newly dead, frantic in passing,
but our hands lanced through them.

I cannot recall where I went, except home
to my kinsmen, who stood in a circle
around the old dining-room table in mourning
as I soundlessly descended the stairs. An anthem

of emptiness bore me, their shining faces rising
to behold what manner of stalking horror
I had become. But they reached up one by one
to touch me as I bound them in one slow circuit

one to another, until I came to my sister,
the youngest, fairest of all. I touched her hands
and gave her all that I had. I transformed then
before her disbelieving eyes, my feathers

the colour of iron-blue slate, my seething eyes
silver as pin-pricks of grief. And I told her
in the language of tales that have no ending
that she would be my cherished one come flood

or come fire. My soul as a bluebird flew
to the mountain of forgetting, where it landed
and stood trembling. The path, steep and foreboding,
had not been cleared. Even winged things know fear.

This is a dream of becoming, as all dreams are.

DOUGALD HINE

Black Elephants
and skull jackets

a conversation with Vinay Gupta

Before I know who he is, Vinay Gupta has started telling me about his plan
to start a small African country. The drug factory is the important part,
apparently – that and the Gurkha mercenaries.

We're sitting on the bare floorboards of a townhouse in Mayfair: five storeys
of gilded mirrors, marble hallways, handpainted Chinese wallpaper and
furniture that looks like it just came out of a skip. In one corner, a large
bracket fungus is growing out of the wall, about two feet below the ceiling. It's
the kind of scene that makes you think the world as we know it already ended,
you just weren't paying attention.

It is January 2009. For months now, the world economy has been visibly in
chaos, and even the politicians are starting to acknowledge that the conse-
quences of this won't be confined to the financial markets. Gupta seems like
a man who relishes chaos.

I'm here because the artists and activists who have squatted this Mayfair
palace are about to open its doors to the public. For three weeks, it will become
the Temporary School of Thought, a free university where anyone can pitch
up and offer classes. Gupta and I have just joined the faculty: I'm offering
lectures on 'Deschooling Everything' and 'Economic Chemotherapy', but this
feels pretty tame compared to his curriculum which takes in 'Infrastructure
for Anarchists', 'Biometrics for Freedom', 'Avoiding Capitalism for the Next
Four Billion' and 'Comparative Religion'.

For some reason, this last one sounds like a euphemism.

He's the kind of character you want to run a background check on. Anyone
who shows up in a squat, wearing a black jacket with a black skull printed on

the back, telling stories about his work for the Pentagon, his plans to fix global poverty and his friendly Gurkha mercenaries deserves a background check.

What makes it worse is when the stories check out. You can find the Defense Horizons paper he co-authored with the former Chief Information Officer of US Department of Defense. Then there's the Hexayurt – the refugee shelter he invented, which can be assembled from local materials, costs less than a tent and lasts for years. Evidence of this turns up in photographs from the park at the centre of the Pentagon to the playa at Burning Man.

Like a one-man Alternate Reality Game, he's conscious of the need to leave a trail of evidence. 'Otherwise, no one would ever believe me!'

The jacket, the hand-printed business cards, the over-the-top invented organisations – for a while, the cards say 'Global Apocalypse Mitigation Agency' – are partly geek humour, the residue of his early career as a software engineer. They're also a strategy for living with the kind of extreme situations Gupta spends his time thinking about.

He works on big problems: how to prevent biometrics becoming a tool for genocide; how to deal with the survivors after a nuclear terror attack on a US city; what to do if H5N1 goes pandemic at a 50% Case Fatality Rate. (His briefing paper on severe pandemic flu contains the advice: 'Do not count the dead. Count the living.')

At the Rocky Mountain Institute, he helped edit two of Amory Lovins' books: *Small is Profitable*, on decentralised energy, and *Winning the Oil Endgame*, on moving the United States to a zero-oil future. The latter was paid for by Donald Rumsfeld's office, when he was Secretary of Defense, and is credited with shaping Bush's State of the Union speech in 2006, with its pledge to end America's 'addiction' to oil.

'I wish they'd followed up that speech with action,' Gupta says, when I mention this.

His real obsession, though, is poverty – something he attributes to his family background, half-Indian, but born and raised in Scotland.

'When I was a kid, my mother and father visited some of our family in Calcutta. I remember them telling me stories of how these relatives – middle class people, teachers – lived in a swanky area of town, but in a really lousy apartment. In the kitchen they kept a brick on top of the chapatis so that rats coming in through the open window wouldn't drag them away!'

The complex cultural awareness bundled together in that story bears unpacking: that people have drastically different experiences of life, that things he – as a child growing up in Scotland – couldn't imagine living with were normal to others. 'And that they were my relatives, people like me.'

A few weeks after the encounter in the Mayfair squat, and after a lot of long conversations over Chinese food, the Institute for Collapsonomics comes into being. Gupta and I are among its founders.

The Institute is at least half a joke, a sister organisation for the Global Apocalypse Mitigation Agency. But it is also a crossing point for people from very different personal and professional backgrounds who, for one reason or another, have found themselves thinking seriously about what happens if and when the systems we're meant to rely on start to fail.

We convene in the back corner of Hing Loon, which does the best eggplant with garlic sauce in Chinatown, or after hours in somebody's office. We invite former hedge fund managers and Ukrainian government officials to discuss the causes and realities of economic collapse. We gatecrash think tank seminars, with mixed results. The two of us spend three hours at a cafe in St James's Park, arguing about pandemic flu and the role of government with a guy from the Cabinet Office. One Friday afternoon we invite ourselves to the National Endowment for Science, Technology and the Arts, turning up mob-handed to what turns into the most chaotic meeting I have ever attended.

On our way back from that meeting, we alight upon a logo which embodies the spirit of collapsonomics. The Black Elephant is an unholy union of two boardroom clichés: the Elephant in the Room, the thing which everyone knows is important, but no one will talk about; and the Black Swan, the hard-to-predict event which is outside the realm of normal expectations, but has enormous impact. The Black Elephant is an event which was quite foresee-able, which was in fact an Elephant in the Room, but which, after it happens, everyone will try to pass off as a Black Swan. We think we have spotted a few of these.

A year on, by the time we sit down to record this interview, two things have happened.

On the one hand, the sense of panic which characterised the early months of the economic crisis has subsided. Stock markets have regained most of their losses, economic statistics inform us that the recession is over – for now, at least.

Yet even as green shoots continue to be spotted, the headlines suggest another possibility. Emergency talks over a bailout for Greece to prevent a Euro collapse. Sarah Palin tells Tea Party activists America is ready for a second revolution. And here in the UK, more news piles up every day about huge cuts in public spending for schools, universities, local authorities.

Reading the papers, it feels less like the crisis is over – more like it became the new normal. Did collapsonomics just go mainstream?

Then again, in the UK, our idea of a crisis is that we have hit Peak Student: the point at which economic reality and funding cuts mean less young people will go to university year-on-year, rather than more. Meanwhile, in Haiti, a country which had little left to collapse, a disaster is playing out on an utterly different scale.

Two days after our interview, Science for Humanity announces that it is raising funds to carry out research into the deployment of the Hexayurt as a shelter solution for some of the million people made homeless by the Haitian earthquake. This would be the first large-scale application on the ground of a project on which Gupta has been working since 2002.

After a year of kicking around together, one of the things that strikes me is his ability to bridge these different worlds, the changes underway in Western countries – inconveniences perceived as disasters, for the most part – and the present day extremes of life and death in the world of the very poor. This is one reason I've been keen to put some of our conversations on the record, to talk about where the kind of practical thinking he's doing connects to the cultural questions opened up by a project like Dark Mountain.

The interview takes place, naturally, in a Chinese restaurant. It is after midnight. Both of us on laptops, talking and typing, so that a transcript is produced as we go. This method seems to work. A flow of other diners come and go, their conversations our backdrop: the Estonian girl who sold books door-to-door for the same company I had done a decade ago, the stand-up comics who just finished a gig, the group of drunk guys who interrupt us to ask if we're playing Battleships.

'Something like that,' we tell them.

DH: Dark Mountain is about what happens when we accept that our current way of living might just not be sustainable, however many windfarms we build. So I guess I wanted to start with your prognosis for that way of living.

vg: Well, firstly, which 'we' are we talking about here? We as in Europeans and Americans? Or we as in people, period, globally? Because the hard part of this problem is actually thinking globally, about all of the people – and the diversity in our ways of lives and exposure to environmental and economic risks is huge.

Some cultures are right at the edge of the envelope already, and washing over the edge: island nations, the Inuit, semi-arid agriculturists in general. Other cultures are pretty bang-centre and fairly stable. Iowa isn't going to stop growing corn any time soon, but the whole of sub-Saharan Africa could be a dustbowl in 20 years.

So it's not regular and uniform, it's all of these little lifestyle niches, some of which will fare better than others against various future scenarios.

dh: So when people think about 'collapse', they should be asking where it's going to happen, rather than whether it's going to happen?

vg: Well, in terms of sustainability, there are two questions. Sustain what? And then, can we sustain those things? Right now, more or less the whole of the debate focuses on whether we can sustain hyperconsumption – and the answer is no, of course not. Something is going to give: oil, climate, topsoil, some other factor we're not even paying attention to. You can't just burn the earth's natural resources like a gas flare on an oil rig forever.

dh: Yes, for me the thing which sums up what's screwed about the discourse of 'sustainability' is Marks & Spencer's Plan A campaign. You remember the slogan? 'Plan A: Because there is no Plan B'. And what I want to know is, well, for whom is there no Plan B? For high-end supermarkets? Or for liveable human existence? Or did we stop making that distinction?

vg: Precisely. And that's the cultural narrowing of the sustainability discourse to mean the American and European lifestyle. There is no possible way in which that standard of living is going to be sustained. It's impossible for two reasons.

Firstly, ecological constraints. Not just climate, but land use patterns in general. We just don't have the ability to keep doing this indefinitely, and climate is just the first of a long list of things that can and eventually will go wrong.

Secondly, and this is less widely understood, even in the most optimistic scenarios globalisation is going to get us. Migration of jobs and capital around the world is making the poor richer, and the rich poorer, with a lot of noise on top of that basic pattern. Another thing that moves wealth around is natural resource scarcity: when people start paying top dollar for oil, the oil states start getting rich. Suppose we wind up with a 'global middle class' of, say, four billion people, we're going to see that same kind of auction pricing and wealth transfer for more or less all natural resources: copper, iron, nickel, even wood.

So one way or another, even with all the new high tech stuff you can think of, we're not going to be so much richer than our neighbours on the planet forever. We're all headed, on average, for a lifestyle about where Mexico is today, and possibly a good deal worse if climate or other factors really start to bite.

If things go wrong, we could wind up anywhere.

DH: One of the questions Dark Mountain opens up is what it takes to make life 'liveable'. This is very much in play from a cultural perspective. For example, a book like Cormac McCarthy's novel *The Road* – leaving aside its literary achievement – subtly reinforces a very common, seldom-stated cultural assumption, that life outside of a continuation of American late consumerism is unliveable.

VG: And that's where most people are already living! Not in *The Road,* but outside of the Western consumerist bubble.

DH: And those are not the same thing. Part of what I find so interesting about your work is that it feels like you've arrived at this question – about how we distinguish what makes life liveable from the way you and I happen to be living right now – from a completely different perspective. I got there by reading Ivan Illich and John Berger. You got there by working with Rocky Mountain Institute and the US Department of Defense.

VG: That and the fact that I'm half-Indian. You can't underestimate the effect of that, even growing up thousands of miles away from India, there was still the curiosity about how the other half lived, combined with the sense that these people were my relatives, some of them. People like me.

So fast forward to my early 30s and I'm involved with Rocky Mountain Institute. Now, RMI is really extremely good at infrastructure. Amory is personally incredibly intelligent and sensitive to how large-scale systems work: he's a master of the complex. I, on the other hand, like simple systems. There was an event called the Sustainable Settlements Charrette in 2002 and what came out of that was a question: can we do a new kind of refugee camp?

And that was where I suddenly found a new angle on things: apply the RMI infrastructure insights, not to the big, complex western cities, but to the refugees!

This turned out to be incredibly fruitful, because refugees are a special case of the very poor. Villagers all over the world share many problems with them, problems like water and shelter. So through thinking about how to make life liveable for refugees, you arrive at practical ideas for all these people.

DH: Ideas which also apply to people in rich countries, when things go wrong?

VG: Absolutely. Like, what happens after a nuclear attack on a US city? The work on that started at a disaster response event called Strong Angel III, run by Eric Rasmussen, an ex-US Navy surgeon who's now running InSTEDD.

A couple of friends and I came as self-supporting American refugees. We swung by Home Depot, picked up about $300 of equipment, and were self-sustaining for shelter, for water, for cooking – and we would've been for sanitation, if they'd let us use our composting toilet. People sat up and took notice, because that opened up a lot of new terrain – decentralised response to extreme crisis situations, where you have to make what you need from what you have.

DH: What strikes me here is that the situations you're talking about are situations which people – even in government or NGOs or the military – prefer not to think about, because they're too alarming or too hopeless. And in that sense, there are very strong parallels to the scenarios we're talking about with serious climate change, resource scarcity, social and economic collapse – take your pick!

The point being that a lot of the people who've been drawn to the conversations around the Dark Mountain Project have reached a place where they no longer find the future offered by mainstream sustainability narratives believable. They're coming round to the likelihood that we're going to outlive our way of living – and that feels like giving up, or like once you face that, you might as well give up. We get accused a lot of defeatism – of being the guys who say 'we're fucked!' – and you're the guy whose job starts at the point where people admit they're fucked!

VG: Well, take the work on nuclear terrorism. What I found was that nobody had actually thought about cleaning up after a one-off nuclear attack in a realistic meat-and-potatoes way. They just hadn't. Worse, the people who looked at my work – senior folks in the kinds of organisations which get to think about this stuff professionally – agreed it was the best plan they had seen, but to my knowledge have not committed to building that response capability. Not because it would not work – nobody's ever suggested it wasn't feasible, efficient and necessary – but because it would.

And that means admitting you might get hit, and are prepared to deal with it. Not a popular position.

DH: Sounds a lot like being in denial.

VG: Yes, absolutely it's denial, and a lot of what I do is denial management. When Mike Bennett and I started Buttered Side Down, we consciously did everything possible to push people out of that denial – branding it as a 'historic risk management consultancy' and the scary, scary homepage, leavened with the humour of the name.

You always hit the denial and cognitive dissonance when dealing with the real world. It's all over everything in our society. TV isn't helping!

DH: So I guess the question for a lot of people is, how do you handle these possibilities? How do you admit that it could happen, without feeling like just giving up?

VG: There's an easy way, and a hard way. Only the hard way produces results.

The easy way is nihilism, which is basically escapist. 'This situation is hopeless,' you say, 'but if something else were true then it wouldn't be hopeless, and then I could re-engage.'

DH: You mean like people who say 'well, the climate situation is hopeless, so I'm not going to worry about it'?

VG: Yes, exactly. They haven't given up on the hope that somehow it's all going to work out and allow them to continue to live (and consume) in their current way. They've abandoned trying to fix the situation, but deep down they still unconsciously expect that it will somehow all be OK in the end.

People who are in that position say they've abandoned all hope, but they haven't really. It's wishful thinking. It's Goth. It's the easy way.

The hard way is mysticism. 'Look, we are all going to die.'

'The question is only when, and how.'

DH: Is that mysticism?

VG: Yep, one way or another. Anybody who thinks about these questions seriously is a mystic. Even atheism, if it's fully informed by a consideration of death, is a mystery tradition. The mystery is 'If we're all going to die, what is worth living for?' And the answer is, must be, everything.

DH: For a lot of people, 'mysticism' suggests escapism – a retreat from reality.

VG: You know, that's largely a cultural issue in the West. There's a legacy here of religion being about a mythical state, a salvation. That's not at all how it worked in pre-Christian traditions, Greek, Roman, Hindu. Those roots go back to something else, not the hope of an afterlife, but a hope for this life.

Stoicism is European Zen, more than anything else. And Diogenes looks a lot like a sadhu.

DH: So how does this help you think practically about dealing with situations in which large numbers of people are going to die – whether that's a climate disaster, or a situation like Haiti right now?

VG: Large numbers of people? 100%. Everybody is going to die. The only question is when, and how. So it's not about saving anybody. Talking about saving lives is perpetuating the illusion of living forever. I cannot save a single life. At best, my work allows people to experience more life before they face death, as we all inevitably must: a universal experience which we all face alone; an initiation or an extinction, we cannot say with certainty.

It's this vision of the certainty of death which is at the heart of my work.

DH: How does that change the way you approach these extreme situations?

VG: There's this model I came up with called *Six Ways to Die*. It's like a mandala, a picture of life and death. In the centre is the individual self: you. At the perimeter of the circle are the six ways to die: too hot or too cold, hunger and thirst, illness and injury. What stands between you and these threats is infrastructure, the stuff that gives you shelter, supply and safety: your house, the power grid, the water purification plant, the sewer pipes, hospitals and Marks & Spencer's.

You can't draw an accurate map of what keeps people alive without having one eye squarely on death, and if you haven't faced your own mortality more or less fully, *Six Ways to Die* is very hard on you. Because you will die.

To fight for people's lives effectively means understanding that you are fighting for something measured in years, in days, in seconds and moments, not in the sense of some abstract salvation from death itself.

'How can I add to the span of your years?' is not the same mindset as 'How can I save you?' If I fail, I failed to buy you five or 10 or 15 or 50 years, made of days and moments. It's this time to live and experience which is at stake, not your life per se.

DH: That shift in mindset – apart from anything else, that's a substantial change in your sense of your role. I think a lot of us who have been activists, or in some way trying to 'change the world', are familiar with the 'How can I save you?' role – whether it's 'saving lives' or 'saving the planet'.

VG: It's all going: us, now; the planet, in a few billion years.

At birth, we leapt from a building, and it takes 70 or 80 years to hit the ground on a good day. On a bad day, you miss the lower 30 or 50 floors!

DH: Now that's dark! But you know, I see a lot of major figures in the environmental movement wrestling with this at the moment. They've spent years telling people, if we just try hard enough and get it together, we can save the planet – or rather, we can save our way of living. And they're no longer convinced, but they feel like if they admit how serious things are, everyone will just give up. And this becomes intensely morally charged.

When Paul Kingsnorth, my Dark Mountain co-founder, debated George Monbiot in the Guardian last year, the key bit in George's argument – the bit that got thrown backwards and forwards endlessly in the comments and the blog posts – was his suggestion that we were passive in the face of (or even enthusiastic about) mass death.

Here's the bit I'm thinking of. He writes: 'How many would survive without modern industrial civilisation? Two billion? One billion? Under your vision several billion perish.'

VG: Look, 'modern industrial civilisation' cannot scale to seven billion people. Two billion people in that ecosystem niche are effectively trashing the entire global ecosystem, with climate going first, followed hard on by oceans, deforestation, topsoil and all the rest. Even if it stabilises, the impact as the poor billions who don't currently use many natural resources pile on to the consumption bandwagon is going to destroy everything.

This is absolutely and completely obvious. Either the poor are going to continue living in their current conditions or worse – conditions which most industrial nations would consider an apocalypse – or they are going to 'develop' and follow us into the burning building.

DH: I wonder, sometimes, whether the absolute focus on climate change in the environmental movement today is partly a way of avoiding thinking about this larger question?

VG: Well, climate hits the rich and the poor. It's scary because it'll flood Venice and Bangladesh at the same time, and nobody can buy their way out of it. Most of the other ecological collapses allow the richest to buy their way to the end of the line – last tuna syndrome.

DH: How much will the last tuna to come out of the sea fetch in a Japanese fish market?

VG: That's the one.

DH: Perhaps. I see something else, though. The focus on climate change allows the implication – which I don't think many environmentalists actually believe – that if it wasn't for the pesky sensitivity of our climate system to CO_2, our way of living, our mode of development, our model of progress would be just fine. I see this in the popular discourse about climate change, from politicians and in the media, and I don't see it being challenged clearly by mainstream environmentalists.

VG: It's all very complicated, and there's a huge, huge amount of stuff going on. We can't master the complexity, we don't have the ability intellectually to master all the science. People are at the edge of their limit to cope. Picking the most pressing problem and screaming about it is an ancient human reflex. TIGER! Climate is our tiger.

DH: That's a good point, about people struggling to cope. It's all very well talking about how someone who comes up with disaster plans for a living handles the possibility of major, discontinuous change – of life being shorter and messier than we grew up expecting it to be – but how about the rest of us?

VG: Well, I'm not proposing a Zen revolution – not yet, anyway!

DH: It is quite a thought! But I have a strong sense of people looking for new ways of thinking, tools to adapt, ways to get their heads round the changes we're likely to live through. I think that's why Paul and I have had such a strong response since we published the manifesto.

VG: Well, a simple humanism gets you most of the way: think about poverty first. The poor are already living without all these things we are afraid of losing. They're too poor to consume much carbon. They eat all organic produce because they can't afford fertiliser. We are afraid of becoming them, if we trash the planet with our insane greed and the standard of living that comes with it. So when you start to get clear about poverty – and I'll show you what that's like in a moment – you start to get clear about limitation.

Here's how this works, the back of an envelope version. Six and a half billion people. Half rural, half urban. Of the urban population, about two-thirds are doing OK or very well. One-third – one billion – live in utter, abject poverty. Of the rural population, you've got about a billion who are OK, a billion who are really struggling, and a billion who are regularly hungry.

With me, so far? Four billion in various states of poor, and a couple of billion of those, a third of the people on the planet, with really serious daily personal problems like no dental care beyond having your teeth pulled with rusty pliers.

This is poverty – and it's everywhere.

And how does it work? Average income in the USA is about $100 per day. Average income for the poorest billion is maybe $1 per day. So at global averages, there are 100 people living on this income.

Now, think about the kind of will-to-blindness it has taken us all to build our consumer paradise while all this is going on around us. That blindness, that wilful ignorance, is what climate change threatens. But it did not start with climate, it started, as everything on Earth does, with poverty.

All of these people who discovered climate recently? They'd been ignoring poverty their whole lives. The denial is cracking, and it's going to be messy, but do not assume that the environment is all that's under the rug.

DH: This is one of the things we tried to do in the manifesto, though I don't know if it was clear enough, to piece these things together: climate, resource scarcity, social and economic instability. All these unpredictable, converging tsunamis that we're facing, all rooted in forms of denial that go generations deep.

VG: The kind of suffering we are afraid of coming from climate collapse is the ordinary condition of half of the human race.

DH: Yes. And here's the question we've been moving backwards and forwards across: once you admit that, what do you do next?

VG: Well, let's talk about what we really need. Back to *Six Ways to Die*: shelter, supply and security. Take water: there's a simple technology, a clay water filter called the Potters for Peace Filtron. It's a few dollars a unit, can be made anywhere in the world, and it takes out all the bugs. There are lots of similar little innovations for other basic needs. Taken together they can make the villages healthy and good places to live.

That's what you need. Everything else is what you want.

DH: Now, this reminds me of Illich. One of the recurring themes in his work is the massive, unexamined extension of our definition of 'need' that has gone on in modern societies: our failure to distinguish between the kind of ground-level needs that you're talking about and the systems and institutions we happen to be dependent on right now.

There's another point from Illich, from one of his essays, 'Energy and Equity' – which feels incredibly relevant today, even though it was written nearly 40 years ago. Here's the passage I'm thinking of: 'A universal social straitjacket will be the inevitable outcome of ecological restraints on total energy use imposed by industrial minded planners bent on keeping industrial production at some hypothetical maximum.' In other words, if we frame the question of sustainability as – how do we achieve the most energy-intensive society we can, within ecological limits – the result is the end of democracy. There is no political choice left about our way of living. Whereas, if we include the range of positions below those limits, we have many possible ways of living.

VG: You're talking about hard optimisation, technocratic maximisation of utility. That's very hard to think through, as you say, without totalitarian control.

DH: Yes, although today it comes disguised as pragmatism. If you read something like *Heat*, for example – to pick on George Monbiot, again – it's not immediately obvious that you're dealing with 'maximisation' of anything. For the purposes of his argument, reducing our emissions to reasonable levels is an almost-impossible task, therefore the least impossible option is the closest we have to a realistic one.

So there, we're still talking about achieving maximum possible consumption – what Illich warned was a social straitjacket – but because of the context, in which we're also talking about such a massive reduction of consumption, it's easy to miss the assumption that we should consume as much as we can.

VG: The problem is that we live without restraint in a limited world.

DH: Also, it's important to acknowledge the extent to which that problem is cultural. It's not simply an evolutionary drive that leads us to unlimited consumption, so that every human who ever lived would be doing the same were they in our shoes. You can find examples of times and places where people have lived very differently – and not necessarily because of local ecological constraints or lack of technology, but because they were not acting on the assumption that the source of meaning or satisfaction in life is the maximisation of consumption.

VG: In general, old cultures get to be old cultures by wisely negotiating with whatever their limits are. In some places it's land use, not wrecking your soil, in other areas it's population. But old cultures get to be old cultures by not doing this or anything like it.

OK, so here's what it boils down to: are we going to get to be an old culture?

DH: And again, which 'we' are we talking about? Is it really about whether Europe or America becomes an old culture? The ecological problems aren't limited by one culture or another: all over the world, we see the same patterns of hyperconsumption emerging in their own local versions. It's a global issue, not just one for us in the West.

VG: Absolutely – and there's a historical context to this. American and European exceptionalism has existed in one form or another since the early days of colonialism. It's hundreds of years of gunboat diplomacy and technological breakouts, as the rest of the world struggled to understand what was happening, and cope with the invaders. And the last cards in that game are going to be played in this present generation.

In the future, we're all Mexicans. That's the standard of living towards which globalisation is driving us. Every country will have its rich and its poor, and some will generally do better than others, but the overwhelming military and technological superiority, which was the foundation of the economic hegemony of America and Europe, is largely at an end.

Europeans and Americans are soon going to live in the same world as everybody else: the world in which you do not have everything you want, and sometimes you do not have enough. That is coming because the plenty we took for granted was based on the absurd political power imbalances that gunpowder and mechanised war brought us, when only we controlled them. As military force runs out as an option, and industrial production becomes available to everybody, America and Europe lose the economic advantages which came with being in control of the majority of resources of the globe.

In the future, all of us on Planet Earth are going to be dealing with the fact that there are seven billion of us. In the future, you do not get a jacuzzi. Not unless you are very, very lucky and are one of the rich, or unless your jacuzzi runs on abundant resources, not scarce ones.

If you live in a hot country, you can use the sun. In a country with abundant biomass, you can burn wood. In a cold country with geothermal springs, you can use the ground. But you are not going to burn natural gas for fun in 50 years time in any scenario I can imagine from here, and that's the end of a brief, short, foolish age.

We can still live well, but it must be wisely and appropriately, as if we were going to live a thousand years, but knowing we will not.

DH: You know, that sounds pretty upbeat, from a man wearing a skull jacket! What's left, though, is the question of how we get there from here?

VG: That's exactly what we don't know. It's where the history of the twenty-first-century is going to be made, in the same way that wrestling with the nuclear bomb was the defining dilemma of the twentieth-century.

We don't have a canned solution for this one, it's a whole culture, and a whole world, engaging with a problem we've never seen before. It's a pass/fail grade on evolution. It's not a problem which can be project-managed.

DH: What's striking is, when you talk about this, you sound hopeful.

VG: The hope starts at the point when you give up. I'm going to die one day, so are you, and the most we can expect from this life is to enjoy the ride. As long as the grass still grows, and the young are optimistic, life will be wonderful.

PAUL KINGSNORTH

Confessions of a recovering environmentalist

'Some see Nature all ridicule and deformity...
and some scarce see Nature at all.
But to the eyes of the man of imagination,
Nature is imagination itself.'
William Blake

Scenes from a younger life # 1:

I am twelve years old. I am alone, I am scared, I am cold and I am crying my eyes out. I can't see more than six feet in either direction. I am on some god-forsaken moor high up on the dark, ancient, poisonous spine of England. The black bog juice I have been trudging through for hours has long since crept over the tops of my boots and down into my socks. My rucksack is too heavy, I am unloved and lost and I will never find my way home. It is raining and the cloud is punishing me; clinging to me, laughing at me. Twenty five years later, I still have a felt memory of that experience and its emotions: a real despair and a terrible loneliness.

I do find my way home; I manage to keep to the path and eventually catch up with my father, who has the map and the compass and the mini Mars bars. He was always there, somewhere up ahead, but he had decided it would be good for me to 'learn to keep up' with him. All of this, he tells me, will make me into a man.

Only later do I realise the complexity of the emotions summoned by a childhood laced with experiences like this. My father was a compulsive long-distance walker. Every year, throughout my most formative decade, he would take me away to Cumbria or Northumberland or Yorkshire or Cornwall or Pembrokeshire or the Welsh marches, and we would walk, for weeks. We would follow ancient tracks or new trails, across mountains and moors and ivory black cliffs. Much of the time we would be alone with each other and with our thoughts and our conversations, and we would be alone with the oystercatchers, the gannets, the curlews, the skylarks and the owls. With the gale and the breeze, with our maps and compasses and emergency rations and bivvy bags and plastic bottles of water. We would camp in the heather, by cairns and old mine shafts, hundreds of feet above the orange lights of civilisation, and I would dream. And in the morning, with dew on the tent and cold air in my face as I opened the zip, the wild elements of life, all of the real things, would all seem to be there, waiting for me with the sunrise.

Scenes from a younger life #2:
I am nineteen years old. It is around midnight and I am on the summit of a low, chalk down, the last of the long chain that wind their way through through the crowded, peopled, fractious south country. There are maybe fifty or sixty people there with me. There is a fire going, there are guitars, there is singing and weird and unnerving whooping noises from some of the ragged travellers who have made this place their home.

This is Twyford Down, a hilltop east of Winchester. There is something powerful about this place; something ancient and unanswering. Soon it is to be destroyed: a six lane motorway will be driven through it in a deep chalk cutting. It is vital that this should happen in order to reduce the journey time for car travellers between London and Southampton by a full thirteen minutes. The people up here have made it their home in a doomed attempt to stop this happening.

From outside it is impossible to see, and most do not want to. The name-calling has been going on for months, in the papers and the pubs and in the House of Commons. The people here are Luddites, nimbies, reactionaries, Romantics. They are standing in the way of progress. They will not be tolerated. Inside, there is a sense of shared threat and solidarity, there are blocks of hash and packets of Rizlas and litres of bad cider. We know what we are here for. We know what we are doing. We can feel the reason in the soil and in the night air. Down there, under the lights and behind the curtains, there is no chance that they will ever understand. We are on our own.

Someone I don't know suggests we dance the maze. Out beyond the fire-light, there is a maze carved into the down's soft, chalk turf. I don't know if it's some ancient monument or a new creation. Either way, it's the same spiral pattern that can be found carved in rocks from millennia ago. With cans and cigarettes and spliffs in our hands, a small group of us start to walk the maze, laughing, staggering, then breaking into a run, singing, spluttering, stumbling together towards the centre.

Scenes from a younger life #3:
I am twenty one years old and I've just spent the most exciting two months of my life so far in an Indonesian rainforest. I've just been on one of those organised expeditions that people of my age buy into to give them the chance to do something useful and exciting in what used to be called the 'Third World', I've prepared for months for this. I've sold double glazing door-to-door to scrape the cash together. I have been reading Bruce Chatwin and Redmond O'Hanlon and Benedict Allen and my head is full of magic and idiocy and wonder.

During my trip, there were plenty of all of these things. I still vividly re-member *klotok* journeys up Borneo rivers by moonlight, watching the swarms of giant fruitbats overhead. I remember the hooting of gibbons and the search for hornbills high up in the rainforest canopy. I remember a four day trek through a so-called 'rain' forest that was so dry we ended up drinking filtered mud. I remember turtle eggs on the beaches of Java and young orangutans at the rehabilitation centre where we worked in Kalimantan, sitting in the high branches of trees with people's stolen underpants on their heads, laughing at us. I remember the gold miners and the loggers, and the freshwater croco-diles in the same river we swam in every morning. I remember my first sight of flying fish in the Java Sea.

And I remember the small islands north of Lombok where some of us spent a few days before we came home. At night we would go down to the moon-lit beach, where the sea and the air would still be warm, and in the sea were millions of tiny lights: phosphorescence. I had never seen this before; never even heard of it. We would walk into the water and immerse ourselves and rise up again and the lights would cling to our bodies, fading away as we laughed.

Now, back home, the world seems changed. A two month break from my country, my upbringing, my cultural assumptions, a two month immersion in something far more raw and unmediated, has left me open to seeing this place as it really is. I see the atomisation and the inward focus and the faces of the people in a hurry on the other side of windscreens. I see the streetlights and the asphalt as I had not quite seen them before. What I see most of all are the adverts.

For the first time, I realise the extent and the scope and the impacts of the billboards, the posters, the TV and radio ads. Everywhere an image, a phrase, a demand or a recommendation is screaming for my attention, trying to sell me something, tell me who to be, what to desire and to need. And this is before the internet; before Apples and Blackberries became indispensable to people who wouldn't know where to pick the real thing; before the deep, accelerating immersion of people in their technologies, even outdoors, even in the sunshine. Compared to where I have been, this world is so tamed, so mediated and commoditised, that something within it seems to have broken off and been lost beneath the slabs. No one has noticed this, or says so if they have. Something is missing: I can almost see the gap where it used to be. But it is not remarked upon. Nobody says a thing.

*

It is 9.30 at night in mid-December at the end of the first decade of the twenty-first century. I step outside my front door into the farmyard and I walk over to the track, letting my eyes adjust to the dark. I am lucky enough to be living among the Cumbrian fells now, and as my pupils widen I can see, under a clear, starlit sky, the outline of the Old Man of Coniston, Dow Crag, Wetherlam, Helvellyn, the Fairfield horseshoe. I stand there for ten minutes, growing colder. I see two shooting stars and a satellite. I suddenly wish my dad was still alive and I wonder where the magic has gone.

These experiences, and others like them, were what formed me. They were what made me what I would later learn to call an 'environmentalist': something which seemed rebellious and excitingly outsiderish when I first took it up (and which successfully horrified my social climbing father, especially as it was partly his fault) but which these days is almost *de rigeur* amongst the British bourgeoisie. Early in my adult life, just after I came back from Twyford Down, I vowed, self-importantly, that this would be my life's work: saving nature from people. Preventing the destruction of beauty and brilliance, speaking up for the small and the overlooked and the things that could not speak for themselves. When I look back on this now, I'm quite touched by my younger self. I would like to be him again, perhaps just for a day; someone to whom all sensations are fiery and all answers are simple.

All of this – the downs, the woods, the rainforest, the great oceans and, perhaps most of all, the silent isolation of the moors and mountains, which at the time seemed so hateful and unremitting – took hold of me somewhere unexamined. The relief I used to feel on those long trudges with my dad when

I saw the lights of a village or a remote pub, even a minor road or a pylon; any sign of humanity – as I grow older this is replaced by the relief of escaping from the towns and the villages, away from the pylons and the pubs and the people, up onto the moors again, where only the ghosts and the saucer-eyed dogs and the old legends and the wind can possess me.

But they are harder to find now, those spirits. I look out across the moonlit Lake District ranges and it's as clear as the night air that what used to come in regular waves, pounding like the sea, comes now only in flashes, out of the corner of my eyes, like a lighthouse in a storm. Perhaps it's the way the world has changed. There are more cars on the roads now, more satellites in the sky. The footpaths up the fells are like stone motorways, there are turbines on the moors and the farmers are being edged out by south country refugees like me, trying to escape but bringing with us the things we flee from. The new world is online and loving it, the virtual happily edging out the actual. The darkness is shut out and the night grows lighter and nobody is there to see it.

It could be all that, but it probably isn't. It's probably me. I am 37 now. The world is smaller, more tired, more fragile, more horribly complex and full of troubles. Or, rather: the world is the same as it ever was, but I am more aware of it and of the reality of my place within it. I have grown up, and there is nothing to be done about it. The worst part of it is that I can't seem to look without thinking anymore. And now I know far more about what we are doing. We: the people. I know what we are doing, all over the world, to everything, all of the time. I know why the magic is dying. It's me. It's us.

*

I became an 'environmentalist' because of a strong emotional reaction to wild places and the other-than-human world: to beech trees and hedgerows and pounding waterfalls, to songbirds and sunsets, to the flying fish in the Java Sea and the canopy of the rainforest at dusk when the gibbons come to the waterside to feed. From that reaction came a feeling, which became a series of thoughts: that such things are precious for their own sake, that they are food for the human soul and that they need people to speak for them to, and defend them from, other people, because they cannot speak our language and we have forgotten how to speak theirs. And because we are killing them to feed ourselves and we know it and we care about it, sometimes, but we do it anyway because we are hungry, or we have persuaded ourselves that we are.

But these are not, I think, very common views today. Today's environmentalism is as much a victim of the contemporary cult of utility as every other aspect of our lives, from science to education. We are not environmentalists now because we have an emotional reaction to the wild world. In this country, most of us wouldn't even know where to find it. We are environmentalists now in order to promote something called 'sustainability'. What does this curious, plastic word mean? It does not mean defending the non-human world from the ever-expanding empire of *Homo sapiens sapiens*, though some of its adherents like to pretend it does, even to themselves. It means sustaining human civilisation at the comfort level which the world's rich people – us – feel is their right, without destroying the 'natural capital' or the 'resource base' which is needed to do so.

It is, in other words, an entirely human-centred piece of politicking, disguised as concern for 'the planet'. In a very short time – just over a decade – this worldview has become all-pervasive. It is voiced by the President of the USA and the President of Anglo-Dutch Shell and many people in-between. The success of environmentalism has been total – at the price of its soul.

Let me offer up just one example of how this pact has worked. If 'sustainability' is about anything, it is about carbon. Carbon and climate change. To listen to most environmentalists today, you would think that these were the only things in the word worth talking about. The business of 'sustainability' is the business of preventing carbon emissions. Carbon emissions threaten a potentially massive downgrading of our prospects for material advancement as a species. They threaten to unacceptably erode our resource base and put at risk our vital hoards of natural capital. If we cannot sort this out quickly, we are going to end up darning our socks again and growing our own carrots and holidaying in Weston-super-Mare and other such unthinkable things. All of the horrors our grandparents left behind will return like deathless legends. Carbon emissions must be 'tackled' like a drunk with a broken bottle: quickly, and with maximum force.

Don't get me wrong: I don't doubt the potency of climate change to undermine the human machine. It looks to me as if it is already beginning to do so, and that it is too late to do anything but attempt to mitigate the worst effects. But what I am also convinced of is that the fear of losing both the comfort and the meaning that our civilisation gifts us has gone to the heads of environmentalists to such a degree that they have forgotten everything else. The carbon must be stopped, like the Umayyad at Tours, or all will be lost.

This reductive approach to the human-environmental challenge leads to an obvious conclusion: if carbon is the problem, then 'zero-carbon' is the solution. Society needs to go about its business without spewing the stuff out. It needs to do this quickly, and by any means necessary. Build enough of the right kind of energy technologies, quickly enough, to generate the power we 'need' without producing greenhouse gases and there will be no need to ever turn the lights off; no need to ever slow down.

To do this will require the large-scale harvesting of the planet's ambient energy: sunlight, wind, water power. This means that vast new conglomerations of human industry are going to appear in places where this energy is most abundant. Unfortunately, these places coincide with some of the world's wildest, most beautiful and most untouched landscapes. The sort of places which environmentalism came into being to protect.

And so the deserts, perhaps the landscape always most resistant to permanent human conquest, are to be colonised by vast 'solar arrays', glass and steel and aluminium, the size of small countries. The mountains and moors, the wild uplands, are to be staked out like vampires in the sun, their chests pierced with rows of 500 foot wind turbines and associated access roads, masts, pylons and wires. The open oceans, already swimming in our plastic refuse and emptying of marine life, will be home to enormous offshore turbine ranges and hundreds of wave machines strung around the coastlines like Victorian necklaces. The rivers are to see their estuaries severed and silted by industrial barrages. The croplands and even the rainforests, the richest habitats on this terrestrial Earth, are already highly profitable sites for biofuel plantations designed to provide guilt free car fuel to the motion-hungry masses of Europe and America.

What this adds up to should be clear enough, yet many people who should know better choose not to see it. This is business-as-usual: the expansive, colonising, progressive human narrative, shorn only of the carbon. It is the latest phase of our careless, self-absorbed, ambition-addled destruction of the wild, the unpolluted and the non-human. It is the mass destruction of the world's remaining wild places in order to feed the human economy. And without any sense of irony, people are calling this 'environmentalism'.

A while back I wrote an article in a newspaper highlighting the impact of industrial wind power stations (which are usually referred to, in a nice Orwellian touch, as wind 'farms') on the uplands of Britain. I was emailed the next day by an environmentalist friend who told me he hoped I was feeling ashamed of myself. I was wrong; worse, I was dangerous. What was I doing giving succour to the fossil fuel industry? Didn't I know that climate change would do far more damage to upland landscapes than turbines? Didn't

I know that this was the only way to meet our urgent carbon targets? Didn't I see how beautiful turbines were? So much more beautiful than nuclear power stations. I might think that a 'view' was more important than the future of the entire world, but this was because I was a middle class escapist who needed to get real.

It became apparent at that point that what I saw as the next phase of the human attack on the non-human world, a lot of my environmentalist friends saw as 'progressive', 'sustainable' and 'green'. What I called destruction they called 'large scale solutions'. This stuff was realistic, necessarily urgent. It went with the grain of human nature and the market, which as we now know are the same thing. We didn't have time to 'romanticise' the woods and the hills. There were emissions to reduce, and the end justified the means.

It took me a while to realise where this kind of talk took me back to: the maze and the moonlit hilltop. This desperate scrabble for 'sustainable development' – in reality it was the same old same old. People I had thought were on my side were arguing aggressively for the industrialising of wild places in the name of human desire. This was the same rootless, distant destruction that had led me to the top of Twyford Down. Only now there seemed to be some kind of crude equation at work that allowed them to believe this was something entirely different. Motorway through downland: bad. Wind power station on downland: good. Container port wiping out estuary mudflats: bad. Renewable hydro-power barrage wiping out estuary mudflats: good. Destruction minus carbon equals sustainability.

So here I was again: a Luddite, a nimby, a reactionary, a Romantic; standing in the way of progress. I realised that I was dealing with environmentalists with no attachment to any actual environment. Their talk was of parts per million of carbon, peer reviewed papers, sustainable technologies, renewable supergrids, green growth and the fifteenth conference of the parties. There were campaigns about 'the planet' and 'the Earth', but there was no specificity: no sign of any real, felt attachment to any small part of that Earth.

*

Back at university, in love with my newfound radicalism, as students tend to be, I started to read things. Not the stuff I was supposed to be reading about Lollards and Wycliffe and pre-reformation Europe, but green political thought: wild ideas I had never come across before. I could literally feel my mind levering itself open. Most exciting to me were the implications of a new word I stumbled across: ecocentrism. This word crystallised everything I had been feeling for years. I had no idea there were words for it or that other people felt it too, or had written intimidating books about it. The nearest I had come to such a realisation thus far was reading Wordsworth in the sixth form and feeling an excited tingling sensation as I began to understand what he was getting at amongst all those poems about shepherds and girls called Lucy. Here was a kindred spirit! Here was a man moved to love and fear by mountains, who believed rocks had souls, that 'Nature never did betray the heart that loved her' (though even then that sounded a little optimistic to me). Pantheism was my new word that year.

Now I declared, to myself if no one else, that I was 'ecocentric' too. This was not the same as being egocentric, though some disagreed, and though it sounded a bit too much like 'eccentric' this was also a distraction. I was ecocentric because I did not believe – had never believed, I didn't think – that humans were the centre of the world, that the Earth was their playground, that they had the right to do what they liked or even that what they did was that important. I thought we were part of something bigger, which had as much to right to the world as we did and which we were stomping on for our own benefit. I had always been haunted by shameful thoughts like this. It had always seemed to me that the beauty to be found on the trunk of a birch tree was worth any number of Mona Lisas, and that a Saturday night sunset was better than Saturday night telly. It had always seemed that most of what mattered to me could not be counted or corralled by the kind of people who thought, and still think, that I just needed to grow up.

It had been made clear to me for a long time that these feelings were at best charmingly naïve and at worst backwards and dangerous. Later, the dismissals became encrusted with familiar words, designed to keep the ship of human destiny afloat: Romantic, Luddite, nimby and the like. For now, though, I had found my place. I was a young, fiery, radical, ecocentric environmentalist and I was going to save the world.

When I look back on the road protests of the mid-1990s, which I often do, it is with nostalgia and fondness and a sense of gratitude that I was able to be there, to see what I saw and do what I did. But I realise now that it is more than this that makes me think and talk and write about Twyford Down and Newbury and Solsbury Hill to an extent which bores even my patient friends. This, I think, was the last time I was part of an environmental movement that was genuinely environmental. The people involved were, like me, ecocentric: they didn't see 'the environment' as something 'out there'; separate from people, to be utilised or destroyed or protected according to human whim. They saw themselves as part of it, within it, of it.

There was a Wordsworthian feel to the whole thing: the defence of the trees simply because they were trees. Living under the stars and in the rain, in the oaks and in the chaotic, miraculous tunnels beneath them, in the soil itself like the rabbits and the badgers. We were connected to a place; a real place that we loved and had made a choice to belong to, if only for a short time. There was little theory, much action but even more simple *being*. Being in a place, knowing it, standing up for it. It was environmentalism at its rawest, and the people who came to be part of it were those who loved the land, in their hearts as well as their heads.

In years to come, this was worn away. It took a while before I started to notice what was happening, but when I did it was all around me. The ecocentrism – in simple language, the love of place, the humility, the sense of belonging, the *feelings* – was absent from most of the 'environmentalist' talk I heard around me. Replacing it were two other kinds of talk. One was the save-the-world-with-windfarms narrative; the same old face in new makeup. The other was a distant, sombre sound: the marching boots and rattling swords of an approaching fifth column.

Environmentalism, which in its raw, early form had no time for the encrusted, seized-up politics of left and right, offering instead a worldview which saw the growth economy and the industrialist mentality beloved by both as the problem in itself, was being sucked into the yawning, bottomless chasm of the 'progressive' left. Suddenly people like me, talking about birch trees and hilltops and sunsets, were politely, or less politely, elbowed to one side by people who were bringing a 'class analysis' to green politics.

All this talk of nature, it turned out, was bourgeois, Western and unproductive. It was a middle class conceit, and there was nothing worse than a middle class conceit. The workers had no time for thoughts like this (though no one bothered to notify the workers themselves that they were simply clodhopping, nature-loathing cannon fodder in a political flame war). It was terribly, *objectively* right wing. Hitler liked nature after all. He was a vegetarian too. It was all deeply 'problematic'.

More problematic for me was what this kind of talk represented. With the near global failure of the left wing project over the past few decades, green politics was fast becoming a refuge for disillusioned socialists, Trots, Marxists and a ragbag of fellow travellers who could no longer believe in communism or the Labour party or even George Galloway, and who saw in green politics a promising bolthole. In they all trooped, with their Stop The War banners and their Palestinian solidarity scarves, and with them they brought a new sensibility.

Now it seemed that environmentalism was not about wildness or ecocentrism or the other-than-human world and our relationship to it. Instead it was about (human) social justice and (human) equality and (human) progress and ensuring that all these things could be realised without degrading the (human) resource base which we used to call nature back when we were being naïve and problematic. Suddenly, never-ending economic growth was a good thing after all: the poor needed it to get rich, which was their right. To square the circle, for those who still realised there was a circle, we were told that '(human) social justice and environmental justice go hand in hand' – a suggestion of such bizarre inaccuracy that it could surely only be wishful thinking.

Suddenly, sustaining a global human population of ten billion people was not a problem at all, and anyone who suggested otherwise was not highlighting any obvious ecological crunch points but was giving succour to fascism or racism or gender discrimination or orientalism or essentialism or some other such hip and largely unexamined concept. The 'real issue', it seemed, was not the human relationship with the non-human world; it was fat cats and bankers and cap'lism. These things must be destroyed, by way of marches, protests and votes for fringe political parties, to make way for something known as 'eco socialism': a conflation of concepts that pretty much guarantees the instant hostility of 95% of the population.

I didn't object to this because I thought that environmentalism should occupy the right rather than the left wing, or because I was right-wing myself, which I wasn't (these days I tend to consider the entire bird with a kind of frustrated detachment). And I understood that there was at least a partial reason for the success of this colonisation of the greens by the reds. Modern environmentalism sprung partly from the early twentieth century conservation movement, and that movement had often been about preserving supposedly pristine landscapes at the expense of people. Forcing tribal people from their ancestral lands which had been newly designated as national parks, for example, in order to create a fictional 'untouched nature' had once been fairly common, from Africa to the USA. And actually, Hitler had been something of an environmentalist, and the wellsprings which nourished some green thought nourished the thought of some other unsavoury characters too (a fact which some ideologues love to point to when witch-hunting the greens, as if it wouldn't be just as easy to point out that ideas of equality and justice fuelled Stalin and Pol Pot).

In this context it was fair enough to make it clear that environmentalism allied itself with ideas of justice and decency, and that it was about people as well as everything else on the planet. Of course it was, for 'nature' as something separate from people has never existed. We *are* nature, and the environmentalist project was always supposed to be about how we are to be part of it, to live well as part of it, to understand and respect it, to understand our place within it and to feel it as part of ourselves.

So there was a reason for environmentalism's shift to the left, just as there was a reason for its blinding obsession with carbon. Meanwhile, the fact of what humans are doing to the world had become so obvious, even to those who were doing very well out of it, that it became hard not to listen to the greens. Success duly arrived. You can't open a newspaper now or visit a corporate website or listen to a politician or read the label on a packet of biscuits without being bombarded with propaganda about the importance of 'saving the planet'. But there is a terrible hollowness to it all; a sense that society is going through the motions without understanding why. The shift, the pact, has come at a probably fatal price.

Now that price is being paid. The weird and unintentional pincer movement of the failed left, with its class analysis of waterfalls and fresh air, and the managerial, carbon-uber-alles brigade has infiltrated, ironed out and re-worked environmentalism for its own ends. Now it is not about the ridiculous beauty of coral, the mist over the fields at dawn. It is not about ecocentrism. It is not about reforging a connection between over-civilised people and the world outside their windows. It is not about living close to the land or valuing the world for the sake of the world. It is not about attacking the self-absorbed conceits of the bubble that our civilisation has become.

Today's environmentalism is about people. It is a consolation prize for a gaggle of washed-up Trots and at the same time, with an amusing irony, it is an adjunct to hyper-capitalism; the catalytic converter on the silver SUV of the global economy. It is an engineering challenge; a problem-solving device for people to whom the sight of a wild Pennine hilltop on a clear winter day brings not feelings of transcendence but thoughts about the wasted potential for renewable energy. It is about saving civilisation from the results of its own actions; a desperate attempt to prevent Gaia from hiccupping and wiping out our coffee shops and broadband connections. It is our last hope.

*

I generalise, of course. Environmentalism's chancel is as accommodating as that of socialism, anarchism or conservatism, and just as capable of generating poisonous internal bickering that will last until the death of the sun. Many who call themselves green have little time for the mainstream line I am attacking here. But it is the mainstream line. It is how most people see environmentalism today, and it is how environmentalists allow it to be seen. These are the arguments and the positions that popular environmentalism – now a global force – offers up in its quest for redemption. There are reasons; there are always reasons. But whatever they are, they have led the greens down a dark, litter-strewn dead end street, where the bins overflow, the lightbulbs have blown and the stray dogs are very hungry indeed.

What is to be done about this? Probably nothing. It was perhaps inevitable that a utilitarian society would generate a utilitarian environmentalism, and inevitable too that the greens would not be able to last for long outside the established political bunkers. But for me, now – well, this is no longer mine, that's all. I can't make my peace with people who cannibalise the land in the name of saving it. I can't speak the language of science without a corresponding poetry. I can't speak with a straight face about saving the planet when what I really mean is saving myself from what is coming.

Like all of us, I am a footsoldier of empire. It is the empire of *Homo sapiens sapiens* and it stretches from Tasmania to Baffin Island. Like all empires it is built on expropriation and exploitation, and like all empires it dresses these things up in the language of morality and duty. When we turn wilderness over to agriculture we speak of our duty to feed the poor. When we industrialise the wild places we speak of our duty to stop the climate from changing. When we spear whales we speak of our duty to science. When we raze forests we speak of our duty to develop. We alter the atmospheric makeup of the entire world: half of us pretends it's not happening, the other half immediately starts looking for new machines that will reverse it. This is how empires work, particularly when they have started to decay. Denial, displacement, anger, fear.

The environment is the victim of this empire. But 'the environment' – that distancing word, that empty concept – does not exist. It is the air, the waters, the creatures we make homeless or lifeless in flocks and legions, and it is us too. We are it; we are in it and of it, we make it and live it, we are fruit and soil and tree, and the things done to the roots and the leaves come back to us. We make ourselves slaves to make ourselves free, and when the shackles start to rub we confidently predict the emergence of new, more comfortable designs.

I don't have any answers, if by answers we mean political systems, better machines, means of engineering some grand shift in consciousness. All I have is a personal conviction built on those feelings, those responses, that goes back to the moors of northern England and the rivers of southern Borneo – that something big is being missed. That we are both hollow men and stuffed men, and that we will keep stuffing ourselves until the food runs out and if outside the dining room door we have made a wasteland and called it necessity, then at least we will know we were not to blame, because we are never to blame, because we are the humans.

What am I to do with feelings like these? Useless feelings in a world in which everything must be made useful. Sensibilities in a world of utility. Feelings like this provide no 'solutions'. They build no new eco-homes, remove no carbon from the atmosphere. This is head-in-the-clouds stuff, as relevant to our busy, modern lives as the new moon or the date of Lughnasadh. Easy to ignore, easy to dismiss, like the places that inspire the feelings, like the world outside the bubble, like the people who have seen it, if only in brief flashes beyond the ridge of some dark line of hills.

But this is fine; the dismissal, the platitudes, the brusque moving-on of the grown-ups. It's all fine. I withdraw, you see. I withdraw from the campaigning and the marching, I withdraw from the arguing and the talked-up necessity and all of the false assumptions. I withdraw from the words. I am leaving. I am going to go out walking.

I am leaving on a pilgrimage to find what I left behind in the jungles and by the cold campfires and in the parts of my head and my heart that I have been skirting around because I have been busy fragmenting the world in order to save it; busy believing it is mine to save. I am going to listen to the wind and see what it tells me, or whether it tells me anything at all. You see, it turns out that I have more time than I thought. I will follow the songlines and see what they sing to me and maybe, one day, I might even come back. And if I am very lucky I might bring with me a harvest of fresh tales which I can scatter like apple seeds across this tired and angry continent.

WILLIAM HAAS

Traffic

Before the car door flattened him, the bike messenger swore he'd never drive. Now his Honda Accord idles in stalled traffic. Stitched along a line of brake lights, his car is a single scale on a steel serpent that straddles the horizon and swallows its own tail. As greenhouse heat gathers, freon cools his skin.

Concrete blood has seized the American Uroboros. A final spasm injects into its veins synthetic stone, crushed seashells, and shale. Time passes. The serpent lies silently, scales tough as bark on a petrified fir. No parasites feast on the stone flesh. Bodies trapped behind windshields have long since dissolved.

A vulture circles, drawn not by the stench – there is none – but by the sudden shape, coiled like a firework snake, carbon black and stiff, one vast and legless trunk. Wind shear shapes the sands beneath – ripples, wavelets, dunes of dust.

CHRIS PAK

Stories of the future

'Where are the novels that probe beyond the country house or the city centre? What new form of writing has emerged to challenge civilisation itself?'[1]

This question, thrown down by the Dark Mountain manifesto, suggests an answer from beyond the mainstream of the literary novel. One genre has long offered a literature of debate about the future, an engagement with civilisation in all its technological complexity and with the impulse to find new relations between the human and the non-human. Science fiction, often stereotyped or dismissed, responds to the questions at the heart of the Dark Mountain Project and deserves to be considered in relation to it.

Science fiction is that form of literature which imagines the future in order to better understand the present, employing a distinctive language to engage speculatively yet critically with our contemporary world. Its central concerns are with ideas of progress, civilisation, technology and science, as well as with change, both to our patterns of living and thought. Examining from a number of perspectives the fundamental bases of what it means to live as part of a global civilisation, it offers us ways in which to question the narratives of progress that have driven technological innovation and underpinned industrialism and modern civilisation.

Yes, there are texts that present galactic civilisations built upon the foundations of a technologised culture's colonisation of nature. But science fiction is also a critical mode; writers employ its language to build worlds that model some aspect of our contemporaneity in order to question and critique them. It looks toward the future and attempts to foresee the problems that progress could create, but most importantly it focuses on the present to ask, 'What is this that we are doing to ourselves?'

There are many competing definitions of science fiction, most of which fail to encompass the diversity of theme, style and form allowed for by the mode's conventions and language. Brian Aldiss, science fiction writer and critic, has suggested that the genre can be defined as:

the search for a definition of mankind and his status in the universe which will stand in our advanced but confused state of knowledge (science), and is characteristically cast in the Gothic or post-Gothic mode.[2]

While it is hard to arrive at a satisfactory definition for a mode as fluid as science fiction, Aldiss' attempt has the benefit of highlighting the central theme of the search for a sense of place and meaning in the universe. Instead of the nature of our world, excluded from the realm of culture and the human, science fiction situates us within the greater space of the universe while acknowledging the confused position that we occupy in relation to it. Science tells us, after all, that we are irrevocably a part of nature.

While science fiction has been popularly associated with the myth of the techno-fix, where technological innovation is presented as the solution to social problems, this underlying belief has always existed alongside a more critical approach. From the earliest American pulp science fiction right through to today's Hollywood, there is certainly no shortage of examples of uncritical optimism. Take *Ralph 124c 41+* (serialised by Hugo Gernsback in his magazine *Modern Electrics* in 1911–12) in which the title character takes his love interest on a tour of the metropolis of 2660, a technological civilisation in which a problem such as food shortages caused by overpopulation is addressed by developing more efficient farms – a whole chapter is devoted to details of the innovations that allow this. Complete control and surpassing of the natural is underscored as the great achievement of this civilisation. Its synthetic dairy products 'are far easier to digest, and are more wholesome than the natural product' because they have eliminated 'all of the disease-carrying microbes and bacteria […] which we can control very easily in our plants.'[3]

This future, with all its technological changes, presents no significant social change to match them. *Ralph* embodies a vision of the future as 'an upgraded version of the present' in its brightest form: more technologically advanced, but with growth stable and social dynamics unchanged. In his introduction to the 2000 reprint science fiction writer Jack Williamson writes:

> As an historical document, it shows the vast shift in public temper from Gernsback's easy assumption of a bright technological future to the Cold War's 'balance of terror' and all the apprehensions of our postatomic age.[4]

Such faith in progress would receive significant attrition in the wake of WWII, Hiroshima and Nagasaki, the Cold War, and Vietnam, all of which been the subject of critical response within science fiction. But, as Williamson also notes, 'H.G. Wells, in his great science fiction written at the turn of the century, had foreseen the limits and penalties of progress.'

In *The Time Machine*, published in 1895, an inventor known as 'the Time Traveller' tells of his journey to the far future, where he encounters two species of evolved humans – the decadent Eloi and the subterranean Morlocks, who treat the Eloi as cattle. Civilisation has collapsed. The Time Traveller's dream of a future where class division has been resolved has not come to pass. 'Instead, I saw a real aristocracy, armed with a perfected science and working to a logical conclusion the industrial system of to-day.' He sees the cause of this as a destructive 'triumph over Nature and the fellow-man.'

At the conclusion of the novel, the Time Traveller's remarkable story is given credence by the narrator's discovery of two flowers described by the Time Traveller in his account as from this future. The narrator tells us in the epilogue that the Time Traveller:

> thought but cheerlessly of the Advancement of Mankind, and saw in the growing pile of civilization only a foolish heaping that must inevitably fall back upon and destroy its makers in the end.

The Time Machine's critique of the Victorian faith in social progress made possible by Industrialism dispels the myth that evolution proceeds from 'primitive' to 'superman' and argues instead that civilisation is a rare and brief – precisely because destructive and unsustainable – development within the human organism's existence on Earth. This is made clear when the Time Traveller continues to transport himself into an ever distant future and observes the final periods of life on Earth. In the last of these, the only organisms he sees are indistinct shapes that flop upon their tentacles under a blood red sky.

In another early science fiction text, *Last and First Men* (1930), Olaf Stapledon employs a similar understanding of evolution and civilisation to portray the development of humans from the present through the next two billion years. While these Last Men are superior to the First, it is by no means a direct progression; humanity at several points evolves into organisms that possess no culture, and only infrequently do they develop a significant civilisation. In 'Time Scale 5', humanity's existence is shown to be too insignificant to measure when compared to cosmic time, while a note immediately following the tag 'End of Man' tells us that 'Apart from accidents Earth would still have been habitable.'[5] Significantly, however, Stapledon still envisions humanity's existence as one of struggle from 'savagery towards civilization'[6] and employs myths of the Noble Savage to characterise pastoral figures and present them as a foil to the corruption of civilisation. Despite this, *Last and First Men* destabilises the meaning of humanity and civilisation. Technology and civilisation cannot avail because of human limitations when compared to the sublime vastness of the universe, of nature, of which he forms but a small part.

Early in the Last Man's account of the history of humanity he comments on the First, contemporary humans, explaining that:

> the actual social constitution of his world kept changing so rapidly through increased mastery over physical energy, that his primitive nature could no longer cope with the complexity of his environment. Animals that were fashioned for hunting and fighting in the wild were suddenly called upon to be citizens, and moreover citizens of a world-community.[7]

Here we have the mismatch between urban civilisation, the mastery over the physical world made possible by harnessing increasingly massive potentials of energy, and humanity's fundamental nature as animals subject to traits that have been inescapably built into the human psyche through evolution. The intellectual and physical advantages possessed by the Last Men when compared to the First, despite efforts to design a new species possessing a mode of consciousness suitable to sustaining culture and civilisation, reveal them to still be 'very small, very simple, very little capable of insight.'[8]

Stapledon imagines many gradients of civilisation over this two billion year timescale, many, though not all of whom construct vast urban civilisations. The Fifth Men live in 'an open forest of architecture. Between these great obelisks lay corn-land, park, and wilderness' and they work to redress the destruction of biodiversity caused by their predecessors, the fourth species of humans, by 'creating a whole system of new types, which they set at large in the Wild Continent' set aside from civilisation.[9] It is the third species of human that receives much admiration from the narrator, who is himself a member of the sixteenth and last species of man:

> Suffice it that the upshot was a very remarkable civilization, if such a word can be applied to an order in which agglomerations of architecture

were unknown, clothing was used only when needed for warmth, and
such industrial development as occurred was wholly subordinated to
other activities.[10]

Here we are given a glimpse of a potential 'uncivilised' community.
Industrialism, architecture, and clothing: these symbols of urban society are
subordinated to a desire for the natural. 'But in this race the interest in live
things, which characterized the whole species, was dominant before indus-
trialism began.' The narrator does not idealise this relationship but notes that
it is their desire to own living things that confers status. They have highly
developed and 'very exact principles of aesthetic excellence in their control of
living forms.' Though admirable for their considered application of technol-
ogy, it is by exerting mastery over nature that this civilisation is able to define
itself and escape the evolutionary influence of social traits at odds with civili-
sation as we understand the term.

Gernsback, Wells and Stapledon established many of the narratives that
science fiction would continually engage with throughout the domination of
the market by American pulp magazines. Although Stapledon was largely
unaware of science fiction and Wells precedes the official establishment of
the genre, both of these British writers were clearly writing science fiction,
and both were eagerly read by its readers. Wells himself was reprinted by
Gernsback in the early issues of *Amazing Stories*. While much science fiction
argued for the benefits of increasing levels of technology and a mastery over
the physical world, there were other voices arguing against an unquestioning
faith in progress. The 'gadgetry' or 'gosh-wow' strand of science fiction –
popular in the pulps in the 1930–1960 period and embodied by Gernsback's
Ralph – was balanced, from the 1960s, by a 'New Wave' of science fiction,
informed by counter-cultural politics, the exploration of the 'soft sciences' and
an increasing critical engagement with the established myths of a 'Western'
culture. Other voices have explored the limits to civilisation and the underly-
ing myths of colonialism that inform them. This division into pre- and post-
1960s blocs should not be taken too far; these dynamics were already at work
in much science fiction of the pulp age. But, with the 1960s generation of
writers, there is a discernable recognition of the untapped potential of science
fiction in challenging the assumption of unremitting progress, and an explicit
shift in politics that moves toward inclusiveness. More recently it has become
clear that modern environmental narratives have been anticipated by science

fiction and that a propensity to engage with human consciousness and its place in the universe, and on Earth, have long been central to the literature.

A key voice in this shift has been that of Ursula Le Guin. Her work is characterised by a focus on nature as a colonised other. While this could be identified as one of the central issues of her science fiction, Le Guin is also interested in other forms of otherness, whether that is racial, sexual or class-based. In fact, she identifies an underlying colonialist impulse as responsible for oppression at all these levels. The genre's special relationship with imagining otherness of many fantastic orders allows it to approach this constellation from an apparently oblique angle, but one that models the machinations of civilisation from perspectives alternative to the dominant representations of civilisation and progress.

Le Guin's 1972 novel, *The Word for World is Forest*, is influenced by the events of the Vietnam War. Athshe, a forested world inhabited by the 'uncivilised' Athsheans is invaded by colonialists from Earth. They wilfully misunderstand or ignore the natives, whom they refer to derogatorily as 'Creechies'. Even Lyubov, alone in his sympathy for what he sees as pastoral and defenceless Athsheans, is unable to fully appreciate them as a people who can respond violently to aggression and so is killed when Selver leads the other Athsheans on a raid of the invader's camp. Davidson, a representative of the worst kind of imperialist vision, hunts the Athsheans as he would animals on Earth, if there were any animals left to hunt. They enslave the population and justify their actions by employing the historically resonant argument that 'this isn't slavery, Ok baby. Slaves are humans. When you raise cows, you call that slavery?'[11] As forests no longer grow on their future Earth, those of Athshe represent a fortune in lumber, even when the prohibitive costs of transportation are factored into their calculations. It is the exploitation of the world's resources that is the greatest single factor behind colonialism, which is in turn driven by the demands of an expanding urban civilisation driven by the myth of progress.

The Athsheans are contrasted with the colonists through a series of living styles influenced by Tao, Native American belief, a greater involvement of women in the governance of their towns and a mode of consciousness drawn from Aboriginal Dreamtime, which conditions every aspect of their existence. 'Selver is a god', but one in the sense used by the Athshean's in the everyday speech of the 'Women's Tongue' (*Sha-ab*), drawn from the 'Men's Tongue' and which 'were not only two-syllabled but two-sided.'

Sha'ab meant god, or numinous entity, or powerful being; it also meant something quite different [...] translator.

[...] 'Might he then be one who could translate into waking life the central experience of vision: one serving as a link between the two realities, considered by the Athsheans as equal, the dream-time and the world-time, whose connections, though vital, are obscure. A link: one who could speak aloud the perceptions of the subconscious. To 'speak' that tongue is to act. To do a new thing. To change or to be changed, radically, from the root. For the root is the dream.[12]

It is to the root of action, to belief, that the conflict of the text is taken. In order to overcome the colonists the once peaceful Athsheans must turn the violence they have learned against their teachers. By such actions the inhabitants are able to regain their freedom and prevent the deforestation of Athshe but, tragically, they are also irrevocably changed. Selver confronts his counterpart, Davidson, at the climax of the story when they have won their freedom and tells him that:

we are gods. [...] We bring each other such gifts as gods bring. You gave me a gift, the killing of one's kind, murder. Now, as well as I can, I give you my people's gift, which is not killing.[13]

In *Always Coming Home* (1985) Le Guin continues her examination of alternative belief systems and the lifestyles they inform. The novel itself is a bricolage of songs, stories, poems, notes from the narrator Pandora and an extended narrative told by Stone Telling, a member of the people called Kesh. In 'A First Note' the author tells us that 'The people in this book might be going to have lived a long, long time from now in Northern California.'[14] In 'Towards an Archaeology of the Future', the narrator, whose identity dovetails with that of the voice of the author-narrator, tells of the difficulties she faces when attempting to build a possible future and to give a voice to a culture who 'owned their Valley very lightly, with easy hands.'[15] The difficulty of creating a space where the voices of a possible future culture could make itself heard is not trivial. Nevertheless the author makes it clear that 'the difficulty of translation from a language that doesn't yet exist is considerable, but there's no need to exaggerate it. The past, after all, can be quite as obscure as the future (*Always* ix).'[16] Imagining a future that presents alternatives to urban civilisation can and should be done.

The people of Kesh are strongly influenced by Native American culture. Many of the pieces collected by Pandora are based on mythology drawn from a tradition of oral storytelling. Because of this she finds it difficult, in her capacity as anthropologist, to recover their history, remarking 'I don't know how to translate 'culture' into his language more exactly, and the word 'civilisation', of course, won't do at all.' Part of the problem is a difference in the way they understand time itself, and like the Dreamtime of *The Word for World is Forest*, this difference conditions their attitude to living. Pandora explains that:

> He doesn't perceive time as a direction, let alone a progress, but as a landscape in which one may go any number of directions, or nowhere. He spatialises time; it is not an arrow, nor a river, but a house, the house he lives in.[17]

To the people of Kesh it is not a self-evident truth that they have progressed since their arrival in Northern California. Implicit in this description is the point that people can choose from a multiplicity of possibilities how they wish to change the way in which they live in the world. This world is itself considered a home, not a field for the exploitation of resources, and so there is attached to this worldview a sense of responsibility to care for it. This is coupled with the fact that 'people' in this language includes animals, plants, dreams, rocks, etc.' We are never told where Pandora comes from but there are hints that she is a contemporary of the reader's. There are more hints that the civilisations we might have expected of the future have fallen due to a complex of factors – war, the depletion of resources, radioactivity and chemical poisoning – though this is never made clear. What is emphasised is that they have had a lasting effect on the people of the future as 'genetic (chromosomal) damage caused by long-lasting toxic or radioactive wastes or residues of the military-industrial era' are major problems in the Valley.[18] When caring for their home the Kesh take into account their impact on all of the people of the Valley.

Stone Telling recounts her experiences as a girl whose estranged father is a general of the Condor people. She meets him for the first time when young and her first impression of him is as someone 'entirely different from the men in the camp. He spoke Kesh, and lived in a household, and was a daughter's father.'[19] He has come to Kesh to establish more efficient transportation networks to enable the Condor to travel south, much against the locals' wishes.

When he returns at a later time he takes Stone Telling back to the city of the Condor to live, allowing her to compare their lifestyle with those of the Valley people. The Condor's attempts to establish these transportation networks are only a prelude to war:

> The Condor people seem to have been unusually self-isolated; their form of communication with other peoples was through aggression, domination, exploitation, and enforced acculturation. In this respect they were at a distinct disadvantage among the introverted but cooperative peoples native to the region.[20]

Against the possibility of a future culture is one that continues many of the traits of modern civilised 'Western' ones. The Condor display all the traits of an exploitative culture that views all otherness as blank space to be colonised and are only prevented from developing the technological infrastructure to support globalised conquest by 'the absence of the worldwide technological web, the 'technological ecosystem,' of the Industrial Age, and on a planet almost depleted of many of the fossil fuels and other materials from which the Industrial Age made itself.' In comparison to the people of the Valley, industrial civilisations are predicated on a series of exploitative relationships that cannot be sustained.

The Kesh are not a primitivist society, however. Advanced technology does exist, but control over it has been ceded to the cybernetic 'City of Mind'. In the language of the Valley people, 'city' (*Kach*) is not a common word and is only used as a compound in *tavkach*, City of Man, and *yaivkach*, City of Mind. In regards to the City of Mind the cybernetic intelligences concern themselves with 'the collection, storage, and collation of data' which is freely accessible to anyone who seeks it. Their goal is 'conscious, self-directed evolution', and 'this evolution proceeded consistently in the direct linear mode.'[21] This is not a concession to the human myth of progress. The City of Mind concerns itself with the world only as an object of study, not as a thing to be interfered with. Technology as a tool of humanity is shown to be another other with its own existence separate from the human world.

The narrator's research points toward the fact that the City of Mind see humans as 'a primitive ancestor, or divergent and retarded kindred, left far behind in the March of Mind' but, because they are not human and possess their own language, TOK, and so their own cognitive faculties, such an explanation is limited by the narrator's attempt to translate their stance into something intelligible to the reader. 'There would of course be no ethical or emotional colour in such an assumption of evolutionary superiority' because the City of Mind quite simply does not care about the direction human affairs take. Technology will not save or destroy human societies – that privilege is reserved for themselves.[22]

The 'City of Man', like that of Mind, is 'outside the world', 'set apart from the community and continuity of human/animal/earthly existence.'[23] The phrase translates as Civilisation and History. The central motif of the hinge, recurring in Kesh architecture and town planning, art and myth, centres around the gap between living inside the world as the Kesh do now, and living outside of it, as does the City of Mind and Man. Two stories given to Pandora, 'The Hole in the Air' and 'Big Man and Little Man' deal with the problem of the hinge between worlds. Both are told in the Kesh style, which draws significantly from a blend of Native American iconography and the science fiction imagining of other possible worlds. They are a pair that tell of the crossing from both perspectives, from within to without and vice versa.

Those outside the world live in a nightmare vision of an urban civilisation populated by people whose heads face backwards and who go about blind to the way in which they poison themselves and the world around them, preoccupied as they are with killing and war. In 'The Hole in the Air' a Kesh man, sick from the poisoned food and pollution outside the world attempts to make his way back into the mountains to find a way to live in the world again, but a new dam has flooded his valley and the place where he found the hole in the air. He can only escape by letting the buzzards, who tell him they are dying of hunger, eat his corpse, whereupon he awakes back in the world again and soon dies of 'grief and poison'.[24]

'Big Man and Little Man' is a Kesh originary myth. Big Man lives outside the world and was 'so big that he filled up the entire world outside the world.' He is like the backward headed people who 'had their heads on wrong'. Failing to find a way to possess the inside world either by getting 'it pregnant with himself' or by eating it he creates Little Man and a mock woman to assuage his fear and populate the inside world. But, the woman not being real, they can only make copies of Little Man. His fear does not diminish and so 'he killed whatever he was afraid of', destroying the landscape and living things. 'Everything was dying ten, everybody was poisoned. The clouds were poison' and the scent of carrion drives Big Man further from the world. But his leaving makes more space where carrion eaters, the fly and coyote, condor, buzzard, vulture and others, all of which have a mythic resonance for the

Kesh, come inside the world where they made food of the dying world. 'There were some human people along with them' who 'were so hungry they weren't afraid to eat carrion with the buzzard and dung with the dogs' and so were able to live inside the world. Pandora comments that 'these figures of lore and superstition seem to have been the literalisation of a metaphor' and contextualises the myths with reference to the urban civilisation that preceded them in California. She suggests that the myth is a coded reference to:

> The permanent desolation of vast regions through release of radioactive or poisonous substances, the permanent genetic impairment from which they suffered most directly in the form of sterility, stillbirth, and congenital disease.[25]

The Kesh would not see these consequences of civilisation as unintended side effects of a developing industry or as accidents. As Pandora explains, 'Accidents happened *to* people, but what people *did* they were responsible for.' While *Always Coming Home* is only partly 'the story of a people who believed, for a long time, that their actions did not have consequences'[26] it is also the story of how some people, at one time, but not for all time, managed to make a home of this world by taking responsibility for their own actions and being mindful of all the people, in the Kesh sense of the word, and of their world seen as a home.

Science fiction, then, is a literature of debate about the future, engaging with civilisation in all its technological complexity and the repercussions this has for a changing social paradigm. At its heart it attempts to open up new ways of thinking about the world by building alternatives and by examining the influence of the intrinsic values that underlie civilisation and culture.

As a body of literature science fiction is a dialogue that examines and redraws the imaginative spaces that we populate with stories of the future in order to provide meaning to our present action. Le Guin, in particular, builds an alternative to the imagined futures of Wells, Stapledon and Gernsback that in some places extend the critique of civilisation found in the former two and opposes the technological optimism of the latter. Here we find a literature which concerns itself with the dangerous but necessary freedom to imagine alternatives to the dark future to which, if they go unexamined, the myths of civilisation may lead.

References

1. Paul Kingsnorth & Dougald Hine, *Uncivilisation: The Dark Mountain Manifesto* (2009)

2. Brian Aldiss, *Trillion Year Spree* (London: House of Stratus, 2001)

3. Hugo Gernsback, *Ralph 124C 41+: A Romance of the Year 2660* (Lincoln: University of Nebraska Press, 2000) pp.140–1

4. Ibid, p.xi

5. Olaf Stapledon, *Last and First Men: A Story of the Near and Far Future* (Middlesex: Penguin, 1930) p.285

6. Ibid, p.21

7. Ibid, p.22

8. Ibid, p.327

9. Ibid, pp.227–8

10. Ibid, p.201

11. Ursula K Le Guin, *The Word for World is Forest* (New York: Berkley Medallion Books, 1972) p.10

12. Ibid, pp.105–6

13. Ibid, p.160

14. Ursula K Le Guin, *Always Coming Home* (Toronto: Bantam Books, 1985) p.ix

15. Ibid, pp.4–5

16. Ibid, p.ix

17. Ibid, p.181

18. Ibid, p.511

19. Ibid, p.32

20. Ibid, p.404

21. Ibid, pp.156–7

22. Ibid, p.159

23. Ibid, p.160

24. Ibid, p.164

25. Ibid, pp.165–7

26. Kingsnorth & Hine, op.cit., p.3

TONY WALTON

In Time of Pestilence

In Time of Pestilence, in a time
of vile collaboration and the flat
incineration of all false hopes
with all false papers, even then there are more
things to admire in a man than to despise,
as Camus well knew, keeping a clean
sheet to the final whistle, like a Long Man
between the Sticks, standing Giant-tall and
all a-splendour in the whirling Door of
Seasons Turning and old realities
overturning in their infinite
alternating possibilities.
At times like these, better take stock, and best
to take a strong shot of whatever works
for you, stiffen the sinew, burnish the
pride, the long ride awaits us. And we do
not go alone: Love rides alongside singing
songs of love; Truth brings up the rear, making
sure all things are clear (including the coast)
and well understood; while Beauty like a
lamb in Spring, like any young and living
thing, dances loose-limbed and proudly prancing
up ahead. What need of false gods? What need
for Codes of Hate and punishments most dreadful?
In a Time of Plague, as Defoe would know,
you know your foes from your friendly faces;
you know just how far you can go, and how
far they will, if they can. In a Time of
Plague it's every man-jack for hisself
'n Divil take the hinder. It would not

from such benchmarking be a blinder
to be kinder than that: a reminder
that your bill of kindness is well overdue
and will be with you shortly. You take out
what you put in, what goes around comes
around and there's still no such thing as a
free lunch, much less a free dinner.
Loving-kindness grows consistently thinner,
must be anorexic, poor thing, the
bulimics splutter, puking in the gutter
and falling in: wouldn't know where to look
for stars or any other fucking item,
worramean? More to admire than despise?
Who's counting? Yet it would be a close accounting,
a neck-and-neck contest, all things roughly
considered. What use are possession stats,
anyroad? The point is, on paper,
Admirable Qualities field the far
stronger team; they play deeper at the back
and far more incisively up front – still,
it's a funny old game, and every dog
has his dog-day starring role, if he lives
that long. And no, Defoe and Camus were
never wrong: the race does go to the strong,
but the victor's cup overflows with
bitter gall and all the curses of the Legions of the
Dispossessed; who will have best yet, just wait
and see: their pain deepens and there is no
help for them, no cure offered. In a Time
of Pestilence, the lepers forsake the
colony and hit the streets and take over:
they eat street sellers of *Big Issue*
using the free paper as a tissue
to wipe their chops. They rampage through the smart shops
and swanky boutiques, all their bits falling off:
it certainly clears the traffic. The cops
won't lay a finger on them. And how would
L'Etranger deal with this invasion?

What mad Raskolnikov Moment exploding
all the rage on a page inside his head,
where the ink is bright red and the pen dipped
in blood: mightier than the sword in deed.
What eugenic cull could cut a swathe wide
enough and deep, for long enough and far
enough, to rid the Earth of this scum-of-
the-earth? Their birth should be outlawed, their people
sterilised or spared only under close
licence. You have No Idea how bad it is
out there in the no-hope dumplands, where
sunlight on the brutal concrete towers
is more tragic than the rain; where grass cries
in its green chains unheard in the sea of
litter and broken machines. What's that sound?
The engagement of magazines, and
flicking-off the safety catch. It's a match
made in heaven: their gun-mentality
rapacity and our common vulnerability.
We have of course the ability
to do something about it, but doubt we
have the moral strength, fraught with our relativist
nightmare: nothing is good, nothing is best,
nothing is right anymore, everything
best is gone, for good, and things make less and
less sense, as though Meaning is an enemy,
Perception a threat. Yet we must love
them, all our moron sisters and all
our thug brothers: the Christians would, or so
they say; and that's another (important)
detail they got (absolutely) right.
In Time of Pestilence – a plague on all
our houses – Innocence flounders, Concord
cracks and One Accord fragments and splinters.
We're backs-to-the-wall and in trouble, boys,
our bubble, boys, is about to burst. What is
the worst that could happen? We may be about
to find out. Give me a call, give me a

shout, any time; speak out and speak clearly:
it's not yet a crime, depending what you say.
But who can condemn what they can't under-
stand? And who can make sense of a Whirling
Dervish? Or pin down the selling-point of
the article in a meteor shower
of streaming particles, and fields of gold
where no bodies go, but where their energy
is, now & always. In Times of Plague and
Pestilence, we do well to reflect
mirrored alternatives, do better to find
the wormhole flume to the bright constellations
and the far-shining galaxies – all that
and rather more through the Whirling Doorway,
over the dancing threshold, across the
Janus step: and – here comes another one
not altogether unlike the other one,
and yet … and yet: we ain't seen nothin' yet.

DOUGALD HINE

Death and the Mountain

John Berger's enduring sense of hope

'The way I go is the way back to see the future.'
Jitka Hanzlová

'How is it I'm alive?
I'll tell you I'm alive because there's a temporary shortage of death.'
A Palestinian[1]

He is a novelist, an art critic, an essayist, a storyteller, but when I picture him with the tools of his trade, it is holding a scythe.

There are two reasons for this. No recent writer in English has been more intimately acquainted with death. And each year, he pays a part of his rent by helping with the haymaking in the field above his house. To grasp the significance of John Berger's work – in relation to literature and to the present situation of the world – both of these facts are essential.

At the centre of his work stands the decision, taken at the height of his career, to settle in the mountains of the Haute Savoie, in a valley too steep for mechanical farming and therefore among the last enclaves of peasant life in western Europe. Almost four decades later, he is still there. Last year, he agreed to donate his archive to the British Library, on the condition that its head of modern manuscripts should lend a hand with the harvest during his visit.

Berger's achievement has been to ground himself within that way of living, an experience which transformed his writing, while remaining a globally-engaged intellectual. More than that, it is the perspective given by that grounding which explains his continuing relevance, his ability to see and name things which other commentators take for granted.

In a particular sense, he embodies the 'Uncivilised writing' called for by the Dark Mountain manifesto. The concept of civilisation is entangled to its roots with the experience of cities. The writing which this project seeks and celebrates is 'uncivilised' not least in the sense that it comes from or goes beyond the city limits: the physical, psychological and political boundaries within which the illusion of humanity's separation from and control over 'nature' can be sustained.

Such writing enters into negotiation with the non-human world on terms which may seem outlandish; it is hospitable to possibilities which civilised philosophy would hardly entertain. And it is in this spirit that I suggest we take the other theme in Berger's writing which I want to address: his sense of the presence of the dead. Fictional as many of them clearly are, his accounts of encounters with the dead – as individuals and collectively – amount to something closer to an uncivilised metaphysics than a literary conceit.

Yet there is nothing fey about this metaphysics. To the extent that philosophical positions emerge from Berger's work, they do so tested pragmatically against the harshness of human experience: not only the tough lives of Savoyard peasants, but those of migrant workers, prisoners, political dissidents, Palestinian families. To list the people he writes about in such categories is misleading, for the relentless specificity of his gaze seldom allows such generalisations. The cumulative effect of his writing, though – and of the relationships from which it emerges – is to test what can be believed against what must be endured.

He would have little time, I am sure, for much of the literature of collapse, fact or fiction, because almost without exception it begins by overlooking the reality of life for most people in the world today, for whom there is little to collapse and who, nevertheless, go on finding ways to make today liveable and get through to tomorrow. Yet, in what I have called his testing of what can be believed, I suspect there is more insight into what will endure when (or where) the certainties of our way of living fail us.

1. From 'Civilisation' to the mountains

When I came here I was mostly with the old peasants, because the younger ones had gone, and they became my teachers. It was like my university, because I didn't go to university. I learnt to tap a scythe, and I learnt a whole constellation of sense and value about life.[2]

To understand the question posed by his decision to settle in the Haute Savoie, it is necessary to know something of Berger's life before that relocation, his politics and his public profile.

His first novel, *A Painter of Our Time* (1958) was withdrawn by its British publishers under pressure from the Congress for Cultural Freedom, an anti-communist lobby group backed by the CIA. His early essays, written as art critic at the *New Statesman*, were collected under the title *Permanent Red* (1960), a statement of political constancy borne out by a piece in his most recent collection *Hold Everything Dear* (2007).

> Somebody enquires: are you still a Marxist? Never before has the devastation caused by the pursuit of profit, as defined by capitalism, been more extensive than today. Almost everybody knows this. How then is it possible not to heed Marx who prophesied and analysed the devastation … ? Yes, I'm still amongst other things a Marxist.[3]

In 1972, he won the Booker Prize for his fourth novel, *G*. He used the platform to castigate Booker-McConnell for the sources of its wealth in the Caribbean sugar trade and gave half his prize money to the Black Panthers as an act of reparation. (The Panther activist who accompanied Berger to the award ceremony was alarmed by his intensity. 'Keep it cool, man,' he whispered, 'keep it cool.')

The same year, he made a television series which turned that same articulate anger on establishment narratives of art history. *Ways of Seeing* was an attack on Kenneth Clark's *Civilisation* (1969), also produced by the BBC. Clark had offered a grand tour of the Western tradition, introduced from the study of his country house, interspersed with globe-trotting location sequences which would become the template for big-budget documentary series. By contrast, Berger stands against a blue-screen in a studio, and this is used not to transport him to any pre-filmed backdrop, but to place the mechanics of television in shot, questioning the ways in which it can be used to lead an audience.

His subject is the mystification of art, the 'meaningless generalisations' by which professional critics deflect attention from the content of a painting and the questions it might open up about the world. His delivery is intense, but also playful, driven by curiosity. You have the sense of witnessing thought in progress, rather than the presentation of a completed worldview. He ends the first episode by warning the viewer to treat his arguments, too, with scepticism.

The series was repeated twice that year on BBC2 and the accompanying book became required reading for a generation of art school undergraduates. In an age when there were three channels to choose between, its presenter had become, if not a household name, at least a recognisable face for a significant part of the viewing public.

So the Berger who settled in the Haute Savoie was a public figure, an acclaimed and controversial writer, an intellectual of the first rank – in as much as such statements can ever be meaningful. When such a figure leaves the city for life in a remote village, this invites questions. What is he going in search of? Or trying to escape from?

In this case, there are facts and statements on the record which provide answers, but I suggest we approach these slowly, with care. What we are after is subtler than a statement of intent or a record of circumstances.

To begin with, we can rule out certain familiar explanations. A Romantic imagination may be drawn to an idealised notion of rural life, but the experiments in self-sufficiency which follow seldom survive more than a couple of growing seasons. Nor does Berger fit the type of the recluse, retreating from the uncomfortable gaze of critics and readers. Those who visit report a household characterised by its broad hospitality: the novelist Geoff Dyer recalls sitting at dinner between the local plumber and Henri Cartier Bresson.

If Berger's move to the Haute Savoie was a search for anything, I would say he was seeking a deeper understanding of hope. Two experiences, in particular, make sense of this: one common among his peers, the other quite unusual – yet, from a global perspective, altogether more widespread.

The first is the historical disappointment of the 1960s.

> In 1968, hopes, nurtured more or less underground for years,
> were born in several places in the world and given their names:
> and in the same year, these hopes were categorically defeated.
> This became clearer in retrospect. At the time many of us tried
> to shield ourselves from the harshness of the truth.[4]

That defeat in its different forms, political and cultural, echoes across the writing of a generation: a great lost love, whose absence exerts a physical force upon the course of their lives and work, with utterly different results. To feel the range of that experience, the extent to which it embraced individuals and movements which had perhaps no more common ground than a sense of possibility – and then of the loss of that possibility – we might put Berger's reflections alongside those of Hunter S. Thompson.

> Strange memories on this nervous night in Las Vegas. Five years later? Six? It seems like a lifetime, or at least a Main Era – the kind of peak that never comes again. San Francisco in the middle sixties was a very special time and place to be a part of …
>
> There was a fantastic universal sense that whatever we were doing was *right*, that we were winning … we were riding the crest of a high and beautiful wave …
>
> So now, less than five years later, you can go up on a steep hill in Las Vegas and look West, and with the right kind of eyes you can almost *see* the high-water mark – that place where the wave finally broke and rolled back.[5]

Plenty of intellectual and literary careers of the late-twentieth century were shaped by the attempt to make sense of that high-water mark, to come to terms with – to find ways of speaking and thinking about – the hopes that failed, whether by renarrating the stories of those events, or deconstructing the possibility of hope itself.

Few writers have engaged more directly in this process of coming to terms than Berger, and some might find here another explanation for his relocation: a retreat, not from public attention, but from history and its disappointments. What is missing from such an explanation, however, is the other set of hopes whose disappointment shaped the development of Berger's thinking and led him to the situation of the peasant village.

Having given half his Booker Prize money to the Black Panthers, Berger used the remainder to fund a study of the experience of migrant workers. The book which resulted from this, *A Seventh Man*, is one of four such collaborations with the documentary photographer Jean Mohr. In these works, words and images meet on equal terms, taking turns to present the stories of their subjects.

In the case of *A Seventh Man*, photography is as much subject as medium. It is where this 'story of a migrant worker in Europe' begins.

He looks for the photo among the over-handled papers, stuffed in his jacket. He finds it. In handing it over, he imprints his thumb on it. Almost deliberately, as a gesture of possession. A woman or perhaps a child. The photo defines an absence. Even if it is ten years old it makes no difference. It holds open, preserves the empty space which the sitter's presence will, hopefully, one day fill again.[6]

Photos, too, are among the items brought back to the village by those who return as 'heroes', whose stories inspire a younger man with thoughts of the city.

He has talked with them. They take him aside as though inviting him into their conspiracy. They hint that there are secrets which can only be divulged and discussed with those who have also been there. One such secret concerns women. (They show him photographs in colour of naked women but they will not say who they are ...)

Whilst listening, he visualizes himself entering their conspiracy. Then he will learn the secrets. And he will come back having achieved even more than they, for he is capable of working harder, of being shrewder and of saving more quickly than any of them.[7]

This leap of the imagination, this conspiracy of hope is – at the personal level, the level of experience – what brings the worker to the city. At the same time, he is brought there by the workings of a world economic system, and the book is an attempt to hold both of these perspectives in view.

For the workers Berger and Mohr meet in Geneva, Stuttgart, Vienna, the reality of life in the city is hellish, a sentence to be served, before the longed for return. Yet even this will be incomplete.

The final return is mythic. It gives meaning to what might otherwise be meaningless ... But it is also mythic in the sense that, as imagined, it never happens. There is no final return.

Because the village has scarcely changed since he left, there is still no livelihood there for him. When he carries out one of his plans, he will become the victim of the same economic stagnation which first forced him to leave.[8]

The stories of the migrant workers are quite different from those of the 1960s radicals; the pattern of hope and its defeat both more and less final. (The book ends with a dialogue between a returned worker and his younger cousin, as the cycle begins again.) Yet if Berger's reflections on hope and its defeats take a different path to his contemporaries, the experience of *A Seventh Man* may explain why.

What can be said for sure is that it was Berger's research with migrant workers which led him to leave the city. The decision was driven by the same engaged curiosity that runs throughout his work:

> ... meeting these men, I began to understand that the majority of them were the sons of peasants. Now certain things about their lives I could imagine as a writer: the city's impact, the solitude. But I couldn't imagine what they had left behind. What were the peasant's values, his view of his own destiny... ?
>
> So it was then I think that I made the decision: I wanted to see if I could write about peasants. Write about what mattered to them. And to write about them in this way – to understand their experience of their world – I'd have to live among them.

To live among them was not simply a matter of location – a rustic farmhouse with a picturesque view – but of participation in the life of the community, which meant its work.

> To a peasant, when an outsider wants to come and to talk, he usually wants to take something, exploit him ... But if you are, as I was, prepared to get dirty with them, clean stables and work the fields and so on – and do these things ludicrously badly, so that they are master and you the idiot – if you can do this, the distance can be overcome, a closeness felt. [10]

It was not only in the fields that Berger became aware of his ignorance, but in his writing. The novel which he had intended to write did not work: the technique of the novel itself proved unable to accommodate the experience of the people whose stories he wanted to tell.

In the peasant village, money plays little role day to day: work is done, needs are met, use value created, entertainment made, within a dense fabric of relationships, habits and practices. There is nothing utopian about this – to be a peasant, as Berger reminds us, means an 'almost unimaginable burden of labour' and the obligation to meet a master's demands '*before* the basic needs of his family'[11] – but nor does it mean the same thing as being without money in a city. The novel, with its best and worst of times, belongs to the age of cities and to the possibilities, the choices and risks of a milieu in which money means everything. These choices and their consequences shape its twists and turns, in a way which is alien to the experience of the village.

> The choices a peasant actually makes are largely ones he is forced to make – choices of reaction. Something happens suddenly, you're up against it, what do you do?[12]

For the Booker prize-winning novelist, it was necessary to begin again, to find a new way of telling. If the books which Berger has written since have often been published as novels, this says as much about the publishing industry as about his relationship to the novel as a form. He is more likely to speak of himself as a storyteller, and of a village as a place that tells stories.

This new way of writing emerges in *Pig Earth* (1979), the first of three books which explore – through stories, essays and poems – the movement from peasant society to the city. Early in the book, he describes the role of storytelling in the fabric of a working village. Stories are told differently, with a certain tolerance, since they inevitably involve those 'with whom the story-teller and listener are going to go on living'.

> Very few stories are narrated either to idealise or condemn; rather they testify to the always slightly surprising range of the possible. Although concerned with everyday events, they are mystery stories. How is it that C . . . , who is so punctilious in his work, overturned his hay-cart? How is it that L . . . is able to fleece her lover J . . . of everything, and how is it that J . . . , who normally gives nothing away to anybody, allows himself to be fleeced?[13]

This earthy sense of the mysterious may be part of the 'constellation of sense and value about life' which Berger says he learned from the old peasants. It is a theme which comes up in his essay, 'A Story for Aesop', when contrasting the contemporary novel with the attitude of the storyteller.

> Everything he has seen contributes to his sense of the enigma
> of life: for this enigma he finds partial answers – each story he
> tells is one – yet each answer, each story, uncovers another
> question, and so he is continually failing and this failure main-
> tains his curiosity. Without mystery, without curiosity and
> without the form imposed by a partial answer, there can be no
> stories – only confessions, communiqués, memories and frag-
> ments of autobiographical fantasy which for the moment pass
> as novels.[14]

In another essay, he writes about the 'traditional realism' of storytelling
culture as having something in common with science.

> Assuming a fund of empirical knowledge and experience, it
> poses the riddle of the unknown. How is it that...? Unlike
> science it can live without the answer. But its experience is too
> great to allow it to ignore the question.[15]

For Hamlet – and, surely, for Shakespeare himself – there were 'more things
in heaven and earth ... than are dreamt of in our philosophy.'[16] The history of
the seventeenth and eighteenth centuries is one of the massive expansion of
knowledge through science – or 'natural philosophy', to use the language of
the time. Yet it is also a history of contraction: the contraction of 'reality' to that
which can be bounded within the nutshell of the scientific worldview.
Hamlet's position, that the world is fundamentally mysterious, ceases to be
intellectually respectable. Mystery has become a territory to be colonised and
brought into the light. That this is possible is not a fact which science estab-
lished, but a belief system with which it has been entangled.

    In this sense, Berger's storytelling epistemology – these ways of knowing
which can live without the answer, but cannot ignore the experience – may be
open to terrain which is shut to the classically modern approaches to reality.
It is with this possibility in mind that I invite you to approach the most mys-
terious aspect of Berger's later writing: his earthy sense of the presence of the
dead.

2. Seeing the Dead

> Until the dehumanisation of society by capitalism, all the
> living awaited the experience of the dead. It was their ultimate
> future. By themselves the living were incomplete. Thus living
> and dead were interdependent. Always. Only a uniquely mod-
> ern form of egotism has broken this interdependence. With
> disastrous results for the living, who now think of the dead as
> *eliminated.*[17]

> Often when I shut my eyes, faces appear before me ... They
> belong to the past. The certainty with which I know this has
> nothing to do with their clothes or the 'style' of their faces.
> They belong to the past because they are the dead, and I know
> this by the way they look at me. They look at me with some-
> thing approaching recognition.[18]

In the first episode of *Ways of Seeing*, Berger contrasts the straightforward-
ness with which a group of schoolchildren talk about what they see in a paint-
ing with the technical language and vague generalisations of professional art
historians. The latter, he suggests, seem intent on masking the images out of
fear of their directness, of the questions they might prompt.

Were we to enter a classroom or seminar in which Berger's later writings
are under scrutiny, I suspect we would find a similar evasion going on. The
situation is hypothetical – I do not know whether anyone is teaching these
texts in English Literature departments – but I do know that, within the
bounds of civilised literary criticism, there is no framework for engaging with
the questions which arise if we take them seriously. Grown-ups are not meant
to see dead people and, if they insist that they do, this is likely to be patholo-
gised.

Poets are a special case: the poetic license is a day pass from the asylum.
Yeats is allowed to be silly, because poetry is not required to make sense. And
to the extent that Berger's writing about the dead is discussed, there is an
attempt to qualify it as poetry. 'The first eleven parts of this essay on the dead
are purely lyrical,' writes Ron Slate of 'Twelve theses on the economy of the
dead.'[19] (The final part is sectioned off, presumably because 'the dehumani-
sation of society by capitalism' is hardly a lyric theme.)

Part of the problem is that our culture lacks a developed discourse about
metaphysics. We still have religion, but in Europe it has been privatised, while

in America – where it persists in a public form – it has been largely bastardised into pseudo-science by those who mistake Genesis for a physics and biology textbook. And so, if I talk about the seriousness of Berger's sense of the dead, this will be misheard: people will think I mean the kind of para-scientific assertions about communication with the dead made by Spiritualism. What characterises such assertions, however, is their claim to direct knowledge: it is in this sense that they mimic science, posing as the colonisation of the unknown. What Berger has to say about the dead is a cohabitation with mystery, not an attempt to enclose or eliminate it. It rests on two assumptions: that the set of things which exist is larger than the set of things which may be talked about directly; and that things which may not be talked about directly, may nonetheless be approached indirectly.

Let us step back for a moment, onto easier ground. John Berger writes about death, again and again. There are essays on the deaths of his friend and mentor Ernst Fischer, his neighbours François, Georges and Amélie, the poet Mayakovsky, the sculptor Zadkine; on a photograph of the corpse of Che Guevara; on drawing his father's body in its coffin and on his final conversations with his mother. These may be personal accounts, but they are not the occasional pieces which many writers offer in tribute to loved ones; rather, they contain the heart of his thinking.

'The day before yesterday a friend of mine killed himself by blowing his brains out,' begins a piece in which he goes on to write about Gabriel Garcia Marquez's *Chronicle of a Death Foretold*. It is here that he first voices the idea of storytellers as 'Death's secretaries,' death as the organising principle which makes sense of a life. Most stories, he says, begin with a death, and that is true of his own fiction. His most beautiful novel, *To the Wedding* (1995), is a love story in which a young woman learns that she is going to die, turns away her lover, only for him – slowly – to convince her that her coming death does not cancel out their love. The characters of the *Into their Labours* series, navigating the survival of peasant society into its absorption into the city, are accompanied by the dead and, in some stories, join them: *Pig Earth* ends with a barn-raising among the dead, *Lilac and Flag* (1992) with a ghost ship sailing away from the city 'to become the mountain'. The autobiographical novel, *Here is where we meet* (2005), proceeds through a series of encounters with the ghosts of family, friends, lovers and heroes.

It is in this book that we find one layer of explanation for the centrality of the dead to Berger's worldview. He is writing of time spent with his father, before he was six years old, by the river at the bottom of their suburban garden.

> Those Saturday afternoons were the beginning of an under-
> taking my father and I shared until he died, and which now I
> continue alone ... An agreement that he could share with me,
> as he could with nobody else, the ghost life of his four years of
> trench warfare, and that he could do so because I already knew
> them ...
>   We fought about my future with no holds barred and no
> exchanges possible, yet neither of us forgot for a second during
> the fight that we shared the secrets of another incommensu-
> rable war. By being himself, my father taught me endurance.[20]

After the war, Berger's father had stayed in the army for another four years, as part of the war graves operation which sought to recover, identify and give dignity to the bodies of the dead. Born in 1926, Berger says of himself, in a poem entitled 'Self-portrait: 1914–18':

> I was born by Very Light and shrapnel
> On duckboards
> Among limbs without bodies.[21]

The sense of duty to the dead is the shared undertaking 'which now I continue alone.'

Yet, as Berger insists in one of his best known lines, 'Never again shall a single story be told as though it were the only one.'[22] So there are other layers of explanation, other partial answers. The endurance his father taught him is also a key term in his description of his peasant teachers. Walking in the mountains, Berger tells an interviewer:

> Here you sense how close the peasant lives to the reality of
> death ... What I mean is that the peasant keeps the dead alive.
> The dead are with him, constantly recalled. Which is to say
> that history is alive for the peasant as it is not for others.[23]

Now, we are returning to the mystery, because we must confront a question which has a deep bearing on Berger's stance towards the people among whom he has lived. The peasant worldview, as he describes it, lives publicly and matter-of-factly with the company of the dead, in a way which stands outside what is socially acceptable as reality among grown-ups in civilised conversation. In relation to these two approaches to reality, where does Berger place himself?

In *Pig Earth*, he acknowledges that he and his family 'remain strangers who have chosen to live here.'[24] Among the things they do not have in common with the peasant families around them is religion. (Though, elsewhere, Berger describes himself as 'croyant', a believer: 'I hate most churches, but that's a different thing.'[25]) The question, however, is not whether he shares their beliefs, but what attitude he takes towards them. Does he carry with him to the mountains, however politely he keeps it to himself, the civilised assumption that these are obsolescent superstitions? Or does he meet his neighbours on equal terms?

The man who emerges from the essays, the stories, the interviews, could only do the latter. Like the anthropologist Hugh Brody, whose work he admires, Berger is incapable of treating people as relics or as marginal. Rather, he encounters them as his contemporaries, dwelling at the centre of their own worlds. This had always been accompanied by a quest for historical understanding, as he writes in *A Seventh Man*:

> To see the experience of another, one must do more than dismantle and reassemble the world with him at its centre. One must interrogate his situation to learn about that part of his experience which derives from the historical moment.[26]

But there is a shift, which seems to date from the start of his 'second education',[27] his initiation into this other 'constellation of sense and value'.[28] Increasingly, history and experience are consciously set in relation to something else, an explicitly metaphysical dimension. Here – in his most intimate book, *and our faces, my heart, brief as photos*, a collection of love letters – he expresses this in relation to the changing understanding of death, once thought of as 'the companion of life':

> Time was death's agent and one of life's constituents. But the timeless – that which death could not destroy – was another. All cyclic views of time held these two constituents together … The mainstream of modern thought has removed time from

this unity and transformed it into a single, all-powerful and active force.[29]

This reassertion of 'the intractable', 'the timeless' unbalances the dominance of history in conventional Marxist thought, and tips in favour of the specific – the present moment, rather than the anticipated future – which Berger's painterly attention and ethical instincts had always leaned towards. 'Let's take our bearings within another time-set,' he writes, 20 years later. 'The eternal, according to Spinoza is *now*.'[30]

All of this constitutes, among other things, a remarkably subtle deconstruction of the concept of progress in Marxism. Revolution – a word which always suggested the cyclical rather than the linear – is now conceived as including 'a break-out from the prison of modern time.'[31] Yet this does not affect the existing obligations of resistance.

'Suppose,' he suggests to his comrades at the Transnational Institute, 'that we ... say that we are not living in a world in which it is possible to construct something approaching heaven-on-earth, but, on the contrary are living in a world whose nature is far closer to that of hell; what difference would this make to any single one of our political or moral choices?' None at all, he answers: 'All that would have changed would be the enormity of our hopes and finally the bitterness of our disappointments.'[32]

The same love letters in which the politics of time first comes to the fore are also the source of Berger's most direct, personal and uncanny writing about the presence of the dead. Over a page and a half, he describes the faces which appear before him when he shuts his eyes. 'I related this experience once to a friend,' he says – and here, too, it is related as experience, not as fiction or parable or metaphor.

> The face looks straight at me and without words, by the expression of the eyes alone, it affirms the reality of its existence. As if my gaze had called out a name, and the face, by returning it, was answering, 'Present!'

At the end of this passage, he says simply, 'They belong to the past because they are the dead and I know this by the way they look at me ... with something approaching recognition.'[33]

I do not believe that I can convince you as to what John Berger may or may not believe about the dead. All I invite you to do is dwell with that passage –

find the book and read it in full – and consider whether or not he is being serious in describing it as 'experience'. Consider, moreover, how different the world might feel if one were to take such an experience seriously, without claiming anything more than a partial ability to explain it.

I am sure that Berger understands the difficulty that we are having here. As he – well, the narrator, but you know what I mean – says in *Here is where we meet*, 'I risk to write nonsense these days.'[34] It is true: we risk to write nonsense when we attempt to acknowledge that reality may not be limited to things which do, or even could, make sense.

3. The luxury of nihilism

> Sometimes it seems that, like an ancient Greek, I write mostly
> about the dead and death. If this is so, I can only add that it is
> done with a sense of urgency which belongs uniquely to life.[35]

If, as I have suggested, Berger's writing is underpinned by a metaphysical position beyond the Pale of civilised modernity (or, for that matter, almost anyone else's brand of Marxism), this could sound like a particularly extreme version of the escapism with which he has sometimes been charged. What I want to emphasise, then, is the context from which his position emerges, because it seems to me that such attitudes to reality may prove to be more enduring and more useful than is generally anticipated in our age of global disruption – and that the opposite may be true of many positions generally assumed to be more advanced, civilised, modern or any of the other terms by which the ways we happen to see the world today imply their superiority over the ways that people have seen it in other times and places.

Because, whatever we make of Berger's ways of seeing the dead, they do not belong with that form of belief in 'life after death' which seeks to distract from or justify present suffering. 'I've always put life before writing,' he tells his mother's ghost. ('Don't boast,' she tells him.) And the man who emerges through these texts is committed to the question of how to live – and how to live well, in the aesthetic and the ethical (which is to say, the political) sense of the word. Specifically, he is driven to explore this question from the perspectives of those whose lives take place outside the walls whose building he sees as 'the essential activity of the rich today.' (Physical walls, as in Palestine, but also walls of unseeing: in the end, Berger's allegiance to the poor is inseparable from his insistence on the importance of seeing, for – he tells us – only the poor can afford to see the world as it really is.)

In the process, it seems to me, his philosophical project – not a systematic philosophy, but an improvised, Jugaad philosophy – is to test our ways of seeing the world, to find those which will hold up against the extremes of human experience.

> Nihilism, in its contemporary sense, is the refusal to believe in any scale of priorities beyond the pursuit of profit, considered as the end-all of social activity, so that, precisely: everything has its price. Nihilism is resignation before the contention that Price is all. It is the most current form of human cowardice. But not one to which the poor often succumb.[36]

Nihilism, it seems – and, perhaps, other positions characterised by a metaphysical vacuum – can only be sustained when backed up by a high standard of material living and the accompanying distractions. Beyond the walls, other ways of seeing do better. The harshness of life for the majority of the world is documented with unflinching anger in his latest essays, but a kind of hope – or, at least, an 'undefeated despair' – remains in people's 'ingenuity for getting by, their refusal of frontiers … their adoration of children … their belief in continuity, their recurring acknowledgement that life's gifts are small and priceless.'[37]

Berger is not concerned with advising those in the rich world who fear the collapse of their way of living. Yet, in another sense, I think he saw all this coming a long way off. Because there is an ambiguity in his explanations of his decision to go and live among peasants.

> You cannot imagine the fatigue and the hardening. No one would wish that traditional peasant life continue exactly as it is. One would wish it to change. But change how? Is the answer simply progress? Does anyone still believe progress solves everything, eliminates all problems and contradictions?
>
> The fact is that progress, as it dawned in the Enlightenment and developed in the nineteenth century, has not paid off on all its promises. And now, a culture, the culture of peasants, a culture that might help us to reassess 'progress' – this culture is simply being eliminated, or at least allowed to disappear.[38]

This sense of watching the final disappearance of peasant culture is balanced, elsewhere, with a sense of its potential resilience.

> If one looks at the likely future course of world history … the peasant experience of survival may well be better adapted to this long and harsh perspective than the continually reformed, disappointed, impatient progressive hope of an ultimate victory.[39]

In contrast to the 'serviced limbo' of the citizen, the 'unprotected' peasant knows how to 'wrest some meaning and continuity from a cycle of remorseless change.'[40] Such a capacity for wresting meaning from the uncontrollable is, for me, at the heart of the cultural challenge laid down by the Dark Mountain Project. And reading that passage, I can't help feeling that Berger's journey to the mountains was not so much a retreat from history, as a long bet on the endurance of those people he defines as 'a class of survivors.' With their refusal of belief in progress, they remain – for him – history's last best hope.

In this, he has much in common with Subcomandante Marcos of the EZLN, a man with whom he has met and corresponded, and of whose writing he once said, '[it] combines modesty with unflinching excess.'

> The excess is not that of political extremism … The excess comes from their conviction (which personally I accept completely) that they also represent the dead, all the maltreated dead – the dead who are less forgotten in Mexico than anywhere else in the world.[41]

It takes one to know one, as they say.

References

1. Both quotations are taken from John Berger's most recent essay collection, *Hold Everything Dear: Dispatches on Survival and Resistance* (2007)

2. John Berger quoted in Lewis Jones, 'Portait of the artist as a wild old man', *Daily Telegraph*, 23rd July 2001

3. John Berger, 'Ten Dispatches About Place' in *Hold Everything Dear: Dispatches on Survival and Resistance* (2007)

4. Berger, 'Between Two Colmars' (1973) in *About Looking* (1980)

5. Hunter S. Thompson, *Fear and Loathing in Las Vegas* (1972) Ch.8

6. John Berger & Jean Mohr, *A Seventh Man* (1975) p.16

7. Ibid., p.29

8. Ibid., pp.216–7

9. John Berger quoted in Gerald Marzorati, 'Living and writing the peasant life', *New York Times* 29th November 1987

10. Ibid.

11. John Berger, *Pig Earth* (1979) p.198

12. Berger quoted in Marzorati, op cit

13. *Pig Earth* pp.8–9

14. John Berger, 'A Story for Aesop' (1986) in *Keeping a Rendezvous* (1992)

15. John Berger, 'The Storyteller' (1978) in *The White Bird* (1985)

16. Hamlet I.v.166–7

17. John Berger, 'Twelve theses on the economy of the dead', *Left Curve* No.31 [ ] 2008

18. John Berger, *and our faces, my heart, brief as photos* pp.13–14

19. Ron Slate, 'On Hold Everything Dear, essays by John Berger' – www.ronslate.com/hold_everything_dear_essays_john_berger_pantheon

20. John Berger, *Here is where we meet* (2005) pp.186–7

21. John Berger, *Pages of the Wound* (1996)

22. John Berger, *G.* (1972); used as an epigraph by Michael Ondaatje, *In the Skin of a Lion* (1986) and Arundhati Roy, *The God of Small Things* (1995)

23. in Marzorati, op.cit.

24. *Pig Earth*, p.7

25. in Jones, op.cit.

26. *A Seventh Man*, p.104

27. John Berger quoted in Kenneth Baker, *The Moment of Truth is Now*, San Francisco *Chronicle*, 6th January 2002

28. in Jones, op.cit.

29. *and our faces…* p.36

30. *Hold Everything Dear*, p.119

31. Ibid., p.140
32. John Berger, 'Leopardi' in *The White Bird*
33. *and our faces...* pp.12–14
34. *Here is where we meet* p.42
35. John Berger quoted in Stan Persky, *John Berger* –
    www.dooneyscafe.com/archives/140
36. 'Ten Dispatches About Endurance', *Hold Everything Dear* pp.93–4
37. Ibid., p.100
38. Marzorati, op.cit.
39. *Pig Earth* pp.212–3
40. Ibid., pp.206–7
41. John Berger, *Photocopies* (1996)

J . D . W H I T N E Y

Grandmother

Grandmother
                        sits
on her sitting-down
spot on the
ground
                surrounded by
trees full of
night
                full of
ghosts
sitting on branches
speaking –
before anything was –
of things not yet
so
     saying
Old Woman Who Never Dies
tell
us
     when
the story will be
told.
Says
     saying what will
happen makes it
so.
Says
Listen.
                Says
here we go.

Grandmother
                                            doesn't like
watching people
die.
     Too much
fuss.
     Oh,
what a bad
surprise!
Pah!
     Bears
know how to do it.
When bears have to
die
     that's
what they do.
Die

Grandmother
                              calls
the sitting-down
council of
                      all
beings –
                  secret
(this time)
from people.
Hears all the
wondering:
                  why those
two-leggeds
can't
dance in the
                  circle
too
      why
they think they're too
good to be
food
      for
anyone else
                  but
get to eat US.
Listens.
Says
      no
no volunteers.
Thinks some.
Says
now
      here –
meet your new
cousins:
                  Mosquito
Black Fly
bloodsucker
Wood-
      tick

Grandmother
              dresses
up.
    Puts what her
friends
left her
        when they
passed on
on.
Birch
   bark.
Necklace of dried
turtle hearts.
Roots.
    Feathers.
Heron
foot.
    Moth-
wing powder.
Milkweed
       pods.
Lichens.
Pussywillow
fur.
    Her
hummingbird
skins
    &
veil
   of webs.
Says:
    there!

ALASTAIR MCINTOSH

Popping the Gygian question

In *The Republic,* which was written nearly two and a half millennia ago, Plato portrays Socrates and his friends as embarking upon an enquiry into the nature of justice. Socrates observes that none of them are very clever, but to determine what justice looks like in an individual is no small feat. He suggests that just as it is easier from a distance to read large lettering than small, so justice might be discerned more clearly if sought at the scale of the state rather than the individual. He therefore proposes a thought experiment. They should set up an imaginary Republic. If they can determine what justice looks like in a city-state, then they might infer its nature in the soul.

What Plato is doing here is inverting the usual idea that we get the politicians we deserve. He's asking, 'If such is our politics, what does it say about us?' *Uncivilisation,* the manifesto of the Dark Mountain Project, proposes a similar exercise. On its final page we are invited to climb the heights together by the poet's pilgrim path, and 'look back upon the pinprick lights of the distant cities and gain perspective on who we are and what we have become.'

I welcome such a taking of perspective while confessing wariness as to what is meant by 'Uncivilisation'. If we are to be useful in this world – if, to express my own values, we are to serve the poor or the broken in nature – then we cannot indulge in the sort of postmodern deconstruction that knocks down the Lego and leaves it scattered on the nursery floor. Our world now has nearly seven billion people. Whether we like it or not, 'civilisation' is held together by a tightly interlocked socio-economic system. The worry is that this arguably has very little resilience. *Uncivilisation* is correct that we walk on lava with a thin and brittle crust.

To take just one example, we now know that in October 2008, British banks came within hours of having to close down cashlines and suspend commercial lines of credit. If this had happened, commerce would have gridlocked. If suppliers think they might not get paid they won't dispatch the goods. But modern supermarkets operate on a just-in-time delivery system. Even a temporary blip in financial lubrication would almost certainly have caused shortages which would quickly have been compounded by panic buying. At such a juncture, social disorder is not far around the corner. Just as it's said, 'If you don't like education, try ignorance,' so we must be resolute but not dismissive in our critique of civilisation. It might be the cause of our woes, but equally, its absence could become the cause of something worse.

For these reasons I welcome the idea of 'Uncivilisation' as a thought experiment. But let us, in such civilised company as we have with one another, ensure that whatever deconstruction we do also has an eye to reconstruction, or replacement with a credible alternative that would not require totalitarian enforcement. What I want to offer here are some footnotes in the footsteps of Plato, because *The Republic* is, in my view, the greatest philosophical study of civil society that we have in the traditions of the West. I realise what outrage that may cause to followers of Popper or Lyotard. But then, I purport to be neither a modernist nor, if such a thing exists beyond the modern, a post-modernist. Like Plato, I am a premodern essentialist.

That does not mean I swallow Plato hook, line and sinker or dismiss the importance of science. Far from it. Many of Popper's criticisms of authoritarian leanings in Plato were highly apposite, especially for our society that has moved on since ancient Greece. But Plato offers some unparalleled insights into the relationship between justice, the individual and the state. In particular, I want to focus here on the visibility or invisibility of power. In so doing I will take it as axiomatic that 'power denied is power abused,' and by 'denied' include that which is 'hidden' – especially when we hide from ourselves our complicity in systems that we may decry. This is where Plato is so challenging. He forces us to look at where we stand in relation to our social systems, and equally to look at our social systems in relation to ourselves. It presses us to engage in the joined-up thinking that is so often deficient in civilisation's discontents. In this, I am minded of a cartoon where all the activists file past with their placards. 'Save the Whale,' says one. 'Down with the Corporations,' another. 'Stop the War,' a third, and they go on and on, until the last which reads: 'I hate my Dad!' Yes, it is challenging to look at outer social structures relative to our own inner psychodynamics, but that is what Plato urges us to do. Without such integrated social and psychological honesty I do not think we can sustain action in the world in ways that build hope and give life.

So, *civilitas*, civilisation. Etymologically, the word contrasts with barbarity: the civilian with the soldier, civil law with criminal law. The problem with it, and thus our need to consider 'Uncivilisation,' comes about when the term gets co-opted by various forms of domination. That doesn't make civilisation bad. It only affirms the badness of domination masquerading as civilisation. We should remember that our civil rights and civic duties are also part of civilisation. So is the duty to civil disobedience in the name of upholding a more civil sense of what is civilised. I don't think we need to engage too much in the displacement activity (displacement from the urgent imperatives of action) in fussing about how we use these words. People who fuss overmuch about words rarely get much done. Let actions speak louder. And in using names and ideas to explore such actions, my touchstone of validity is what I call the 'Crofter Test'. If something cannot credibly be explained to a Hebridean crofter who works the land and fishes the sea, and who functions as an individual in community with others, then we should think twice about its worth. Here from where I write in Glasgow this has its urban equivalent in the 'Govan Test'. If it can't pass muster with folks in this hard-pressed part of town, then we should question whether it is merely an elite conceit from the ivory tower as distinct from fruit from the elementally down-to-earth groves of academe.

Plato founded his Academy in a grove, and in the *Republic* this tension between the two reference points – town and country, as it were – is quickly apparent. He first puts Socrates to the task, setting up an imaginary utopia wherein to discern justice. Socrates pictures a Republic identical with what we today might think of as an eco-village. For him, right livelihood wasn't rocket science. Justice consists in everybody acting in fitting relationship to the wider community – a holistic balance environmentally, intergenerationally and with neighbours. Such a Republic is community writ large. Fulfilment comes from matching the providence of outer life with an inner life capacity to be satisfied. It embraces frugality but avoids destitution. As such, Socrates said he would have men and women spending their days doing honest pastoral and artisanal work. They would feast with their children on vegetarian meals, drinking wine in moderation, and spending their spare time not watching television but singing hymns to the gods, 'so they will live with one another in happiness, not begetting children above their means, and guarding against the danger of poverty or war.' In such a way they will 'at death leave their children to live as they have done.' The Brundtland Commission's famous definition of 'sustainable development' was presaged by Plato!

But on hearing all this, young Glaucon springs to his feet and pours derision on it. He accuses Socrates of setting up living conditions suitable only for fattening pigs. Instead, his version of the Republic would have rich foods in profusion. They'd have nannies to keep the kids at bay, every mod con to make life comfortable, and decorations of gold, ivory and all the latest Britart fads from Charles Saatchi's gallery plus Damien Hirst's diamond encrusted skull.

'Very well,' says Socrates, letting go of his Ecotopia, 'If you wish let us also inspect a city which is suffering from inflammation.' And so he sets in train a discourse of brilliant Socratic questioning. He draws out the consequences of Glaucon's Republic and concludes, 'Then if we are to have enough ... we must take a slice from our neighbour's territory. And they will want to do the same to ours, if they also overpass the bounds of necessity and plunge into reckless pursuit of wealth?'

'Certainly,' admits Glaucon, but becoming less sure of himself.

'Then,' concludes Socrates: 'Let us only notice that we have found the origin of war in those passions which are most responsible for the evils that come upon cities and the men that dwell in them.'

Through Socrates, then, Plato has shown how the collective culmination of our personal values can result in unforeseen emergent social properties finding expression. The hapless Glaucon ends up a little shocked by the implications that Socrates draws from his greed. Equally, a society will only be able to rein in its 'inflammation' if it carries out political reform in parallel with a deepening of the inner personal values necessary to drive transformation. This is especially true in democracies and in economies that allow freedom of purchasing choice to create demand. Under such conditions we may blame the governments, the corporations, or civilisation itself, but if we look in their mirrors, we might be disturbed to see how much it is our own distorted faces that reflect back. Except where our hands are tied, we have to own our decisions, and own up.

The would-be revolutionary in her fashion-branded clothing or his designer suit is a case in point. Sometimes, when I'm challenged on saying this during a talk, I'll reply: 'Will everybody who is wearing a corporate product kindly take it off?' The threat of naked exposure pretty quickly brings home the truth of complicity. And nearly all of us are in this position. My own biggest eco-sin is addiction to eating more than my ecologically sound share of meat and fish. Such complicity in the global problematique is not something to be proud of. But by facing fair and square our own contradictions and confessing them, we at least avoid putting out our own eyes as the price of denial. That way we stay in touch with reality, even though it will be a more uncomfortable reality. And that's a start on the path to transformation, both personal and political in an iterative process. It reduces the hypocrisy and diminishes the likelihood of projecting our inner conflicts onto the outer world, thereby unconsciously abusing the very causes we espouse.

The ability to see clearly, to see both truths and Truth is therefore pivotal. In *Uncivilisation,* the bottom line is that 'there is an underlying darkness at the root of everything we have built ... which feeds the machine and all the people who run it, and which they have all trained themselves not to see.' I do not propose that we should make the category error of pathologising every political structure as if it were our personal responsibility. But I am suggesting that we seek to build a greater understanding of the emergent properties of what it means for us, as individuals, to be covenanted (and not merely contracted) into a body politic. We should seek better to understand power as both the fuel and the lubricant between individuals and structures of power. And in my experience, where we can unveil our own connivance in the Powers That Be, it helps to defuse the self-righteousness that would otherwise keep our opponents closed to us. An open-handed and open-hearted confessional path thereby paves the way for deeper mutuality in the discernment of problems. It legitimises our challenges because we have laid ourselves equally open to challenge. It oils the wheels of both hindsight and foresight, consecrating their bridging in the present. At the deepest level, such clear seeing opens us to 'participation in the harmony of the rhythm of Being,' which is the great religious philosopher Raimon Panikkar's definition of peace.

This question of power's visibility or invisibility is therefore at the heart of transforming what it means to be civilised. But if we are going to use a word like 'transformation', we have to think what we are transforming from, to what, and by which legitimate pathways. Too often the revolutionary overlooks these steps and violence, which is always the recourse of impatience, fills the gaps, numbs the soul, and intergenerationally poisons the soil from which justice might grow.

Again, Plato presses us on the connections between visibility, violence, power and justice. We see it in one of the less remarked-upon narratives of *The Republic* where he tells the story of the Ring of Gyges. It's a tale that, like a pair of cover-flaps to the main story, pops up early in Book 2, just before the philosophers agree to embark upon their republican thought experiment; and briefly resurges again near the end of Book 10, forming part of Socrates' triumphant *coup de grâce.*

Again Glaucon is centre stage and playing devil's advocate with the old master. He puts it to Socrates that justice is nothing more than concealed self-interest. To illustrate he tells of Gyges of Lydia – a shepherd in what would today be western Turkey and the ancestor of King Croesus, who was the richest but not the happiest man in the world. The story variously refers to Gyges' ancestor but also to the 'Ring of Gyges', so to keep it simple I'll just attribute it to Gyges.

One day Gyges was tending the king's flocks when there was an almighty deluge of rain followed by an earthquake. The ground opened to reveal a chasm that turned out to be an ancient tomb. Venturing inside, Gyges found a hollow bronze horse with windowed trapdoors along its sides.

Peering through these he could see the body of an almost superhuman-sized warrior wearing a gold ring. Gyges opened a trapdoor, climbed in, and made off with the ring.

His next stop was for a monthly meeting that all the shepherds had with the king's officials to account for their flocks. While waiting for it to start he played with the ring. Amazingly, he found that when the bevel was turned inwards it made him invisible. On turning it outwards again he'd reappear. In this way he could wander freely amongst his colleagues and overhear everything they said about him.

When the meeting ended, Gyges merged with the cortege and followed them back to the palace. He entered the royal quarters, seduced the queen and with her help, slew the king and seized the crown.

And that's all there is to the story. But just imagine, Glaucon says to Socrates, that there had been two such rings. Imagine that the other had fallen to a just man instead of to a tyrant-in-waiting like Gyges.

We ourselves might pop the Gygian question. What would you or I do if we came by a Ring of Gyges?

Glaucon argues that no matter how principled when the opportunity to act otherwise had been lacking, the finder of such a ring would most likely behave henceforth exactly like Gyges. Would not anybody, Glaucon suggests, use it 'to steal anything he wished from the very marketplace with impunity, to enter men's houses and have intercourse with whom he would, to kill or to set free whomsoever he pleased; in short, *to walk among men as a god?*'

Because justice, he continues, is only held a virtue when working to our advantage. If we possessed a Ring of Gyges but refrained from exploiting it, others would certainly praise us to our faces. However, they would do so merely out of relief at not being in danger of suffering injustice. Secretly, they'd despise our folly. It's like the moral psychology of bankers and their bonuses. Those who do (which is not all bankers) do because they can. In their circular social reference group they'd reckon one another fools to do otherwise. Worse still, as the folklorist Hamish Henderson once said, 'The non-genuine person cannot believe that the genuine exists.' The fruits of Truth and truthfulness themselves are relegated beyond the Pale.

For me, the power of Glaucon's story goes deeper than just the obvious question as to whether good can ever come from knowledge acquired, or actions engaged in, by deceit. It is a cogent reflection on the manifold meanings of invisibility and with it, our complicity and often, self-deception in many of the things that we profess to hate. We may hate, for example, capitalism. But how much are we willing to go out of our way and stretch our pockets to seek out the alternative, as embodied in fairly or co-operatively traded products? We may hate what bankers do, but are we willing to take a lower rate of interest from ethical investment, or even go the full Muslim way of decrying usury full stop? We may shun the casino economy of the stock exchange, but how's your pension? And behind so many of these questions lurks consumerism – not the rustic economy of Socrates but the inflamed one of Glaucon – and its invisible Gygian gas, CO_2.

And so, did Copenhagen fail in 2009 because the UN's politics failed? Or would it be more honest to say that politics actually succeeded; politics covertly did what the majority of people really wanted? By keeping CO_2 invisible, by side-stepping the imperative to act on the rich world's complicity in profligate consumerism, it sanctioned the ongoing Gygian theft of our children's ability to live as we have done.

And where does that leave matters now? My view is that civilisation – because that is what we are talking about when addressing the world at UN level – must reconnect to the soul. It must do all the outer stuff – all the political, economic and technical approaches to tackling a meta-problem like climate change – but it must also address the inner life. It must tackle what drives the relatively rich to consume so much 'stuff' in the first place and acknowledge that the relatively poor cannot ignore temptation. A Persian proverb says that behind every rich person is a devil, but behind every poor one are two. The rich have the devil everybody sees. The poor have the devil that's known plus the one that might emerge given half a chance. Assuming that the consensus science is broadly correct, when it comes to an issue like climate change we're all in this together.

I conclude with Socrates' lines from Book 10, where he returns to Glaucon's story. 'We have proved,' he says, 'that justice in itself is the best thing for the soul itself, and that the soul ought to do justice whether it possesses the Ring of Gyges or not.'

Such is the challenge of our times.

'Most true,' replies a mellowed Glaucon.

ANTHONY MCCANN

A gentle ferocity

A conversation with Derrick Jensen

I met Derrick Jensen once. I was living in Washington DC at the time and he was giving a talk, so I went along. When I got there, a few people were starting to gather for the event. Being a little shy, I moved on through and headed for the carrot sticks and cucumber at the back. I dawdled there for a while, rocking on my heels, waiting for the talk. I noticed someone else standing quietly in the corner, keeping to himself, not taking up very much space in the room. I generally feel more comfortable meeting people one-on-one, and I sidled over to say hello. It was Derrick Jensen.

To his critics, or even his admirers, this picture of Jensen as a gentle, retiring figure might come as a surprise. He has a hardcore reputation. Books such as *Endgame* (2006) have made him arguably the most prominent contemporary 'critic of civilisation', if we can talk about such a category. But Jensen does not only offer critique, he advocates actively bringing down the systems on which we currently depend. He reports conspiratorial conversations with ex-military personnel and hackers who discuss ways of bringing global trade to its knees. He champions direct action against an industrial system which destroys the natural world – perhaps most famously in his calls for people to blow up dams to save salmon rivers. His anger is directed, too, at those who say there is no room for violence in activism: he enjoys 'deconstructing pacifist arguments that don't make any sense anyway.'

In my own writing and teaching, I work to challenge dynamics of coercion, violence, domination and oppression. I would like to understand when and how people desire to commit violence against violence, and there are elements in Jensen's thinking which challenge and sometimes trouble me. Yet I also see a combination of vulnerability and purpose in his writing which is a long way from the caricature of the dam-busting eco-warrior. Though, since he admits that he has never blown up a dam, or even attempted to, I also wonder about his relationship between argument and action. Is it enough to say,

'I am a writer, writing is what I do'? And how does this relate to his identification with violent resistance?

What I find so powerful in books like *A Language Older Than Words* (2000) and *Walking on Water* (2005) is his commitment to honesty, to working through what it might mean to be human, and what it can mean to make a difference in the face of social, political and environmental violence and catastrophe. I frequently find myself disagreeing with him, but I have never questioned his integrity. To read his work is often to feel the presence of beauty in the crafting of thoughtful anger.

His focus on 'the culture of civilisation' – a language not dissimilar to that of the Dark Mountain Project – starts with the definition he offers in *Endgame*:

> I would define a civilisation … as a culture – that is, a complex of stories, institutions, and artefacts – that both leads to and emerges from the growth of cities (civilisation: from *civis*, meaning citizen, from Latin *civitatis*, meaning city-state), with cities being defined … as people living more or less permanently in one place in densities high enough to require the routine importation of food and other necessities of life.

In this analysis, the Tolowa, on whose land he now lives, were not civilised. They lived in villages and camps, he explains, and were able to do so for 12,500 years without destroying the place. Our current culture, on the other hand, has largely destroyed the place in 150 years. Civilisation, for Jensen, is a way of life that is inherently unsustainable.

'If your way of life', he suggests to me, 'is based on the importation of resources, it can never be sustainable. If you require the importation of resources it means you denuded the landscape of that particular resource. The way to live in place forever is to improve your habitat by your presence. It's what salmon do. It's what redwoods do. It's what indigenous humans do. You don't survive in the long run by exploiting your surroundings, but by actually improving your surroundings.

'Dolores LaChapelle taught me that it's not survival of the fittest, it's survival of the fit -how well you fit into your surroundings. It doesn't really matter whether you're living in a city or you live in the country, in this culture, because this culture is inherently unsustainable. You can be living in a groovy eco-village, and if you've got electricity, you've got copper wiring, which means that you are based on a mining and transportation infrastructure.

'I look around right now and I see there's some plastic, and there's some hardwoods, and there's some more plastic, and there's some metal and there's a painting on the wall, and what about the pigments, where's that from? What are the resource inputs for all those?'

As I listened to Jensen describe his surroundings, I recognised something which I have always found powerful in his writing, which is an appeal to specificity. In *Walking on Water* (2004), Jensen writes that 'specificity is everything, it's the only thing we've got.' Is cultivating that sense of actually being present, being in place, and being connected to what's around you, one of the core challenges for him?

'Yeah, I think the first thing is to acknowledge that place actually *exists*. Westerners generally view the world as consumable resources to be exploited, as opposed to other beings to enter into a relationship with. The notion that the non-human world has anything to say is central to every indigenous culture, and it's absolutely anathema to this culture, which believes that we're the only ones who have subjective existence.

'Canadian lumbermen have a great line, 'When I look at a tree I see dollar bills.' If all you see when you look at trees is dollar bills, then you're going to look at them one way. If you look at the trees and see trees, you'll look at them another way. It doesn't matter if we're talking about trees or fish or women. If I look at women and see orifices, I'm going to treat them one way. If I look at this particular woman and see a particular woman, I'll treat her differently.

'How we perceive the world affects how we behave in it, and this culture has systematically driven us insane. John Livingstone wrote about how people perceive cities as being a place where you get overloaded with sounds and sights, but he believes it's the opposite, that actually they're places of sensory deprivation. In this moment, right now, look around and ask yourself, how many things do you see? How many beings do you see? How many machines do you have a daily relationship with and how many wild beings, plants or animals? We're living in an echo chamber, and you can start to believe your own hallucinations.

'In order to survive, the real world must be primary. The humans that come after are not going to give a shit about whether we were pacifists or not pacifists. They're not going to give a shit whether we voted Democrat or Republican, Green, Whig, Tory, whatever. They're not going to care if we recycled. They're not going to care about any of that stuff. What they're going to care about is whether they can breathe the air and drink the water. We're fighting for life on the planet here, and people are worried about the economy?'

Jensen's views have brought him quite a bit of attention. Some follow him as a visionary, some peg him as an extremist. Where does the hostility generally come from, I wondered?

'I routinely get 400 to 600 people at talks, and I get notes from people every day saying, 'Thank God, I thought I was the only person thinking these things, and I'm so glad.' Most of the hate mail I've gotten has been what I call horizontal hostility. In ten years, out of more than a thousand pieces of hate mail, only two were from right-wingers. The others were from vegetarians because I eat meat, anti-car activists because I drive a car, pacifists because I don't believe in pacifism. In one sense or another, they're all lifestylists – people who believe that lifestyle change equals social change, and that's where most of the vituperation towards me has come.'

One possible response to Jensen's work is fear – fear of the future, fear about what we might do next. In *Endgame*, he asks, 'Do we believe that our culture will undergo a voluntary transformation to a sane and sustainable way of living?' It seems obvious that his answer is 'definitely not.' Is it any wonder, then, that the most common response he has got from environmentalists is 'we're fucked!'?

'Which is great, because … hold on a second, I handwrote this the other day: 'Before we can begin to use power on our own terms we must realise we are powerless on theirs. Much of the brilliance of the democratic experiment is 'to con the powerless into believing they have power. What has finally become clear to even the most obtuse is that we the people are powerless in this great democracy. The next turn of the screw was to con us into believing that our power lies in our power to consume, or in our inner power to be enlightened. But only when we realise that we are powerless in all these ways, will we be moved to use power in ways that do affect change.' One of the things I'm trying to do is to help form a culture of resistance that will move us towards effectively stopping this culture. Because, once again, we're talking about life on the planet here. This is not some fricking computer game.'

Jensen's handwritten statement seemed to point to the tendency of the dominant understandings of power to render us invisible and politically irrelevant. But was he also trying to find other ways of thinking about power that will be helpful to us?

'I think we need to ask ourselves, what do we want? What is our goal? And that will help determine the ways we can manifest power. I think for a lot of mainstream activists, their goal is to attempt to maintain civilisation – they say so explicitly. I'm very clear in what I want. I want to live in a world with wild salmon. I want to live in a world with wild sturgeon. I want to live in a world with migratory songbirds. I want to live in a world with more large fish in the oceans every year than the year before, with less plastic, with less dioxin in a mother's breast milk.

'So that's the first issue – I want people to think about what they want. And the next question is, what are the steps to getting there? We have to make some conscious choices. This is one of the areas where I have got into it with pacifists, because every moment we are making a choice. There is culpability in inaction as well. Standing in the face of a complex situation and doing nothing or acting in your own personal way does not absolve you.'

These discussions about culpability lead us to another of Jensen's often repeated positions. He thinks it is time we gave up on hope. He has a definition of hope, one which came out of an audience discussion at one of his talks: 'Hope is a longing for a future condition over which you have no agency. It means you are essentially powerless.'

'That's how we talk about hope in everyday language,' he tells me. 'I don't hope that I eat something today, I'm just going to do it. But when I go on a plane, I hope it doesn't crash, because I've no agency in that situation. If it is going to crash there's nothing I can do about it.

'I'm not a hope fascist. I attempt to be very clear, it's about what we do and don't have control over. A friend of mine whose brother was dying of cancer said to me, 'So you're telling me that I can't hope that my brother survives?' and I said, 'No, of course you can. What you can't do is stand there with the car keys in your hand and say 'Dear brother, I hope you make it to the hospital.' You have to drive him.'

'The thing is to figure out what we do and don't have agency over, and to expand the areas over which we do have agency but don't perceive. Because one of the central points of any oppressive system is to attempt to get you to believe that you are powerless.'

It is well known that Jensen is committed to physical sabotage in principle. Could it not be said, though, that the blowing up of dams to save wild salmon demonstrates the same kind of false hope that he critiques amongst mainstream environmentalists? Very few people are ever going to do this kind of thing, and if they do they will be caught and jailed very quickly. Eco-sabotage has been tried before many times. How could it ever reach the stage where it starts to bring civilisation apart?

'Well, first off, if you have a defeatist attitude like that, it's never going to happen. The best way to ensure it doesn't happen is to pretend it can't happen. Second, it actually is working right now. I have eight words for you.

Movement for the Emancipation of the Niger Delta. MEND. People in Nigeria have been able to reduce oil output by 40%, and they've done this by sabotage and kidnapping oil workers, and they've done this against the full might of the Nigerian government, oil companies, and of course the support of other governments around the world.

'It's absolute nonsense to say that sabotage doesn't work. What about the Pankhursts? What about the IRA, for God's sake? What about resistance against the Germans in World War II? The turning point for the French Resistance was a recognition that the German military was not invincible. As long as people propose that myth of the absolute omnipotence of the oppressors, we will remain oppressed to precisely that degree.

'I've a friend, and he's great, he's just this normal guy who didn't like the coverage of the invasion of Iraq and so instead of complaining about it, he just went to Iraq, and started reporting what was happening. I love this. Instead of sitting on his ass and thinking 'they can't do it', he just did it himself. That goes to the heart of the whole hope thing. There's this line by Thomas Jefferson, 'in war, they shall kill some of us, and we shall destroy all of them.' And that's one of the reasons that the dominant culture always wins, because that's the attitude that it has taken, always, and the attitude the resistance has taken has been the one you mentioned – oh, if we do something they'll catch us.

'Well, you know what? Fuck that, because there will be casualties in war, but we need to take on the attitude, 'they may stop me, they may stop you, but we're going to take out every last dam, we're going to take out every last corporation.' What happens if we match their relentlessness with our own? Because the truth is, they want to win more than we do. They have this insatiability. Most environmentalists don't know what the fuck we want. What do we want? Maybe we want to live in a world that uses a bit less electricity and the electricity is made by wind farms, never mind what that does for bats? Let's get clear on what we want, and let's do it.

'And there will be generations. These struggles last a long time, and that's how any social change comes about – you lose, you lose, you lose, you lose, and then you win. I mean, the Pankhursts went three generations. There's generation after generation in the Irish struggle. The leaders of the civil rights movement in the 50s and 60s were the grandchildren of the Pullman Porters, and they themselves were the children and grandchildren of slaves. We have to dedicate ourselves to the struggle and we have to say, hey, yes, we'll have setbacks, but in time it will be you that grows tired.'

I come from Northern Ireland, so I feel drawn to pick him up on his use of the Irish example. 'For many of us living here,' I tell him, 'to talk about 'the Irish struggle' is so incredibly simplistic. You look at the complexities of reality, the things that people have lived through, and it's just too neat to fit all this into the binary oppositions of war metaphors, to fit it into ...'

Jensen interrupts. 'I don't give a shit about war metaphors,' he says. 'There is an enemy, and those enemies have names. Salmon don't get conflicted. Indigenous people I know don't get conflicted, 'Oh, we can't get into a binary system of us and them.' It's like, fuck that! Tecumseh knew who the enemy was, and yes, there is a binary system. The enemy is the capitalists, and the first thing we need to do, and every indigenous person says this to me, the first thing we need to do is to decolonise our hearts and minds. As soon as we do that, as soon as we switch our allegiance to where we live, it becomes very, very clear. There are enemies, and they are my enemies, and the capitalist system and the capitalists themselves are my enemies, and I've got no problem saying that.'

At this point, Jensen's intense certainty reminds me of something he says in *Endgame*: that violence flows in one direction down the social hierarchy; violence done by those higher up to those lower down is 'invisible', while violence done in the other direction is 'unthinkable', causing shock and horror. I wonder whether such certainty makes it too easy to justify our own violence, to see ourselves as on the side of the angels?

'Gosh, do you think that after 15 books I haven't thought of this? Frankly, these questions have been really bugging me. I deal with this at length. In how many books have I mentioned Robert Jay Lifton's 'claims to virtue?' Lifton talks about how before we can commit any mass atrocity you have to convince yourself that what you're doing is actually in fact beneficial. So the Nazis had themselves convinced that they were not committing genocide, they were purifying the Aryan race. Likewise, capitalists can convince themselves that they are not destroying the world, instead they're developing natural resources. And this is true on a personal level. I myself have never once in my life been an asshole. Every time I've been an asshole I've had it fully rationalised.'

One of the reasons I admired *A Language Older Than Words* was precisely because of its core of self-critique, the deeply personal way Jensen explored the logics of committing violence against violence. The questions he asked were often questions I had asked myself. It was easily the most honest self-interrogation I had come across. I find myself prodding him now because I know he is capable of such self-criticism. Clearly he sees himself as a writer, but I wonder how that fits with the calls to action he makes in his work? If he feels this strongly about it, shouldn't he be out blowing up dams?

'A friend of mine asks this question, 'what are the most pressing problems you can help to solve, given the gifts that are unique to you in all the universe?' I have a gift for writing and I need to use that. Like my friend in Iraq, I saw a hole in discourse and I tried to fill it.

'I was watching *The Battle of Algiers*. It's a great movie about the Algerian resistance against the French, and I said to my friend, 'So, who would I be in this movie?' And my friend said, 'Oh, you'd be dead.' I said, 'Oh, thank you very much.' 'No,' he said, 'you've been dead for 30 years and your books are on the bookshelves of the insurgents.'

'My role is to get little pieces of wood and kindling and paper, to pile them up, and to put some lighter fluid on that, and it's somebody else's job to light the match. My job is to get bringing down civilisation to pass the lab test, you know?'

In thinking of himself as something of a backroom revolutionary, he has also been tough on those who believe that violence is never an acceptable tool to bring about social change.

'I have a good time bashing pacifists in *Endgame*, but the truth is that pacifists were very, very important to the abolition struggle, for example. Harriet Tubman carried a gun, but many of the people in safe-houses along the underground railroad did not. They were run by pacifists. My problem is not with someone being pacifist at all. I don't give a shit what your personal proclivities are. The important thing is, I think, to recognise that we need a range of resistance which includes everything from military resistance to absolutely non-military resistance.

'At some point we need to talk about self-defence. I've known some transition town people who combine relocalisation with firearms skillshare, and with making self-defence on both a personal and a community level a priority. I think that's great. What I'm really suggesting is that we need it all.'

In 2007, Jensen wrote a preface to a new edition of Ward Churchill's *Pacifism as Pathology*, an important text in the long-running argument over whether violence has a place in activism. My own work has been about resisting violence, but it seems to me that if pacifists don't take the work of people like Churchill and Jensen seriously, then how are they going to realistically clarify their own positions?

'The same thing has happened the other way,' Jensen agrees. 'I've been able to hone a lot of these arguments by having those disagreements with pacifists, or whatever. That's one of the reasons I wrote *Endgame*, because I got in so many arguments with pacifists that I just wanted to write out the arguments once and for all so I could be done with it.

'I really like the definition of violence that violence is any act that causes harm to another. It shows the ubiquity of violence, and it demystifies it, and it leads to other questions. So, every time I defecate I'm killing gazillions of bacteria and every time I eat a carrot I'm killing a living being there, too. I think that most of us under most circumstances would agree that it's morally acceptable to commit an act of violence against a carrot, to eat it. I think most of us under most circumstances would agree that it's not morally acceptable to commit an act of violence against a human being.

'What I want to find out is, where do we draw the lines? Is it morally acceptable to raise a carrot in a factory farm situation? Is it morally acceptable to kill a chicken? Is it morally acceptable to raise a chicken in a factory farm situation? Is it morally acceptable to kill Ted Bundy? Is it morally acceptable to kill Sarah Palin? Is it morally acceptable to kill me?

'And if somebody says it's never acceptable to kill a human being under any circumstances, it's like, okay, let's start throwing out ... what about Hitler? In 1939, Georg Elser's assassination attempt? I would like to make these questions as conscious as possible, because our discourse surrounding violence is just so squishy and ridiculous, and harmful, frankly.'

Jensen has written that he doesn't 'provide alternatives because there is no need.' But I suggested to him that one of the strongest parts of his work is that he is constantly providing alternatives, not in terms of what we should do, but in terms of other ways of looking at things. For me, Jensen stands out as an important writer because of the questions he is willing to ask. I may not share his responses, but I am inspired by his questions. I suggest to him that he is inviting people to a more honed ethical awareness.

'Well, thank you. That's one of the nicest things you could say. When I say I'm not telling people what to do, there are a few reasons for that. One is that I don't know people and, frankly, I've been approached by some people who want to blow up dams who are either crazy – literally crazy, as in think they're Marie Antoinette or something – or who are very young. It's one thing to talk to an adult, to have a discussion with someone who is capable of making decisions for themselves, and it's quite another thing to have a discussion with someone who is either very young or otherwise has problems.

'I used to say that I'm a recruiter for the revolution, but that's not true.

Military recruiters basically try to con people into joining up. What I want people to do is to make informed decisions about what they need to do with their life.'

This is interesting, because it touches on one of the challenges of being a writer. You may hope that readers lift up the words and look underneath to see the attitude of the person who wrote them, but often they will just take the words and run. You can't count on people being that interested in the bigger picture that the words suggest, they are as likely to take a particular page or a particular sentence as a banner to wave.

'Absolutely, I can say something that I think is pretty clear, and somebody will just take it wherever they're going to go, and it's like 'Gosh, I never actually said that.' I get pegged a lot of times as a 'violence' guy, but I'm not at all. What I'm recommending is that we need a full range of resistance.'

If it's not all about violence, what are the other tactics that play a part in the deconstruction of civilisation? In another of his books, *Walking on Water* (2004), he talks about the relationship between education and activism. What role do we have as educators of each other in the unweaving of civilisation?

'It's like I said, the first thing we need to do is decolonise, and I think that we can help each other through that process. It can help to have validation, to have a friend with whom you can have a conversation, and say, 'Hey, the stock market went down 300 points today', and say 'Yes, that's great', as opposed to having to explain why that's not bad. I used to question whether maybe I was just wrong about all of this stuff, but probably around writing *Culture of Make Believe* (2004), I thought, no, my analysis of the culture is right-on. There are other things that I still question, but I don't question that any more, and part of that is being surrounded by friends with whom you don't have to say why it's bad for a creature to be driven extinct.'

In spite of the intensity of his positions and the ferocity of his thought, from speaking to Jensen and from his writing, I often also get a sense of a person who is very gentle. So it's interesting that I have heard him characterised by people who don't know him as anything but gentle.

'It's pretty funny, when *Endgame* came out I did this radio interview and about 10 minutes in, the hosts just burst out laughing and said, 'You're a nice guy! We were kind of expecting you to be pounding and spitting.' On a personal level, I'm pretty non-violent. I'm not naturally a bellicose person. It used to kind of disturb me that I was writing about these issues, but then I thought, no, actually, I think I'm the person who should be writing about these issues, or one of the people who should. I'm not actually inherently an angry person at all. I'm pretty even tempered. I can get annoyed or whatever, but I think I've only shouted at two people, and one of those was my sister.

'Somebody said in a review of one of my books that I was 'almost pathologically unsentimental', and I like that. Not unemotional, obviously. I don't really know what it means, but I like it.'

RAN PRIEUR

Beyond Civilised & Primitive

Western industrial society tells a story about itself that goes like this: 'A long time ago, our ancestors were 'primitive'. They lived in caves, were stupid, hit each other with clubs, and had short, stressful lives in which they were constantly on the verge of starving or being eaten by sabre-toothed cats. Then we invented 'civilisation', in which we started growing food, being nice to each other, getting smarter, inventing marvellous technologies, and everywhere replacing chaos with order. It's getting better all the time and will continue forever.'

Western industrial society is now in decline, and in declining societies it's normal for people to feel that their whole existence is empty and meaningless, that the system is rotten to its very roots and should all be torn up and thrown out. It's also normal for people to frame this rejection in whatever terms their society has given them. So we reason: 'This world is hell, this world is civilisation, so civilisation is hell, so maybe primitive life was heaven. Maybe the whole story is upside down!'

We examine the dominant story and find that although it contains some truth, it depends on assumptions and distortions and omissions, and it was not designed to reveal truth, but to influence the values and behaviours of the people who heard it. Seeking balance, we create a perfect mirror image:

'A long time ago, our ancestors were 'primitive'. They were just as smart as we would be if we didn't watch television, and they lived in cosy handmade shelters, were generally peaceful and egalitarian, and had long healthy lives in which food was plentiful because they kept their populations well below the carrying capacity of their landbase. Then someone invented 'civilisation', in which we monopolised the land and grew our population by eating grain. Grain is high in calories but low in other nutrients, so we got sick, and we also began starving when the population outgrew the landbase, so the farmers conquered land from neighbouring foragers and enslaved them to cut down more forests and grow more grain, and to build sterile monuments while the elite developed technologies of repression and disconnection and gluttonous consumption, and everywhere life was replaced with control. It's been getting worse and worse, and soon we will abandon it and live the way we did before.'

Again, this story contains truth, but it depends on assumptions and distortions and omissions, and it is designed to influence the values and behaviors of the people who hear it. Certainly it's extremely compelling. As a guiding ideology, as a utopian vision, primitivism can destroy Marxism or libertarianism because it digs deeper and overthrows their foundations. It defeats the old religions on evidence. And best of all, it presents a utopia that is not in the realm of imagination or metaphysics, but has actually happened. We can look at archaeology and anthropology and history and say: 'Here's a forager-hunter society where people were strong and long-lived. Here's a tribe where the 'work' is so enjoyable that they don't even have the concept of 'freeloading'. Here are European explorers writing that certain tribes showed no trace of violence or meanness.'

But this strength is also a great weakness, because reality cuts both ways. As soon as you say, 'We should live like these actual people,' every competing ideologue will jump up with examples of those people living dreadfully: 'Here's a tribe with murderous warfare, and one with ritual abuse, and one with chronic disease from malnutrition, and one where people are just mean and unhappy, and here are a bunch of species extinctions right when primitive humans appeared.'

Most primitivists accept this evidence, and have worked out several ways to deal with it. One move is to postulate something that has not been observed yet, but that if it were observed, would make the facts fit your theory. Specifically, they say 'The nasty tribes must have all been corrupted by exposure to civilisation.' Another move is to defend absolutely everything on the grounds of cultural relativism: 'Who are we to say it's wrong to hit another person in the head with an axe?' Another move is to say, 'Okay, some of that stuff is bad, but if you add up all the bad and good, primitive life is still preferable to civilisation.'

This is hardly inspiring, and it still has to be constantly defended, and not from a strong position, because we know very little about prehistoric life. We know what tools people used, and what they ate, but we don't know how many tribes were peaceful or warlike, how many were permissive or repressive, how many were egalitarian or authoritarian, and we have no idea what was going on in their heads. One of the assumptions I mentioned above, made by both primitivism and the dominant story, is that stone age people were the

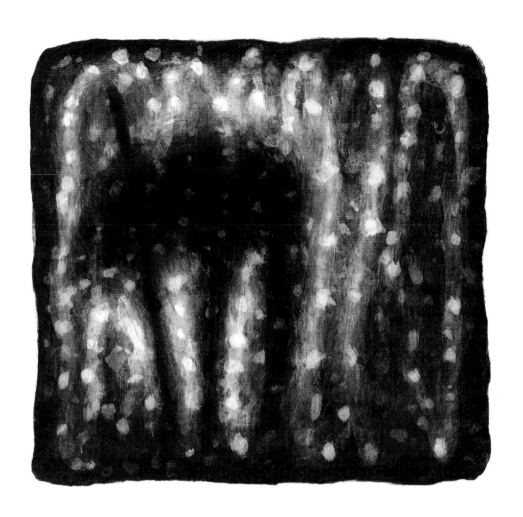

MAT OSMOND

Drawing on Sand

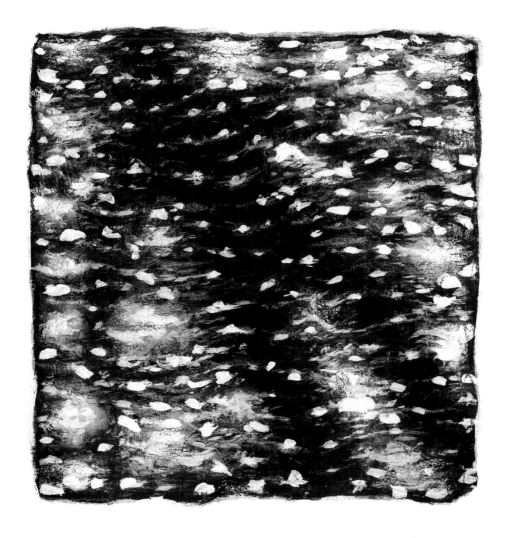

Again and again
he redrew the lines,
combing them, sorting them
over and over. The lines
tangled in the sand,
they tangled in the fronds
of weed, they tangled in
the spidering ribbons left
by the sea's retreat.

They tangled in the smooth
white stones until he could
no longer tell the one from
the other. They tangled in
the flowing rock, in the
deep carpet of shattered
and polished shells.

same as tribal forager-hungers observed in historical times. After all, we call them both 'primitive'. But in terms of culture, and even consciousness, they might be profoundly different.

A more reasonable move is to abandon primitive life as an ideal, or a goal, and instead just set it up as a perspective: 'Hey, if I stand here, I can see that my own world, which I thought was normal, is totally insane!' Or we can set it up as a source of learning: 'Look at this one thing these people did, let's see if we can do it too.' Then it doesn't matter how many flaws they had. And once we give up the framework that shows a right way and a wrong way and a clear line between them, we can use perspectives and ideas from people formerly on the 'wrong' side: 'Ancient Greeks went barefoot everywhere and treated their slaves with more humanity than Wal-Mart treats its workers. Medieval serfs worked fewer hours than modern Americans, and thought it was degrading to work for wages. Slum-dwellers in Mumbai spend less time and effort getting around on foot than Americans spend getting around in cars. The online file-sharing community is building a gift economy.'

Identifying with stone age people is like taking a big stretch. Then if we relax, we find that a lot of smaller stretches are effortless, that we can easily take all kinds of perspectives outside the assumptions of our little bubble. We could even re-invent 'primitivism' to ignore stone age people and include only recent tribes who we have good information about, and who still stack up pretty well against our own society. We could call this *historical primitivism*, and a few primitivists have taken this position. The reason most don't is, first, our lack of knowledge about prehistory forms a convenient blank screen on which anyone can project visions to back up their ideology. And second, stone age primitivism comes with an extremely powerful idea, which I call the *time-line argument*.

The timeline argument convinces us that a better way of life is the human default, that all the things we hate are like scratches in the sand that will be washed away when the tide comes in. Often it's phrased as '99% of human history has been that, and only 1% has been this.' Sometimes it's illustrated with a basketball court metaphor: It's 94 feet long, and if you call each foot 10,000 years, then we had fire and stone tools for 93 feet, agriculture for one foot, and industrial society for around a quarter of an inch.

The key word in this argument is 'we'. Where do you draw the line between 'us' and 'not us'? Why not go back a billion years, and say that 'we' were cell colonies in the primordial oceans? Call a billion years a football field, and the age of agriculture can dance on the head of a pin! This would seem to be a much stronger argument, and yet I've never seen a primitivist draw the line even as far back as *Homo habilis* two million years ago – or as recently as *Homo sapiens sapiens* 130,000 years ago. Why not?

This is a difficult and important question, and it took me a long time to puzzle it out. I think we've been confusing two separate issues. One is a fact, that the present way we live is a deviation from the way of all biological life. If this is our point, then a million year timeline is much too short – we should go back at least a thousand times further.

The other issue is a question: Who are we? When you get below the level of culture, down to the level of biology or spirit, what is normal for us to do? What is possible? What is right?

If you're talking about who we are, then the million year timeline is much too long. The mistake happens like this: 'We are human, and we can plausibly call *Homo erectus* human. Therefore our nature is to live like *Homo erectus*, and the way we live now is not our tendency, not our normal behaviour, but some kind of bizarre accident. What a relief! We can just bring down civilisation, and we'll naturally go back to living like *Homo erectus*, but since we don't know exactly how they lived, we'll assume it's like the very best recent forager-hunter tribes.'

Now, I'm not disputing that many societies have lived close to the Earth with a quality of life that we can't imagine. Richard Sorenson mentions several, and explores one in depth, in his essay on 'Preconquest Consciousness'.[1] What I'm disputing is: 1) that we have any evidence that prehistoric people had that consciousness; 2) that that consciousness is our default state; 3) that it is simple for us to get back there; and 4) that large-scale technologically complex societies are a deviation from who we are.

Who we are is changing all the time, and new genetic research has revealed shockingly fast change in just the last few thousand years, including malaria resistance, adult milk digestion, and blue eyes. According to anthropologist John Hawks, 'We are more different genetically from people living 5000 years ago than they were from Neanderthals.'[2]

Now, you could argue that some of these changes are not really who we are, because they were caused by civilisation: without domesticating cows and goats, we would not have evolved milk digestion. By the same logic, without inventing clothing, we would not have evolved hairless bodies. Without crawling onto dry land, we would not have evolved legs.

My point is, there is no place you can stick a pin and say 'this is our nature', because our nature is not a location – it is a journey. We crawled onto dry land;

we became warm-blooded and grew hair; we moved from the forests to the plains; we walked upright; we tamed fire and began cooking food; we invented language; our brains got bigger; our tools got more complex; we invented grain agriculture and empires and aeroplanes and ice cream and nuclear weapons.

Primitivists want to say that all the steps up to the last few are who we are, and the last few are not who we are. But it's a difficult argument, because we really did those things! So they say that the last few things, although we did them, were extremely unlikely. The word they usually use is 'fluke'. We would have lived in balance until the sun burned out, except that some wild grain seeds happened to fall in the mud at the edge of one camp during a food shortage, and someone noticed that they sprouted into new plants, and had a clever idea.

If civilisation began with a fluke, we would expect to see it begin only once, and spread from there. But instead we see grain farming and explosions of human social complexity in several places at about the same time: along the Tigris and Euphrates, and also in Africa, India, and China. You could still argue that those changes spread by travel, that there was one accident and then some far-flung colonies – unless we found an early civilisation so remote that travel was out of the question.

That civilisation has been found. Archaeologists call it the Norte Chico, in present day Peru. From 3000 to 1800 B.C. they built at least 25 cities, and they had giant stone monuments earlier than anyone except the Mesopotamians. Even more shocking, their system was not based on grain. All previous models of civilisation have put grain agriculture at the very root: once you had grain farming, you had a denser, more settled population, which led to a more complex society, and also you had a storable commodity that enabled hierarchy.

The Norte Chicans barely even ate grain, but they did have a storable commodity that enabled hierarchy, something that allowed small differences in wealth to feed back into large differences, and ultimately entrenched elites commanding slaves to build monolithic architecture. It was cotton. So we have people on opposite sides of the world, in different geographies, using different materials, falling into the same pattern; but that pattern is not about food. It seems to be about economics, or more precisely, about human cognition. After thousands of generations of slow change, human nature reached a tipping point that permitted large complex societies to appear in radically different circumstances.

Now it's tempting to call 'civilisation' the new human default, but of course, in many places these societies did not appear. Also, they all collapsed. And then new ones appeared, and those collapsed. I don't think it makes sense to talk about a human default, any more than it makes sense to talk about a default state for the weather. But the range in which we move has widened.

My information on the Norte Chico comes from Charles C. Mann's book *1491*, a survey of recent findings about the Americas before the European conquest. Mann is neither a primitivist nor an advocate for Western civilisation, but an advocate for, well, *Far* Western civilisation, which was a lot more like Western civilisation than we thought. At its peak, the Inca empire was the largest in the world, with exploited colonies, massive forced resettling of workers, and bloody power struggles among the elite just like in Europe and Asia. The Maya deforested the Yucatan and depleted its topsoil only a few centuries after the Romans did the same thing around the Mediterranean. Aztec 'human sacrifice' was surprisingly similar to the English 'public execution' that was happening at exactly the same time. Even North America had a city, Cahokia, that in 1250 was roughly the size of London. In 1523, Giovanni da Verrazzano recorded that the whole Atlantic coast from the Carolinas up was 'densely populated.' In the 1540s, De Soto passed through what is now eastern Arkansas and found it 'thickly set with great towns.' Of course, that population density is possible only with intensive agriculture. Mann writes, 'A traveller in 1669 reported that six square miles of maize typically encircled Haudenosaunee villages.'

By the time the conquest really got going, all these societies had been wiped out by smallpox and other diseases introduced by the first Europeans. Explorers and conquerors found small tribes of forager-hunters in an untamed wilderness, and assumed it had been that way forever. In a blow to both primitivism and 'progress', it turns out that most of these people were not living in the timeless ways of their ancestors – the 'Indians' of American myth were *post-crash societies!*

The incredible biological abundance of North America was also a post-crash phenomenon. We've heard about the flocks of passenger pigeons darkening the sky for days, the tens of millions of bison trampling the great plains, the rivers so thick with spawning salmon that you could barely row a boat, the seashores teeming with life, the deep forests on which a squirrel could go from the Atlantic to the Mississippi without touching the ground. We don't know what North America would have looked like with no humans at all, but we do know it didn't look like that under the 'Indians'. Bone excavations show that passenger pigeons were not even common in the 1400s. 'Indians' specifically targeted pregnant deer and wild turkeys before they laid eggs, to eliminate competition for maize and tree nuts. They routinely burned forests to keep them convenient for human use. And they kept salmon and shellfish populations down by eating them, and thereby suppressed populations of other creatures that ate them. When human populations crashed, nonhuman populations exploded.

This fact drives a wedge between two value systems that are supposed to be synonymous: love of nature and love of primitive humans. We seem to have only two options. One is to say that native North Americans went too far – of course they weren't nearly as bad as Europeans, but we need to return to even lower levels of population and domestication. I respect this position morally, but strategically it's absurd. How can the future inhabitants of North America be held to a way of life that the original inhabitants abandoned at least a thousand years ago?

The other option is to say that native North Americans did not go too far. The subtext is usually something like this: 'Moralistic ecologists think it's wrong that my society holds nature down and milks it for its own benefit, but if the *Native Americans* did it, it must be okay!' This conclusion is nearly universal in popular writing. Plenty of respectable authors would never be caught idealising simple foragers, but when they find out these 'primitives' hunted competitors like neolithic Microsofts and cleared forests to plant grain, out comes the 'wise Indian' card.

There is a third option, but it requires abandoning the whole civilised-primitive framework. Suppose we say, 'We can regrow the spectacular fecundity that North America had in the 1700s, not as a temporary stage between the fall of one Earth-monopolising society and the rise of another, but as a permanent condition – and we will protect this condition not by duplicating any way our ancestors lived, but by inventing new ways. We can do this because human nature continues to evolve. Just as the old model of civilisation became available to us as we changed, we are changing again and new doors are opening.'

Well, they're only open a crack. To grow biological abundance for its own sake, and not for human utility, is still a fringe position. But my point is that the civilised-primitive framework forces us to divide things a certain way: On one side are complexity, change, invention, unstable 'growth', taking, control and the future. On the other side are simplicity, stasis, tradition, stability, giving, freedom and the past. Once we abandon that framework, which is itself an artefact of Western industrial society, we can integrate evidence that the framework excludes, and we can try to match things up differently.

The combination that I'm suggesting is: complexity, change, invention, stability, giving, freedom, and both the past and the future. This isn't the only combination that could be suggested, and I doubt it's the easiest to put into practice, but it's surprisingly uncontroversial. Al Gore would probably agree with every point. The catch is that Gore is playing to a public consciousness in which 'freedom' means a nice paint job on control, and in which no one has any idea what's really necessary for stability.

To understand what's necessary for both freedom and stability, we need to go deep into a close ally of the critique of civilisation: the critique of technology. Now, as soon as you say you're against technology, some nit-picker points out that even a stone axe is a technology. We know what we mean, but we have trouble putting it into words. Our first instinct is to try to draw a line, and say that technologies on one side are bad, and on the other side are good. And at this point, primitivism comes into the picture as a convenience.

It reminds me of the debate over abortion, which is ultimately about drawing a line between when the potential child is part of the mother's body and when it's a separate person with full rights. Drawing the line at the first breath would make the most sense on Biblical grounds, but no one wants to do that, and almost no one wants to draw it at passage through the birth canal. But if you go further back than that, you get an unbroken grey area all the way to conception! Fundamentalists love to draw the line at conception, not only because it gives them more control over women, but because they hate grey areas.

In the same way, primitivism enters the debate over good technology with a sharply drawn line a long way back. We don't have to wrestle with how to manufacture bicycles without exploitation, or how to make cities sustainable, or what uses are appropriate for water wheels, or how to avoid the atrocities of ancient empires, if we just draw the line between settled grain farmers and nomadic forager-hunters.

To be fair to primitivists, they still have to wrestle with the grey areas from foraging to horticulture to agriculture, and from camps to villages to towns, and with arguments that we should go back even further. The real fundamentalists on this issue are the techno-utopians. They say 'technology is neutral,' which really means 'Thou shalt not ascribe built-in negative effects to any technology,' but of course they ascribe built-in positive effects to technologies all the time. So it ends up being not a statement of fact but a command to action: 'Any technology you can think of, do it!' This is like solving the abortion debate by legalising murder.

We must apply intelligent selection to technology, but we aren't really worried that the neighbouring village will reinvent metalworking and massacre our children with swords. We just want bulldozers to stop turning grassy fields into dreadful suburbs, and we want urban spaces to be made for people not cars, and we want to turn off the TV and take down the surveillance cameras and do meaningful work instead of sitting in windowless office dungeons rearranging abstractions to pay off loans incurred getting our spirits broken.

We like hot baths and sailing ships and recorded music and the internet, but we worry that we can't have them without exterminating half the species on Earth, or exploiting Asian sweatshop workers, or dumping so many toxins that we all get cancer, or overextending our system so far that it crashes and we get eaten by roving gangs.

But notice: primitive people don't think this way. Of course, if you put them on an assembly line or on the side of a freeway or in a modern war, they would know they were in hell. But if you offered them an LED lantern made on an assembly line, or a truck ride to their hunting ground, or a gun, most of them would accept it without hesitation. Primitive people tend to adopt any tool they find useful – not because they're wise, but because they're ignorant; because their cultures have not evolved defences against tools that will lead them astray.

I think the root of civilisation, and a major source of human evil, is simply that we became clever enough to extend our power beyond our empathy. It's like the famous *Twilight Zone* episode where there's a box with a button, and if you push it you get a million dollars and someone you don't know dies. We have countless 'boxes' that do basically the same thing. Some of them are physical, like cruise missiles or ocean-killing fertilisers, or even junk food where your mouth gets a million dollars and your heart dies. Others are social, like subsidies that make junk food affordable, or the corporation, which by definition does any harm it can get away with that will bring profit to the shareholders. I'm guessing it all started when our mental and physical tools combined to enable positive feedback in personal wealth. Anyway, as soon as you have something that does more harm than good, but that appears to the decision makers to do more good than harm, the decision makers will decide to do more and more of it, and before long you have a whole society built around obvious benefits that do hidden harm.

The kicker is, once we gain from extending our power beyond our seeing and feeling, we have an incentive to repress our seeing and feeling. If child slaves are making your clothing, and you want to keep getting clothing, you either have to not know about them, or know about them and feel good about it. You have to make yourself ignorant or evil.

But gradually we're learning. Every time it comes out that some product is made with sweatshop labour, a few people stop buying it. Every day, someone is in a supermarket deciding whether to spend extra money to buy shade-grown coffee or fair trade chocolate. It's not making a big difference, but all mass changes have to start with a few people, and my point is that we are stretching the human conscience further than it's ever gone, making sacrifices to help forests we will never see and people we will never meet. This is not simple-minded or 'idealistic', but rational, highly sophisticated moral behaviour. And you find it not at the trailing edge of civilisation but at the leading edge, among educated urbanites.

There are also growing movements to reduce energy consumption, to eat locally-produced food, to give up high-paying jobs for better quality of life, and to trade industrial-scale for human-scale tools. I would prefer not to own a car, but my motivation is not to save the world – it's that the continuing costs of owning a car put me in a different economic niche, where I am more connected to the impersonal world of money, and less connected to friends and family. On my land I don't use power tools, except for a chainsaw when I have a huge amount of wood to cut. In general I'd rather do work in a way that exercises my body, allows me to hear birds, and does not make me dependent on an industrial system that gives me no participation in power.

When I look at the discourse around this kind of choice, it's positively Satanic. People whose position is basically 'Thundersaw cut fast, me feel like god,' present themselves as agents of enlightenment and progress, while people with intelligent reasons for doing something completely new – choosing weaker, slower tools when high-energy tools are available – are seen as lizard-brained throwbacks. What's even more tragic is when they see themselves that way.

This movement is often called 'voluntary simplicity', but we should distinguish between *technological* simplicity and *mental* simplicity. Primitive people, even when they have complex cultures, use simple tools for a simple reason – those are the only tools they have. In so-called 'civilisation', we've just been using more and more complex technologies for simple-minded reasons – they give us brute power and shallow pleasures. But as we learn to be more sophisticated in our thinking about technology, we will be able to use complex tools for complex reasons – or simple tools for complex reasons.

Primitivists, understandably, are impatient. They want us to go back to using simple tools and they don't care why we do it. It's like our whole species is an addict, and seductive advanced technologies are the drug, and primitivism is the urge to throw our whole supply of drugs in the garbage. Any experienced addict will tell you that doesn't work. The next day you dig it out of the garbage or the next week you buy more.

Of course there are arguments that this will be impossible. The most common one goes like this: 'For civilisation, you need agriculture, and for agriculture, you need topsoil. But the topsoil is gone! Agriculture survives only by dumping synthetic fertilisers on dead soil, and those fertilisers depend on oil, and the easily extracted oil is also gone. If the industrial system crashes just a little, we'll have no oil, no fertiliser, no agriculture, and therefore no choice but foraging and hunting.'

Agriculture, whether or not it's a good idea, is in no danger. The movement to switch the whole planet to synthetic fertilisers on dead soil (ironically called 'the green revolution') had not even started yet when another movement started to switch back: organic farming. Present organic farmers are still using oil to run tractors and haul supplies in, but in terms of getting the soil to produce a crop, organic farming *is* agriculture without oil, and it's the fastest growing segment of the food economy. It is being held back by cultural inertia, by the political power of industrial agribusiness, and by cheap oil. It is not being held back by any lack of land suitable for conversion to organic methods. No one says, 'We bought this old farm, but since the soil is dead, we're just going to leave it as a wasteland, and go hunt elk.' People find a way to bring the soil back.

The other common argument is that 'humanity has learned its lesson.' I think this is on the right track, but too optimistic about how much we've learned, and about what kind of learning is necessary. Mere rebellion is as old as the first slave revolt in Ur, and you can find intellectual critiques of civilisation in the Old Testament: From Ecclesiastes 5:11, 'When goods increase, they are increased that eat them: and what good is there to the owners thereof?' And from Isaiah 5:8, 'Woe unto those who join house to house, and field to field, until there is no place.' If this level of learning were enough, we would have found utopia thousands of years ago. Instead, people whose understanding was roughly the same as ours, and whose courage was greater, kept making the same mistakes.

In *Against His-story, Against Leviathan*, Fredy Perlman set out to document the whole history of resistance to civilisation, and inadvertently undermined his conclusion that this Leviathan will be the last, by showing again and again that resistance movements become the new dominators. The ancient Persian empire started when Cyrus was inspired by Zoroastrianism to sweep away the machinery of previous empires. The Roman empire started as a people's movement to eradicate the Etruscans. The modern nation state began with the Moravians forming a defensive alliance against the Franks, who fell into war-like habits themselves after centuries of resisting the Romans. And we all know what happened with Christianity.

I fear it's going to happen again. Now, the simple desire to go primitive is harmless and beneficial – I wish luck and success to anyone who tries it, and I hope we always have some tribal forager-hunters around, just to keep the human potential stretched. And I enjoy occasional minor disasters like black-outs and snowstorms, which serve to strip away illusions and remind people that they're alive. I loved the idea in *Fight Club* (the movie) of destroying the bank records to equalise wealth. That's right in line with the ancient Jubilee tradition, where debts were cancelled every few decades to restabilise the economy and prevent a hard collapse.

What I fear is that some writers are trying to inspire a movement to actively cause a hard collapse, and if they attract enough followers, they could succeed. This would be a terrible mistake – not just a moral mistake but a *strategic* mistake – and the root of it is old-fashioned authoritarian thinking: that if you force someone to do something, it's the same as if they do it on their own. In fact it's exactly the opposite. The more we are forced to abandon this system, the less we will learn, and the more aggressively we will fight to rebuild something like it. And the more we choose to abandon it, the more we will learn, and the less likely we will make the same mistakes.

The really frightening thing is when people fantasise about destroying libraries and museums, as if this would prevent a complex society from ever getting started again – just as if thousands of years ago, without libraries or museums, people didn't start complex societies about fifty times. In the addiction metaphor, burning libraries is like not only throwing the drugs away, but also erasing all memory of being an addict, and then going back to the same tempting environment with the same addictive personality. It's such a perfect mistake that I can only conclude that these people subconsciously want to repeat the whole cycle of pain.

Of course we will not have another society based on oil, and per-capita energy consumption will drop, but it's unlikely that energy or complexity will fall to pre-industrial levels. Hydroelectric and atomic fission plants are in no immediate danger, and every year there are new innovations in energy from sun, wind, waves, and ethanol crops. Alternative energy would be growing much faster with good funding, and in any case it's not necessary to convert the whole global infrastructure in the next 20 years. Even in a general collapse, if just one region has a surplus of sustainable energy, they can use it to colonise and re-'develop' the collapsed areas at their own pace. Probably this will be happening all over.

I don't think there's any escape from complex, high energy societies, so instead of focusing on avoiding them, we should focus on making them tolerable. This means, first, that our system is enjoyable for its participants – that the activities necessary to keep it going are experienced by the people who do them as meaningful and freely chosen. Second, our system must be ethical toward the world around it. My standards here are high – the totality of biological life on Earth must be better off with us than without us. And third, our system must not be inherently unstable. It might be destroyed by an asteroid or an ice age, but it must not destabilise itself internally, by having an economy that has to grow or die, or by depleting non-renewable resources, or by having any trend at all that ratchets, that easily goes one way but can't go the other way without a catastrophe.

These three standards seem to be separate. When Orwell wrote that the future is 'a boot stamping on a human face – forever,' he was imagining a system that's internally stable but not enjoyable. Techno-utopians fantasise about a system that expands into space and lasts billions of years while crushing any trace of biological wildness. And some paranoids fear 'ecofascism', a system that is stable and serves nature, but that represses most humans.

I think all these visions are impossible, for a reason that is overlooked in our machine-worshipping culture: that collapse often happens for psychological reasons. Erich Fromm said it best, in *What Does It Mean to Be Human?*:

'Even if the social order can do everything to man – starve him, torture him, imprison him or overfeed him – this cannot be done without certain consequences which follow from the very conditions of human existence. Man, if utterly deprived of all stimuli and pleasure, will be incapable of performing work, certainly any skilled work. If he is not that utterly destitute, he will tend to rebel if you make him a slave; he will tend to be violent if life is too boring; he will tend to lose all creativity if you make him into a machine. Man in this respect is not different from animals or from inanimate matter. You can get certain animals into the zoo, but they will not reproduce, and others will become violent although they are not violent in freedom ... If man were infinitely malleable, there would have been no revolutions'.[3]

In *1491*, Mann writes that on Pizarro's march to conquer the Incas, he was actively helped by local populations who were sick of the empire's oppression. Freddy Perlman's book goes through the whole history of Western civilisation arguing for the human dissatisfaction factor in every failed society. And it's clear to me and many other Americans that our empire is falling because nobody believes in it – not the troops in Iraq, who quickly learn that the war is bullshit; not the corporate executives, who at best are focused on short term profits and at worst are just thieves; not the politicians, who are cynically violating every supposed American principle for lobbyist money; and not the people who actually do the work, most of whom are just going through the motions.

Also, America (with other nations close behind) is getting more and more tightly controlled and thus more unbearable for its participants. This is a general problem of top-down systems: for both technical and psychological reasons, it's easy to add control mechanisms and hard to remove them, easy to squeeze tighter and hard to let go. As the controllers get more selfish and insulated, and the controlled get more frustrated and depressed, and more energy is wasted on forcing people to do what they wouldn't do without force, the whole system seizes up and can only be renewed by a surge of transforming energy from below. This transformation could be peaceful, but often the ruling interests block it until it builds up such pressure that it explodes violently.

The same way the ruling interests become corrupt through an exploitative relationship with the people, we all become corrupt when we participate in a society that exploits the life around it. When we talk about 'nature', we don't mean wheatfields or zoo animals – we mean plants that scatter seeds to the wind and animals that roam at will. We mean freedom, raw aliveness, and we can't repress it outside ourselves without also repressing it inside ourselves. The spirit that guides our shoe when it crushes grass coming through cracks in the driveway, also guides us to crush feelings and perceptions coming through cracks in our paved minds, and we need these feelings and perceptions to make good decisions, to be sane.

If primitive life seems better to us, it's because it's easier for smaller and simpler societies to avoid falling into domination. In the best tribes, the 'chief' just tells people to do what they want to do anyway, and a good chief will channel this energy into a harmonious whole. But the bigger a system gets, and the longer a big system lasts, the more challenging it is to maintain a bottom-up energy structure.

I have a wild speculation about the origin of complex societies. The Great Pyramid of Giza is superior in every way to the two pyramids next to it – yet the Great Pyramid was the *first* of the three to be built. It's like Egyptian civilisation appeared out of nowhere at full strength, and immediately began declining. My speculation is: the first pyramid was not built by slaves! It was built by an explosion of human enthusiasm channelled into a massive cooperative effort. But then, as we've seen in pretty much every large system in history, this pattern of human action hardened, leaders became rulers, inspired actions became chores and workers became slaves.

To achieve stability, and freedom, and ecological responsibility, we must learn to halt the slide from life into control, to maintain the bottom-up energy structure permanently, even in large complex systems. I don't know how we're going to do this. It's even hard for individuals to do it – look at all the creative people who make one masterpiece and spend the rest of their life making crappy derivative works. The best plan I can think of is to build our system out of cells of less than 150 people, roughly the number at which co-operation tends to give way to hierarchy, and even then to expect cells to go bad, and have built-in pathways for dead cells to be broken down and new ones to form and individuals to move from cell to cell. Basically, we'd be making a big system that's like a living body, where all past big systems have been animated corpses.

Assuming that our descendants do achieve stability, what technological level will they be at? I want to leave this one wide open. It's possible in theory for us to go even further 'back' than the stone age. I call this the *Land Dolphins* scenario – that we evolve into super-intelligent creatures who don't use any physical tools at all. At the other extreme, I'm not ruling out space colonies, although the worst mistake we could make would be expanding into space before we have learned stability on our home planet. I think physical travel to other solar systems is out of the question – long before mechanistic science gets that far, we will have moved to new paradigms that offer much easier ways to get to new worlds.

The 'singularity' theory is also off the mark. Techies think machines will surpass humans, because the mechanistic model tells them that we're nothing but machines ourselves, so all we need to do is make better machines, which according to the myth of 'progress' is inevitable. If we do get a technological transcendence, it's more likely to involve machines *changing* humans. My favourite scenario is time-contracted virtual reality: suppose you can go into an artificial world, have the experience of spending a week there, and come back and only a day has passed, or an hour, or a minute. If we can do that, all bets are off!

The biggest weakness in this vision is that innovation can go with stability, that we can continue exploring and trying new things without repeatedly destabilising ourselves by extending our power beyond our understanding. But it's equally implausible that we could somehow transform ourselves out of being a curious and inventive species, or that we could drive ourselves to extinction – we are by far the most mentally adaptable species on Earth, and not bad at physical adaptation.

One possibility is that we will diverge into multiple species. It happens all the time in nature, and for most of the history of hominids there were several kinds of us walking around. This could happen through biotech or through ordinary evolution, which we still don't understand. Scientists have spent decades bombarding fruit flies with radiation, trying to produce a random mutation that would lead to a new species, and totally failed. But in another experiment, fruit flies were put through a maze with different exits depending on environmental preferences, and they formed distinct populations that refused to interbreed. It's a good guess that this is already happening with humans, and that our accelerating evolution is being driven not by our high population, but by increasing diversity of human environments, which is likely to continue. Maybe we will spin off subspecies that overspecialise themselves into extinction, while a few generalist core species survive.

If I had to guess, I'd say that we're just going to keep making mistakes and falling down forever, and in that case the best we can do is minimise the severity of the falls. I think we're doing a pretty good job even in the present collapse, which is shaping up to be a big one. Innovations in efficient farming and water filtration and small-scale alternative energy are going to give many regions a soft landing. Even in America, which has a long way to fall, we might escape with no more than a severe depression, a mild fall in population, and a much-needed shakeout of technology and economics. Life will get more painful but also more meaningful, as billions of human hours shift from processing paperwork and watching TV to intensive learning of new skills to keep ourselves alive. These skills will run the whole range, from tracking deer to growing tomatoes to fixing bicycles to building solar-powered wi-fi networks – to new things we won't even imagine until we have our backs to the wall.

I think we can see the future in popular fiction, but not the fiction we think. Most science fiction is either stuck in the recent past, in the industrial age's boundless optimism about machines, or it looks at the present by exploring the unintended consequences of high tech. Cyberpunk is better – if you put a 1950s Disney version of the year 2000 through a cyberpunk filter, you would get very close to the real 2000. The key insight of cyberpunk is that more technology doesn't make things cleaner – it makes things dirtier.

Fantasy, while seeming to look at the past, might be seeing the future: elves and wizards could represent the increasing diversity of humans (or post-humans) after the breakdown of the industrial monoculture, and 'magic' is clearly a glimpse of post-mechanistic scientific paradigms. And I think steampunk does the best of all, if you factor out the Victorian element. Like cyberpunk, it shows a human-made world that's as messy and alive as nature, but the technological system is a crazy hybrid of everything from 'stone age' to 'space age' – thus refuting the very idea that we are locked into ages.

Primitive people see time as a circle. Civilised people see it as a line. We are about to see it as an open plain where we can wander at will. History is broken. Go!

References

1. E Richard Sorenson, 'Preconquest Consciousness' in *Tribal Epistemologies: Essays in the History of Anthropology* ed. Helmut Wautischer, 1998.

2. Quoted in 'Evolution getting faster by the millennium', Sydney Morning Herald 12/12/2007.

3. 'What does it mean to be human?' in Erich Fromm, *The Revolution of Hope: Towards a humanized technology*, 1968.

MELANIE CHALLENGER

The Thorn

The tree cracks into me or my purpose and gravity
Crack against it – each blames the other.
The tree's argument plants its first rejoinder above my knee.
Under the surface of the puncture, the natural ideas begin
To persuade. How the brute flint struck their shiftless ankle
For the soundness of hot nights; and the godless
Outrage of unstopped wind across moors made myth of these tall,
Silent heroes that once stooped through no lack of pride.

                                    And the base
Dreams of partisan or pike tossing death like the careless arrival of sin.

I kneel as before a crowned head, the thorn's nativity palled as a bride.
It is so swiftly branching, green as a teenager, this tongueless child –
The infant cry of its roots knocks my heart, lungs, guts up into a wild
State. As a doddering saint's hand, a hundred years old, the rootstock
Grips my mind. Its thoughts made mine. Its thirst, its patience all mine.

MARIO PETRUCCI

Three hot drops of salmon oil

Let me begin with a rendition, by writer-poet David Whyte, of the Celtic story of Finn and the Salmon. Finnegas, an old man, had fished for seven years in a certain pool, knowing that whoever ate the salmon would acquire all knowledge. At last he caught it and, rejoicing, gave his young apprentice (aptly named Finn) strict instructions to cook it just right and not, on any condition, to eat any of it. But, being a boy, Finn was distracted, staring into the dark woods. The salmon got burned. A blister the size of his thumb rose on one side of the fish. Terrified of failing his master, he pressed a thumb against the blister, hoping to press it back in. It burst, and three hot drops of salmon oil dripped onto Finn's thumb, which – instinctively – the boy thrust into his mouth. And so it was that Finn the boy, not Finnegas the old man, gained knowledge.

Early in 2002, I had something of a near-Finn experience. The fish in my case was an astonishing book, *Voices from Chernobyl*, translated by Antonina Bouis and edited by Svetlana Alexievich. These remarkable women allowed the eyewitness accounts of ordinary people to pass directly onto the page. Peasant and teacher; wife, soldier; fireman and cameraman; the official and the child: common voices, uncommonly eloquent. I found *Voices* purely by chance. Upon opening it, I did not receive instant knowledge – but I was most certainly burned. A key testimony, for me, was that of Ludmila Polyanskaya. 'Where are our intellectuals? Writers? Philosophers?' she cried, 'Why are they silent?' Still, with Seamus Heaney's warning not to 'rampage permissively in other people's sadnesses' ringing in my ears, I was reluctant to pick up my pen. But, again from *Voices*, Alexandr Renansky reassured me that art, like 'the plasma of an infected person, can serve to inoculate.'

I began to realise that, one way or another, we were all infected by Chernobyl. It was still active, in the air we use to speak about it, in the blood we need to think about it. I resolved, as far as I could, to listen. Indeed, writing poetry on the subject often felt like taking dictation. Those men and women; their children, whose words prise open your heart even as they shatter it: they were so insistent.

Heavy Water (Enitharmon Press) and *Half Life* (Heaventree) ensued: a diptych of books, two facets of a single, extended poem. Then, in 2005, I was approached by Bethan Roberts at Seventh Art Productions, an independent film company based in Brighton. The directors David Bickerstaff and Phil Grabsky used the poetry as primary material for a new film. I recall a particular intensity surrounding this film during its production phase, partly because we needed to meet deadlines for Chernobyl's twentieth anniversary. It occurs to me, too, that I was keen for my books to be launched, together, on 26 April 2004, to mark the eighteenth anniversary. Strange how we need 'anniversaries' in order to think or feel our way through such events, to validate them. In the UK, leading up to April 2006, Chernobyl's media currency suddenly got a substantial lift. That will probably happen again, one imagines (somewhat cynically), after 50 years. But these calendar units of historical consumption rarely spill over into any significant re-evaluation in a population largely disenfranchised from personal activism; rather, all that is usually achieved through anniversaries (of such a difficult kind) is a sense of public sympathy mixed with resignation, or a notching-up of background anxiety levels. What, then, is the point of post-apocalyptic or anniversary art?

Well, in the case of poetry, there is no doubt that language constantly falls short of experience – but miraculously so. I say miraculously, because language (particularly the heightened language of poetry) can provide a penetrating experience in its own right. Not merely a substitute experience, nor even a parallel one; but a gateway – a series of gateways – into fields of transformation. A poem has the ability to alight in the mind, in the heart, not unlike an angel. I wonder, was Finn's salmon a water-borne angel; or even a poem? Either way, it is rather in vogue these days to suggest that Old Testament angels were neither sweet nor pure, but more like Jehovah's henchmen. Their plumage came not in white, but in shades of grey. There is something in that, though, because angels – like poems – are agents of difficulty as much as of peace.

This agency embodied by poems, their messy grey-scale angelic impetus, is impoverished by post-enlightenment attempts to categorise literature and science as, at best, the most distant of relatives and, at worst, tribal arch-rivals. Science and art are kissing cousins. John Dewey (in *Art as Experience*) signals this when he writes: 'The odd notion that an artist does not think and a scientific inquirer does nothing else is the result of converting a difference of tempo and emphasis into a difference in kind.' I tend to agree. Both the scientist and the artist ask deeper questions of what is superficially observed; in their respective ways, they each pay the world full attention. And awareness, paying attention – that, at the bottom of it, is what art is really all about. Through art, a civilisation stays awake.

As an ecologist and lapsed physicist, I sense that interfaces such as those between poetry and ecology/science/war hold key 'alertness nutrients' for our world. Think of potatoes: we know the skins are good for us, and yet so often we peel them. But I am sanguine about interfaces, those places in the body politic where the skin is thinner, where knowledge can more successfully seep through – as the pulse does, at the wrist. Great poetry, like all great art, can take the complex pulse of a culture. But if art/poetry can deliver a prognosis on society, can it save the patient? Come to think of it, can any government or organisational policy do so? I say this not to demoralise us, but to remind myself that my first call must be to 'save' the self: that is, to open this self to challenge and support, to empathy and sensitivity – to interfaces. Without that, nothing much is possible, however failsafe my machines may become, however persuasive or creative my organisational response may be.

Nuclear energy is evidence of immense creativity; but creativity, we know, has its negative as well as positive incarnations, which come about through failing to engage the entire self. If we respond to Chernobyl personally, positively, only then can sustainable and sustaining collaborations and activities be discovered. I am not suggesting that, if we had Plato's philosophers running the Republic, material entities such as plutonium and nuclear bombs would be inconceivable. All I am saying is that the potency of self-response *is* very real and extremely present – at least potentially – in society. This 'fuller self' is not to be confused with a bigger ego; nor should it be dismissed as inappropriate (as it often is) in the context of pragmatics, organisations and committees. As Dostoevsky shows us, humans must have a point at which they stand against the culture and positively assert the self. Art provides interfaces: it can help us to access the self, can assist us in transcending formalities so we are able to operate more powerfully than with intellectual efficiency alone. Art inoculates us against the temptation to short-circuit the self, which is what happens when we sink our responsibility and vitality entirely into the formal, the technical, the industrial response.

Konrad Lorenz wrote: 'I believe I've found the missing link between animal and civilised man. It is us.' This is nowhere more evident than in our love-hate relationship with industry. I am narrowing my eyes, of course, in the direction of the nuclear industry – but not that industry alone. David Bohm, the great philosopher and radical scientist, has written: 'We now have the entertainment industry, and practically have a culture industry and an education industry; similarly, we... have the nature industry.' *[On Dialogue]*

Yes, the environment too is becoming an industry. To address Chernobyl, or our environment, without first unravelling this preoccupation with industries is rather like entering the Minotaur's labyrinth without Ariadne's thread. Britain (partly impelled by James Lovelock) hurtles towards a vision of nuclear stations studded along its coasts, black as flies around a rind, whilst remaining as much in thrall to oil as the Neanderthals were to the first cudgel or camp-fire. Through all this – in spite of what we believe as individuals or groups, or even what a Prime Minister or President may say seemingly to the contrary – industrialised and industrialising nations still behave largely as though ecology were 'out there'. Einstein's promising definition of the environment as 'everything that isn't me' is, on closer inspection, flawed. Let us say instead: 'the environment is everything, *including* me.' Perhaps the only global organisation able to take decisive action on the environment will be the planet herself. Gaia – however you interpret that concept – is set to become our greatest revolutionary. Many of us have mixed feelings about revolutions. Gaia's is unlikely to be a bloodless one.

Some of my concerns so far may seem, at first, peripheral or distracting to the core subject of Chernobyl. But Bohm reminds us: 'Studying the distractions is part of the process.' Art can transport us to the periphery, where we can discern its crucial relevance to any (so-called, or apparent) 'centre'. Moreover, what most industries have in common is *their* ability to distract us from a truly central issue: the empowered, engaged self. Indeed, some industries have taken on the quality of a new priesthood or religion. See how their proponents and experts defend their credos against anything but the most irresistible tide of evidence or social will, while their advertisers constantly assure us of paradise (albeit an earthly one). Of course, certain sections of the anti-nuclear lobby can be just as forcefully partisan. I am reminded here of Quentin Crisp's visit to Northern Ireland, where he declared himself an atheist. A woman in the audience instantly stood up and asked: 'Yes, but is it the God of the Catholics or the God of the Protestants in whom you *don't* believe?' The energy debate is similarly locked into sectarianism, a nuclear/non-nuclear dichotomy which allows the deeper, more pertinent issues to lie unaddressed.

There is, in all this, a danger of creating a Chernobyl industry too. One of the best antidotes, perhaps, is the act of 're-membering': effectively, the putting back together of sundered or broken parts. This is a civilised and civilising act, even when understanding or focussed activity is in short supply. For Chernobyl, how else to honour those who were unable to speak, who were rendered see-through by political, social or intellectual neglect, than to remember them – first and foremost – through and with the self?

I must speak, too, of imagination. Many of the risks associated with nuclear energy are (if the industry's claims are reliable) very small indeed; but the immensity of impact of certain forms of human/system failure in nuclear processing and power stations, and the lengths of time for which these impacts may apply, are difficult to conceive. How to bring home, for instance, *in the imagination*, the idea that if the builders of Stonehenge had used conventional nuclear reactors, we would now probably still be actively engaged with their radioactive waste? Art can catalyse the imaginative leaps required to engage with time and space on a scale beyond our usual ken, helping to balance that tendency for the low-risk localised 'now' to dominate. Art also exercises the imaginative faculties, which are essential to a full appreciation of facts: imagination is crucial when contesting or challenging any accepted interpretation of data, just as it is to those who seek to disguise the facts or skew the analysis.

Furthermore, there is no such thing as a 'detached' machine, or instrument. Each object we create, whether fanciful or rooted in cast-iron physical-mathematical precepts, is an extension of our imagination. Industry and commerce are every bit as adept at creating powerful myths as the bard, novelist or film maker. In a profound sense, then, Chernobyl is not merely something that went wrong or that happened *to* us, but a material expression of the collective human self; of what makes us *us*. Which is why the quantification of Chernobyl and its after-effects, important as it is, can never become our sole aim. Chernobyl stands to remind us that knowledge is as much qualitative as quantitative.

One of the chief outcomes of the disaster will be what we allow it to tell us about ourselves, as an expression of our negative imagination and its myths. Why, for instance, do so many countries insist on nuclear power regardless of the complex levels of defence required to render it 'safe'? As John Steinbeck said, 'an animal which must protect itself with thick armour… is on the road to extinction.' Let us not imagine he was referring merely to organic or military shielding.

In understanding Chernobyl, intellect can therefore only ever provide one tool. Einstein said: 'We should take care not to make the intellect our God; it has, of course, powerful muscles, but no personality.' I would extend his warning to rhetoric. Politicians and experts are too easily tempted by it. As for the artist, to play the prophet or rhetorician in the streets, or in books, is merely to lose one's head.

But if not intellect or rhetoric, then what? At the risk of saying what I really mean (and an even greater risk of sprouting the visionary rhetorician's beard as I say it), I believe it a fundamental truth of our species that suffering – and a genuine empathy with suffering – serves to re-orient us in a better direction. Chernobyl is far more than a scientific mistake or a folly of Soviet zeitgeist; more, too, than yet another increment in our capacity to generate tragedy and environmental stress. On some plane – one that is more instinctive and felt than arcane – exists the chance to transform Chernobyl from wound to opportunity, to move from scientific progress measured scientifically to human progress whose values are rooted firmly in compassion.

This, I realise, is all very easy to say – particularly in such vague terms. And please, do not think I treat lightly the various ways in which Chernobyl has already stirred up many people to challenge a merely technical response. Nor is it lost on me that I am among the world's beneficiaries of industrialism. I also admit that I am sometimes sceptical about my own arguments. As a long-term stumbler on the *via negativa*, I have often doubted whether that warm April night in Pripyat was anything other than a horrific instance of needless suffering, scheduled for repetition, over and over, in the future. At least some of you, I feel sure, will identify with those doubts. But what has changed for me recently is that I am now willing to apply that scepticism more consistently: that is, to be sceptical, too, about my doubts. Perhaps, in this narrow corridor of 'doubt doubted', a door – several doors – may open.

One such door leads to vulnerability and, with it, honesty – particularly with ourselves. This doorway feels draughty and uncomfortable. And not without reason, given the negative manner in which vulnerability is so often met by our institutions. But the story of knowledge is, in the end, all one story. *We* are one story, together, as individuals, organisations, nations – even as industries. We can let Chernobyl demonstrate the supremacy of negative imagination, or we can repossess our potential to meet it with wisdom and growth. This is nothing like a bland acceptance of facts, saying some stoic 'Yes' to past or future Chernobyls. As Karl Barth reminds us (via Seamus Heaney), the immense *Yes* of Mozart's music has potency precisely because it encompasses and overwhelms a *No*. Barth's is the kind of *Yes* I mean.

We have both that *Yes* and that *No* within us. In the words of Montaigne, 'I have never seen a greater monster – or miracle – in the world than myself.' Our species is not here merely to service the *Nos* of industrial or economic growth but, surely, to overwhelm them, transcend them, to fully engage the *Yes* of the human spirit. Easier said than done. As Eric Hoffer points out, 'every new adjustment is a crisis in self-esteem.' This is where one of the great insights of psychotherapy might help us. Namely, that if you act *as though* you were well, you start to *become* well. So, let us at least act as though we were beginning. We can voice a *Yes*, even if we are not quite sure, yet, what it represents. There are appalling events throughout history against which we cry that *No* of: 'This must never happen again.' Truth is, without thoroughgoing openness and a deep re-membering, without that *Yes*, it does happen again. If we refuse to transform, we have silently made that choice.

Einstein, when asked how he worked, replied: 'I grope.' We are a young and groping species – artists and industrialists alike. Science, including nuclear science, tells us we have caught the big fish of knowledge: all we need to do is prepare it properly, then consume it. But, through Chernobyl, we find ourselves in the aftermath of a terrible blunder. For me, it represents the largest and most scalding drop of the threesome it makes with Windscale and Three Mile Island. I hope, here, the notion of Finn sucking at his thumb conjures not an image of bungling childishness, but of child-*like*ness. Either way, we have been left in charge of the salmon. Whether by accident or design, we have pressed our thumbs firmly onto a hot blister. Have we now the courage to put it in our mouths?

Further reading
Heavy water: a poem for Chernobyl; Mario Petrucci, Enitharmon Press, 2004.
Half life: Poems for Chernobyl; Mario Petrucci, The Heaventree Press, 2004.
Voices from Chernobyl; Svetlana Alexievich; tr. Antonina Bouis, Aurum Press, 1999 [reprinted, 2005: Dalkey Archive]

in hay waist deep
uncle who said he saw
lash of rain snap
upward viper-
sharp to bite
the coming-down
tail – another tending
eaves from top-notch ladder
felt on his back
drops
worse than
wasps to a sack
while wife with foot
hard on bottom rung
kept her face of
tinder – yet
another
watched brown
slick of cloud a few
metres up suck back its
centre like a seam
in the roasted
bean – till it
split with blue &
for an hour all air smelt
of coffee – last it came to
me   i said   once
i stood
in rain so
ferocious streams
front & back – down
shallow contour of
nipples & ravine
between each
half of arse –

met at my pizzle
till i knew to my balls
how it felt to piss like
Orion: i said this
happened –
but they
laughed & took out
scythes & said the hay was
dry enough

Mario Petrucci

JEFF OLLERTON

W(h)ither science?

One letter can make one hell of a difference:
Substitute A for T or C for G, and you change the coding of DNA, the
structure of the resulting protein, and a person's life: GAG to GTG is all it
takes to transform a healthy individual into a sufferer of
sickle
cell
disease.

Add an h to a word in a punning title and we question whether science can
save us or if it will simply shrivel as global environmental change diverts its
funding into shoring up Western civilisation against the onslaught of a
rapidly
transforming
world.

As a child of the sixties, and as a professional scientist, I have been brought
up to believe that Science Will Save Us, will provide solutions to the
problems created by technological leaps and human avarice. Science gave
us the green revolution in agriculture, genetically modified organisms, solar
power generation. It will give us carbon neutral technology, 'sustainable'
urban environments, an internet with a direct mind interface:

Perhaps it will.
Perhaps it won't.
I don't know;
You don't know;
She, he and it does not know.
Scientific knowledge is not predictable.
But the scientific process may help us to recognise and comprehend
What and where we are.

This is the best of times and the worst of times to be a scientist. Unprecedented levels of funding are being pumped into the global science budget, allowing us to see further and deeper and closer, bringing a level of respect that elevates scientists to a quasi-priesthood. This has spawned a public interest in science that regularly finds scientific news stories at the top of the BBC News website's list of 'most popular stories now.'

But in a strange, twisted paradox, science and scientists are also among the least trusted individuals in society, whilst science itself (the process by which we obtain 'factual' knowledge about the universe and our place in it) is hopelessly misunderstood by the media and politicians. It only takes a raft of hacked and de-contextualised emails to float the reputations of scientists, and science itself, down shit creek with no method of propulsion:

Boredom is a big part of what drives human creativity, by which I mean the full spread of creativity, from the fine arts, through written forms and music, to the sciences:– it's all part of the same drive to prevent our brains from becoming mired in that choking ennui that tastes like stale tea and soggy biscuits.

Boredom is the neuronal curse of a cognitive, self-aware consciousness. It is the reason we invent our stories of gods and heroes.

Boredom is a tax we pay for being human.
Boredom has driven understanding.

Science cannot save us. But it can allow us to understand where we are in relation to the rest of the universe and to appreciate that we are part of the natural world, not separate from nature. And perhaps that will save us, perhaps that is science's lasting contribution to the future of our species. My personal science studies interacting assemblages of co-dependent species, trying to comprehend the processes that maintain these interactions, how they have evolved and what the implications are if they disappear, for both the ecosystems they are part of and for *Homo sapiens*.

We are only just beginning to understand how we are wholly dependent upon the 'ecosystem services' provided by pollinators, decomposing fungi, plants that protect against floods and tsunamis, pest-eating animals, and more, and more. An overriding message from this body of knowledge is that ecosystems are more stable, resilient, and function better if they contain a diverse, richly connected, highly interacting set of animals, plants, fungi, bacteria and other organisms. That includes, I believe, the human ecosystem that forms a nexus within the set of ecosystems that make up the biosphere:

> *We are part, not separate.*
> *We are linked, we require*
> *All the rest of the links*
> *To survive.*

Science has traditionally been seen as responding in a linear fashion to economics: throw enough money at a problem and the problem will be solved. But we are reaching the limit of that linear response when we consider ecosystem services: a scientific asymptote beyond which we cannot purchase what we need to live. Collaborations of ecologists and economists have sought to assign a dollar value to the environmental capital upon which we depend, though these are things that cannot be bought and their value is greater than the GDP of several planets, even if we had the technology to make, or replace, all that the planet provides.

In one of my first year undergraduate lectures on biodiversity, I ask the students to imagine that they are stranded in a remote forest in Britain, lost with no map, no water and no food. It doesn't matter how they got there; could be a plane crash, or the end of civilisation. They may even have been abandoned by their evil step-parent. Doesn't matter: the point is survival. The weather has been cool and wet and there are mushrooms and toadstools in abundance, various species sprouting from every fallen log, pile of dung and grassy ride. It's a long way to anywhere and the stranded students are hungry; very hungry. Would they risk eating these fungi? What are the chances of them being poisoned and dying? My purpose is to get them to think about our engagement with the natural world, our ability to understand how dependent we are upon the environment around us and what it provides for us.

Our ancestors would have known the answer. They would have known that very few (about 1%) of fungi in the British Isles are deadly poisonous. A larger number (some 6%) will make you sick, but it's still a small proportion compared to the number that are edible and good, which is about one fifth. The remaining 70% or so are inedible: they are slimy, woody, bitter or otherwise unpleasant; they might make you gag as you try to swallow their vile caps and stems, but they won't kill you.

This is not an exhortation to go and randomly try eating every toadstool and bracket that you see. But my students, almost without fail, tell me that they would not risk eating any of those wild fungi because they have been told that they are 'bad for us' repeatedly by parents and as part of the collective mass of stories that we tell each other about nature: that it is dangerous, poisonous, destructive. So it is, but rarely, not all of the time. So are we, also not constantly, but infrequently. Because we are a component of the natural world, and we reflect our origins, but most people do not know it. The question I ask my students is thus not just about human understanding of biodiversity, it is about the natural world and our place as part of it:

To be a part, and not apart, we need to understand.
Understanding may come from a life of trial and error, as it did for our ancestors,
Or the observational and experimental trial and error of the scientific method.
One of the myths that we tell ourselves is that we are the Earth's stewards,
Looking after a fragile and delicate planet.
This is the reverse of the fact: the Earth is OUR steward,
And it is our species that will fall if our ecosystems fail.
Science does not have all of the answers, but it does have a lot of the questions.

SEAMUS BRADY

At Pencarrow Lighthouse, a dirge

'All the rivers run into the sea, yet the sea is not full.'
– Ecclesiastes, 1.7

there are six billion of us
in each head sixty five thousand thoughts in a day
that is three hundred and ninety trillion thoughts
every day
and on this cliff top
overlooking the Pacific Ocean
I am adding one more thought –
that wisdom
is like a whale in the sea
a great size when seen
from a small boat
but perhaps to a lighthouse keeper
who knows that the sea
is vast and terrible
when it rattle his doors
and screams oblivion
through the cracks in his windows
perhaps to a lighthouse keeper
a whale is one more reminder
that the sea holds everything
and claims everything
it unthinks all thoughts
and that in time
even the sea forgets

CHRISTINE BOUSFIELD

White Out

No satellites here. Even the old telegraph pole up the hill
is swathed in ivy, hops, waving bindweed,
footed by rhododendron gnawing into its wires.
At night we are pitch black, cut off from
the information highway. Dark matter has gravitational effects:
light, too, draws everything to it like these moths
and ginny spinners banging against my window.
From space, we're a scattering of light across the cold
Northern Hemisphere – we see only stars, collisions
a thousand thousand years old, a history of accidents,
who did what to whom, and in what circumstances,
how best to father and mother an Olympic hurdler, or a king.
But I have no time for celebrities, feel only the enveloping dark,
briar rose petals scattered across disappearing hills,
one rook calling to another in the aspens.

SIMON LYS

The Wanderbuch of Christopher Jansen

A small black body falls from the sky. Broken and coated in tar, rainbow feathers crown its bloodied scalp. A beauty totem stripped and snapped, it lies on the grey pavement, its crisscross bones hopscotching in a shadow of bonfire chars. I look up at the pale blue faceless giant. Streaking white lines map new territories, new battlegrids across the apparent emptiness. The bodies fall like bombs over our blitzed city and the street walks on. Black stilettos and scuffed doc martens stamp past the smashed stick legs in dirty rags. I stare at the faces gliding by. Blindly their lives run on as they step over a bag of rubbish blown over in the wind. But I know. I saw it fall.

I pick up the dead child in my arms, wrap the bones in my coat and hold them to my chest. Cradle them. Cradle him. And set off.

The plastered face of the sky cracks. Rain cries and shudders its thunder. Convulsive gods fit in their thrones. The tiny people below hurry under umbrellas, a swaying field of beaten down fungus.

I walk north. Alone on the street in the downpour. Past empty shadow of house and man. Rose petals are thumped off, stoned in punishment for their beauty, as they trail for sun on the walls of the castles of the well-to-do.

A red balloon floats buffeted through the grey sky.

The west of Highgate cemetery. Overgrown graves and dancing ghosts. Shallow figures dart through the sleeting drizzle. I join them and duck between ivy and under leaves. In the hiding places, in the shelter of trees and standing stones, I take a lightning snapped branch and dig. I use my hands too, I let the earth fill the nail bed. I dig a grave for the unknown child and I lay him to rest.

The eyes, obsolete. The pupil has swallowed the iris and everything is black, moated by a thin yellow sea. I close the lids and I cover the sleeping child with blankets of dirt.

DANIEL FORD & MARK DICKSON

The Lesson

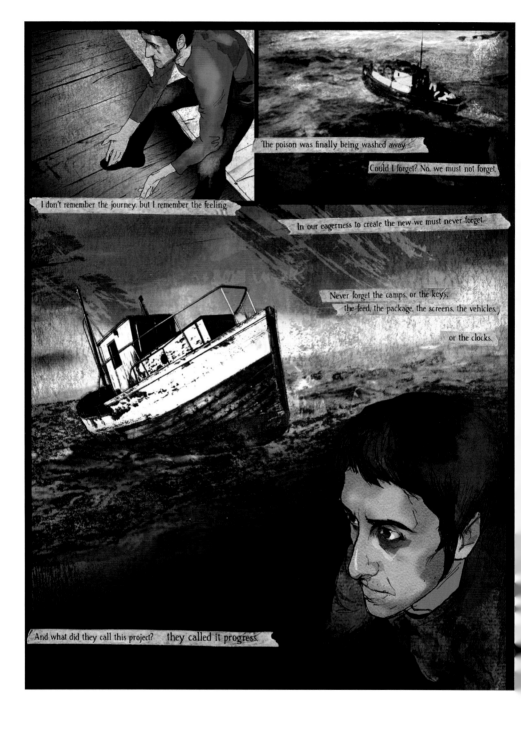

The poison was finally being washed away.

Could I forget? No, we must not forget.

I don't remember the journey, but I remember the feeling.

In our eagerness to create the new we must never forget.

Never forget the camps, or the keys,
the feed, the package, the screens, the vehicles,

or the clocks.

And what did they call this project? they called it progress.

And so we invented new stories.

My children grew stronger.

They knew new thoughts.

There was never time.

There was making, shifting, moving, lifting, treading.

They would speak for the trees,

they would speak for the rivers,

they would speak for the wolf.

We must share this. We could not help but share it

and if they would not listen, if they would not listen what then?

We would make them.

Clumsily man gave names to all things,

he choked the bird when he called it finch, eagle, sparrow, wren, and then the creature fell silent.

He named them so he wouldn't have to listen.

Who can forgive man his symbols and his concepts?

FIN

REINHARDT SØBYE

Innocence is God's only face

Anxiety is Awe for Nothingness

The Worried Angel

The Phony King

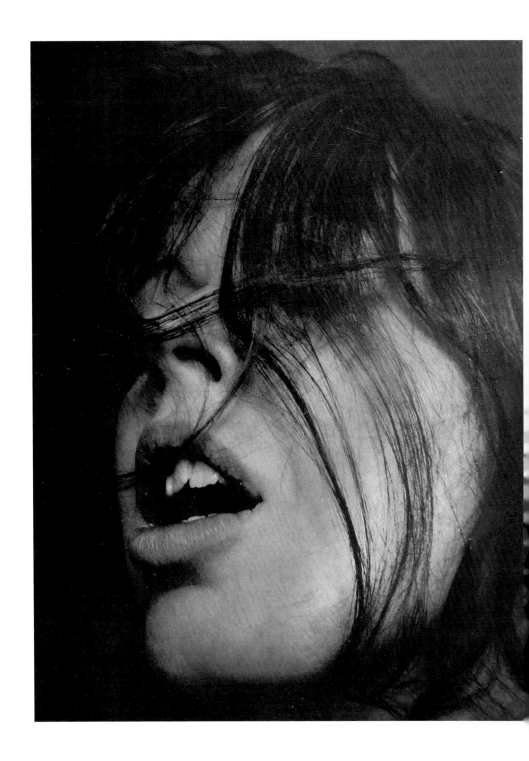

Eternity

Invisible in the full black sky, another plane blasts its anonymous hum and shudder. The mud over the corpse jiggles at the rumble.

I place my hands on the earth, palms flat to still the resting place. I wait for the tremors to pass, for the ground to fall silent and calm. And even when stillness does return, I fear that the quaking will come again.

The red balloon pops on a branch and I jump at the bang.

I entrust the child to the trees. I tell them to feast well.

I walk out through the wet leaves. From the darkness to the light. I hold my hands up into the rain and let the sky wash them clean. Father, pelt me, cleanse me, make me pure. Take death away. Mother, keep safe your children, find life within and let it burn.

Night is coming with its men in uniform trying to close the gates. I hurry out avoiding eye contact. I walk to the tube. I sit on sticky cushions and ride back and forth to the ends of lines. Carriages empty, carriages fill. People look away, hiding behind tales of gossip and exploitation. They stagger and stumble when they get too close. I am something to be avoided. I may contaminate. I have the plague.

I save the travelling souls and get out into the night. Somewhere in the suburban south of the line.

There is a carnival of sorts. Drunken dancing and tin drums. Lost teenagers stagger high in each others arms. Empty ritual, meaning long forgotten in a fog of alcohol and drug. I watch a pack of them wander aimless and confused, smiles smashed into their faces. But their eyes are looking for the horizon, searching for a way out.

I leave the party and I go back to the place I live. Sanitised white, ripped of any connotations of homely. Sterile and separate, I live in a mechanical world, without dust or dirt. Plastic drip dry wipe clean shininess.

I smile at the neighbour who does not know me. Awkward shuffles. Averted eyes.

The lights are on in the flat. The television still natters from this morning. Economic crises and third world flooding. Two separate items. No correlation. I take one of the Habitat dining chairs and smash the screen. It's not glass and so does not shatter satisfyingly. Instead it Dali drips from its frame, viscous media thick as tar.

The room is still too bright, too noisy. I turn off the lights and get candles. That calms things. The place begins to feel sacred.

I take my laptop and hurl it down into the Thames. It does not even try to float. I stand on the balcony and I wish it well. It is eaten fast by the water and the creatures of the mud, three-eyed fish with tumoured jaws that dwell in the skeletons and shopping trolleys of the deep.

I look to the books on my bookcase. I long for them to speak to me. I long for the ghosts of Blake, Whitman and Ginsberg. Ballard, Vonnegut and Bowles. Cowper Powys, Burroughs and Orwell. I call to you all now. Celine and Hesse. Garner and Hoban. Atwood and Hulme. Rise spirits from your pages, wrap your arms and guide me in the darkness. I apprentice myself before you. Show me the way.

The bookcase is silent and still. I run a sweeping arm along, avalanching words to the floor. I kick them out onto the balcony and through the banisters down into the river. Take these words and feast, krakens of the depths. Washed white faces and empty eyes, helpless stoneblank pages, they mean nothing. They speak in silence. So feast, leviathans, feast!

I change out of my suit into warmer clothes and leave the flat. I do not bother locking the door.

I walk and I walk until there is no longer tarmac beneath my feet.

I stop in the field in the midmorning sun. My soles are blistered. I take my shoes off and blood is dripping through my socks. I peel back the cotton. My big toe is swollen and yellow. Burst skin. The nail is black. A fault line runs across it.

I lie on the meadow grass, amongst the cornflowers and harebells. Butterflies loop infinity equations in the sun, iridescent dances in mathematics. Another plane slices overhead, cutting the blue in two. A plague of dead children rain down. Thunder and lightning and pestilence, skeletons on horseback gallop in the storm.

I walk without shoes the rest of the way. Until I reach a place I never knew I was heading for. When I get there my feet are pulp. Soft like melted cake.

I live in the woods under the guidance of the trees. Old wisdom keepers with their gnarled faces and tired eyes.

I travel with the roaming people and they share their stories and I share mine. Tales of creation, tales of death, rebirth, renewal and change.

We keep to the backways, to the forests and the pastures. I leave them and come back and leave them again.

And now I stay here with the trees. I have learnt skills from them. How to work with willow and straw. With the soft woods and the hard. With the leaves, with the fruits. I have learnt to see what is around me. To craft. To build. To make shelter for the night. Wise peoples of the woods and the land have taught me these things.

The days have grown shorter and longer. Time is forgotten.

The children have stopped falling from the sky. I am out of the flightpath here. The towns though are still waking with the bodies on the streets. Before the sweepers get out, first thing, before the alarm clocks and the daily commute.

But even here, away from it all, the leaves are dripping black tar where the sap once ran.

I band together with others who have seen the bodies fall. We campaign politely at first. And nothing happens. We grow violent, angry. We become addicted to the excitement of the lawlessness we revel in. We become addicted to the slamming door of defeat, the paternal turn away in ignorance to us. And it dawns that underneath, we need the status quo to remain. So that we can remain who we are. To keep doing what we are doing. But there is no status quo. Everything is changing. Growing and dying. Waxing and waning. Whether the world sinks further into the shitpit or it rises flapping dry its stinking wings, I will carry on. I am many people in my life. I travel from body to body. I learn things. I forget things. I hear things. I am deaf. Always trying to master. Always the journeyman. That is my destiny. That is the way I am on this earth. The path I have chosen to follow. Though I had no choice.

And right now I am alone in the forest. The old forests of this land before the farmers came. Before the fighters and the followers of Christ. There are witches in these trees, they scream under the moon and unleash their phantoms hounds. Spittle toothed, I hear them snuffling towards me in the blue. I shake in the night and I drink wine that I have made. And the hunger gnaws regrets. I am empty and craving. I shiver in my hole in the wood. Drugless addict cold turkeying in an English winter. I long for healing herbs and trance spells.

I long to wrap myself in plastic and jerk off to screens and technology and the smell of burning oil.

Still the children drop from the planes. Still the leaves drip their slow black sap. Everything is clogging to standstill. My wine is thick in my throat. It tastes of raw liver, jellied blood.

This winter is arctic. The sun has deserted his children this year. Ice forms in my beard at night. My toes have turned black. I can snap the nails off. And then one full mooned night, I have no energy left to howl.

I slice my skin with flint. I take moss from the earth and I push it into the cut. Injected green, infused with life, I run through the frost brittle wood. It snaps and screams. Cracking branches, falling leaves. Tendrils and burrs, ivy and thorn. But nothing can snare me. I am free. I can always run.

I find an unoccupied house on the edge of a village. A terraced row of coun-

cil ugliness. Rotting corpses of car and van litter the driveways. I keep low for
a few days, twitching behind curtains. I tidy myself up and am taken by the
neighbours as the new tenant. I nod at them and make mumbled comments
about the weather.

I steal money. Wallets and bags from elders in the local town. The
wisdomless elders who sit on their passive arses in tea shops, politely boring
themselves to death.

An apprentice needs a master. But there are no wisdom carriers here. So I
take from them what I can. I fill the house with electrics and pulsing wires.
With technology and flashing lights. I spend whole days flicking, clicking,
absorbing information. I buy a car. I drive around the country roads. I kill
rabbits under the wheels. Heavy rubber leaving its tracks in the bloodied body.
I smell of exhaust fumes and red rancid meat

I lock the door of the house. Bolt and chain. I only leave to get in the car. I
drive to the shopping centre in the industrial grey. Weeds grow, pushing up
along the grid lines of the car park.

I light a cigarette to get me through the outside. The bleak trees scream in
their gravel beds. I dive into the bright, through the electric doors to heaven.
Two Saint Peters in uniform, blank black faces, speak into intercoms on a
direct line to God. I gorge myself in the shops. I buy and buy and buy.

Full to sickness I go home. I sit fat and lazy and plug myself into the equip-
ment I have bought. I like the voltage. I turn it up, let it pulse through my
ears, my eyes. All orifices open and set to receive.

I sate myself with this new pleasure until I fear my flesh will burst. And
then – epiphany. A moment of clarity in the barrage and I realise I no longer
want to spend a life downloading from machines. I want instead to upload
myself. I into the machine. Not the other way round. Let them take me.
There, anything is possible. There, there will be a freeness unimaginable. A
new learning.

I float in the ether that night, swirling through naked bodies and infor-
mational overload. I assimilate encyclopaedias, music injects itself, layering
harmony upon harmony. I am fucked in the ass by burly motorcyclists who
rant about conspiracies. I see murders, I do murders, I am murdered. I run
drunk away from cops, through medieval forests, wielding my sword against
orcs and dragons. I gorge and gamble and slaughter and rape. I trip on high
clouds and fall in the dark places. I open up to miracles and I shun the man
next door.

In the morning I wake up slumped naked in an armchair. Dried cum crisps in my pubic hairs. The screens swirl words and numbers and constant chattering faces. My hands are covered in dried blood. I walk out into the kitchen and run the tap. It splutters a few coughs of black before running dry. I rub my hands on a tea towel and slam the door to the living room, shutting away the noise and the glare. And I stand still in the kitchen.

I grow hard. I let the morning sunlight hit me through the glass. Warm me, caress me until it starts to burn.

I grab a dirty tracksuit from the washing machine. A thick fleece coat and my shoes and I walk out through the garden, over into the field. The cows stare at this early morning intruder, ruminating on grass. I start to run. And they follow. Stampeding multi-hooved beast. I duck through the barbed wire, snagging fleece and skin, into the shadow of the still damp wood.

My breathing is heavy. Panting like a feral dog. The cows have stopped running. They chew the grass again. Slowly. Stupidly.

I walk in the woods. Spring is trying to come. The first drips of daffodil-yellow rash in the green. But winter still clings tight.

I walk and I know I am searching for something. I know this morning I will find it. In the orange glowing wood.

Birds are still singing. Welcoming the dawn. Welcoming me and my discovery. A hymn of celebration.

It is not long before I find it. The morning sunrays lighting it for me, so it gives off its power like a beacon.

I see it and I walk towards it.

The smiling bone.

Propped on the moss floor between two roots of beech that twist serpentine and bury themselves back in the earth.

At first I think it is snow. The last of the dying season, when the moon was bright and feathers fell in flurries and buried our secrets in a muffled white.

But it is not snow. It is the smiling bone. A jawbone. Thick strong and beautiful. It is sunbleached and radiates a whiteness alien to the greens and browns that dwell here. It's the length of my forearm, as wide as my outstretched fingers. Snaggle-toothed and giant.

I lie down in front of it. In worship. I reach my hands out, so the tips of my fingers brush its smoothness.

The wetness of the earth soaks through my clothes.

I bury my face down in the mud and inhale. Must and dirt, a rich soup in my throat. The ground pushes up hard against me, stirring sex.

I sit up on my haunches.

I place my hand on the bone and I can feel the heart beat. I can feel the warm breath dripping out over the wet teeth. The spittle and meat stuck to the gums.

I hear its roar. Its song for the stars.

I unzip my fleece. I place the bone inside next to my naked chest.

I walk out of the wood into the light of the open fields. Patches of snow lie collected in the dips at the bottom of tumuli. Spring has run away, and the world has skipped on to winter again.

I feel the jaw stirring inside my coat. Searching, nuzzling, to suckle at my breast.

The teeth are sharp. They must draw blood as well as milk. I am woman and man. I am human and animal. I am rocks and water. I am earth and sky.

I get back to the house. Next door's dog is barking.

The bone is pulsing inside my coat.

I close the back door. Lock and bolt. I tramp frozen mud into the kitchen. I unzip my fleece. I expect a child, I expect a creature struggling for rebirth.

I lay the bone on the kitchen table. It is beautiful. I see the creature it has come from. She lies on the table in front of me. Her arms are long and hang limply at the side. She looks at me saucer eyed. She coughs. And black jelly drips from her mouth.

A crash outside.

I jump and spin. The dog has vaulted the fence and is leaping up at the window. Barking snarling snout smears at the glass.

I jab the broom, smashing out into the dog's face. Shards fly at it, the broom handle jabs into the roof of its mouth and it lets out a shattered shriek.

It continues to bounce at the broken window. Blood dripping. A cold wind shoots in.

I grab a stained tea towel, wrap the bone in it and duck out of the front.

The dog is soon round, running at me.

The car is old and I hold out little hope for the thing starting in this weather. It groans at me. Hard cold oil drips through rusty arteries. The dog jumps over the car like a monkey at a zoo. Its claws skating skids on the bonnet, the paint work scratching and shrieking. The car shudders as I turn the ignition. It threatens to flood as it rattles and judders and refuses to spark.

The dog gets a grip in the grill at the base of the windscreen. Its claws stick in the holes. It butts its head against the glass again and again. Dull thumping over the asthmatic splutter of the engine. Blood is smearing like spread jam on the glass.

It lowers its head and looks at me. Eyes locking. It pushes its furred crown against the glass. Blood seeps along the fontanelles. The glass creaks. And bends. And bulges. As the glassmasked head of the dog pushes in towards me. I growl back it at it. Barking, howling.

The engine starts. Exhaust coughs out into the winter air. The car jerks forward. I drive fast out onto the road without looking. As I spin left the dog topples. Its claws snap off in the grill and it falls and rolls on the tarmac. Flailing like a woodlouse it curls on itself and flips back to standing. I watch in the mirror. Not looking where I am going. The black dog running behind me. The rear window is steaming up, obliterating it.

I drive. The bone on my lap wrapped in the towel. I push up against the weight. We go faster. The car smells of petrol.

My foot is down. My cock is hard. My name is Christopher Jansen. I have been running and searching since I was spat out into medical arms 30 years ago. I have run from parents and lovers and jobs and lives. I will be running until the end. The end of me or the end of everything. We are all running. None of us can stop.

My face is hurting. Along the jawline on the left side. My teeth are screaming. I fear they will pop like corks. The dog is dead. Burning in the red place of my closed eyes. Exhausted body collapsed and burst. Already feasted on. Birthing maggots. My teeth grind in their sockets, working loose.

I beep the horn. I hold it down. Screaming at the other dead faces in their charging metal beasts. I stare at them and I see the numbers written on their flesh. We all race together. Migrating. Swooping and diving in and out of our formation. Sketching patterns on the earth for the birds to decipher.

The sky is bruising darker. Purple scar tissue and open black wounds.

I drive through stroke victims of industry. Vast boarded up hangers of metal and brick stare blankly as I pass by. Kids play football against a crumbling wall and paint pictures of their new gods. Secret codes and hieroglyphs that only they can read.

I drive until the tank is empty. The engine smokes and rasps as the last drops burn away into the air. The car abandons me on empty moorland that stretches to the moon.

She hovers full and low, engorged with light. She beckons me on, me and the bone. We walk out across the gorse, away from paths, away from cars and roads and other man made things. The world is blue and brightening.

A circle of stone sprouts up around me like a ring of toadstools. Hard earth blooming. In the beginning. Before all this. The only life just rock, and it bubbles and breathes and forms itself animate.

I lay the bone at the centre of the circle and step away.

The moon swings lower and offers suck.

The earth rumbles and slips its mooring. Dry mud rises, locking to the bone, forming face. It rolls and jumps and makes substance.

The figure comes to its knees and rises to standing.

I bow before the form. Before my teacher. Before my god.

Sexlessness dissolves into genitals. Female into male and back and forth in an ever changing harmony. It settles itself male for my benefit and I feel the lost power and learning of generations of fractured men shining like a sun. Snapped spined fathers and lost women. Wasted lives of fighting and subjugation. Revenge, humiliation, bitterness. All dissolve and the power, the strength of the unbroken line surges through the figure and I bask in the light.

We spend the night dancing together. And then he tells me stories. Long rambling myths. I have not tasted their like before. We shred the old tales and burn them on a fire for warmth. The fire is hungry and eats them fast, laughing as it scoffs them down. It mocks me for hanging on to them for so long.

We sing out these new legends to the moon. And the moon sings them back. We sing them at the gorse and the grass and the stones. They tingle up my arms like impending heart attacks.

I am the storyteller, says my teacher. I come when the myth well has dried. It is clogged with poisonous corpses. The water is not fit to drink. It is choking the children. Killing the elders with its toxins. The young and fit are battling on blind, unaware of what is happening in their bodies.

You must change, says the story giant. You must all change. Otherwise there is no future. A dead end. Huge bricked concrete wall which you will hurtle into at speed. Smashing. Breaking. Painful slow death looking up at the sun, bleeding from all over your body. It is time to stop running.

Once a father walked out into the land looking for his son. He had to walk the path alone. Leaving the woman, the mother, the lover at home. The man had to find his son again.

I drift in valleys of sleep as the storyteller continues. But the tale is not lost on me. It soaks through me. Every pore. Every hole. In dreams, I run with the boy and the father through the heavy drifts of adventure. There are fires and fighting and screaming pain. The revolution is not bloodless.

I am the boy and I come to an encampment on the edge of a burning city. This is a time of great crisis. A time of shortages after too much greed. A time of bloodied hands and dead dogs. There are fires blazing on the rooftops. Buildings drip like wax. But here in the encampment with my fellows, I am safe.

I am searching for a miracle cure. I am searching for the moon to lodge itself in my solar plexus. To burn with that great womanly wisdom within me. I have tooled up and skilled up and armed myself, but still I shiver at the prospect of the war. I am not equipped.

But only a man has made this. A confused old man that does not know how to tend his garden. I walk down the overgrown path towards him. He is blind. I take him by the arm. We touch the leaves of the plants together. We learn their names. By feel. By smell. We learn what they need to live. We learn what they can give us. And what we must give in return.

I wake from sleeping on the stone. It is frozen. My trousers are wet and iced to the rock. I yank myself free.

I am only a few yards from the road. By a group of fenced off standing stones. A small brown sign registers that they are not mine but are the property of a charity and I am not to touch them. An old jawbone lies in the tre of the circle. I pick it up and slip it into my coat.

I sit in my car and try the key in the ignition. But the monster is dead. Rust is racing around the windows. Eating up through the rubber matting.

I see light in the distance. Through the morning fog a glowing pair of eyes. Coming towards me. I get out of the car and start to wave. I flag them down.

It is a young family with one child, a small boy. They are driving an orange campervan. They are friendly and open.

I say how I have run out petrol. They welcome me on board. They give me a blanket and I wrap up. They have a dog. She licks me over enthusiastically. She sniffs at my coat but then gives up and lies down again in her bed.

We drive. The little boy smiles at me. He has no words yet but he speaks clearly.

The family tell me they are heading on holiday. They come from London. But they are moving out soon. Going to live in a community. They want to be more sustainable. They want a future for their child. They have petrol guilt for driving the van. I ask them if the bodies are still falling on London. The little boy nods and says they are. We all talk some more and listen to Bob Dylan.

They drop me at a service station back up by the main road. We wish each other farewell and wave with smiles and tears.

I cannot walk into the service station. It all seems too absurd. I have spent my days in the wilderness. I have seen the earth walk tall. The giant has told me stories. The giant that we have tried to subdue, a metal noose around its neck. We have dragged it by chains, forced it to do unspeakable acts for our enjoyment. I have seen the giant cry at its degradation as we stand around the ring and laugh and point and pat ourselves on our backs. I have been to the wild places and now I have returned. And I stand outside a Little Chef with steamed windows and posters about their free range eggs. And I start to cry.

It all seems too much. It all seems as if everyone is against me. As if everything is looking the other way. But the boy in the van knew and that gives me hope.

The sun is setting. My hands have gone numb in the chill wind. I have been standing here all day.

A woman looks at me as she walks past. She has a sneer across her painted lips.

Don't think me mad, I say softly.

She looks away.

Don't brush me off as insane. I call after her. She quickens her pace towards the electric doors of the restaurant. Look at yourself, I call. Look at yourself in the eye. Tell me that you're not the mad one. Swear it to me on your mother's life. I dare you!

A man has appeared next to me. He tells me to shut up. He jabs at me with his finger. 'Fucking watch it', he says.

'I've seen the truth', I say. 'I've stared it down and it burnt at my retina.

'Fucking nut job', he says. And he pushes me to the ground. The woman is hovering by the doors. They are sliding open and shut and open again. She tells him to leave it. He prods me with his boot and they go inside.

And out here, in the loud silence of the blowing wind, I sit and shiver and I know that I am not mad.

I wait for them to come back again. I wait so so long, a lifetime, before they re-emerge. She holds him tight as they walk past me. I do not look up at them. I keep my eyes on the tarmac. On their feet. On their black stilettos and scuffed doc martens.

And when they are at a distance, I stand. I reach into my coat. I take out the bone. And I charge.

I roar as I run. The woman turns first. She sees me and screams. The man is too late, I club the bone across the back of his scalp. He topples like a young sapling. He is not sturdy. His roots do not dive deep enough. Blood explodes, bursting through his hair and brown paper skin. The skull splits open like a puffball and spores of brain bloom on the tarmac.

There is more screaming.

The man lies on the ground, swimming to stillness in red. He holds his car keys in his hand.

People are running behind me. They are wearing black. They are dressed the same. An army of avengers. The woman is standing still like a statue. I fear she will remain like that forever, petrified in the lava of time.

I am not made for this violence. My arms are shaking, hurting from the shock of the impact. I hold tight the bone, I twist my hands around it, wringing out the jolt.

In the blood on the ground, the car keys glint. I pick them up and run. I zap them. The hazard lights flash on a large Toyota and I run towards it.

I am destined to win. I will outrun the hunters. I have been running for so long, it is easy for me.

I drive the car through them. They scatter like chickens, flapping at the air with their burnt and stunted wings.

I am in the fast lane. There are sirens drawing closer. I turn off at the next junction. I head into the wildness of the English countryside. That is my home now. This is my land. I am England. I am Albion risen. I will hide myself in my own flesh. My own green and bark and soil. They will not find me. And soon, like weary dogs, they will give up the hunt, they will think I am not important. They will search for easier prey. But they do not know what I hold inside of me. They do not know what power has lodged itself in my gut. And soon I must unleash that power. That is what I have to do. My mission. My journey.

The sirens have stopped. The engines are dead. And the world has gone quiet. A soft breeze blows through the leaves.

The seasons are changing. Autumn has mulched into winter and spring is coming again. And I know that this spring will be bonny. The fruits will hang heavy and rich on the boughs. The flowers will be rainbow bright and glow like stars and we will think that we have landed in paradise. And that is why my job is so important. Because the brightness of the spring is just surface. In the core of the apples, the maggot is eating the seeds. And without the seeds it does not matter how bright, how shiny, how crisp, how juicy that apple is, because that apple will be the last apple. And that sweet cidered taste will be gone forever. Our lips will be dry from then on. We will have nothing else to do but sit and wait for them to crack.

I hear a clock ticking. It sounds fast to me. I listen to a small wind up radio. It tells of bodies falling from the sky. It tells of a new runway for the city. It tells of war in distant lands, in countries of sand and sun. It tells of fights dressed up as sport. It tells of men and women and forgets the children.

I have a small stove that I have made from an oil drum. It keeps me warm. But I must keep feeding it or it will die.

I sit in a cabin in the woods. A cabin that I have made. From trees I have felled. I sit in the cabin. Lit by a candle. And I have to write the stories. I have to listen to the trees. To the rivers. To the winds. I have to channel the myths they whisper and turn them into words. I know there is not much time. I know this all I can do. This is what I have been studying for. This is why I have been in training.

I have paper in front of me. I have ink. On the wall behind me, like a trophy, like an altar, hangs the bone. Its whiteness is fading. It looks like it is turning to wood. Hollow like blasted oak.

LEWIS BASSETT

three poems from the sequence

words like axes

frank
new york sounds like some porno supermarket
i hear inhaling the contents of neon lightbulbs gets you
high
cheese burgers sounds fun
and i guess it was
what a cool show!
nature was boring
and we showed those chimps how to party
im going to miss all these rhymes and these songs
o! and i don't think crying will do it
maybe one day someone will find our home pages
and click through

*

i lay down a spade
the reaction of a victorian crowd
(potatoes boiling lift the lid of the pot)
led to this poem*

that is wat karl referred to as das capital
but has later been called
by the names of a thousand taxis
interjecting down coloured streets
and to bring it home
(you are invited)
there would be orange lit
prostitutes and damp
    avocadoes in an empty fridge

dreamers they were
never the less they brought back
trays of unsold carob and soy
of which i built these foundations

yes the victorians had their say
and carl was right about something
too bad no one can see nowadays
for the smog

*

* I had intended to write a homage to trees.
  This has become a tribute to traffic.

'in a world where you are possible
my love
nothing can go wrong for us, tell me'
Frank O'Hara, *Song*

i can lift weights
i can lift your body above my head
i could check my watch
could tell you the time for years
i could buy ropes and glue
prepare sandwiches

(we could have a dog and children

i could starve myself
spend days in a cold bath
try to forget all the things i know
all the meals i ever ate

i could throw away all my photos
tear up my passport
climb a tree
light a fire
cut my hair
(we could have a boat
we could have a boat
we could climb a tree
we could give away our food
we could surrender our keys
we could throw out the water
the maps, the locks,

the past

i would sing to you:

1987 to 2009
zero up to now
charles darwin and our cousins
300 million years of sunlight
several decades captured on video
a swimming pool at the foot of a mountain where we had
ice cream and let the sun pass over our bare legs

2030
2050
80%
90%

GLYN HUGHES

Poetry's compost

I graduated from Manchester Art College in the late 1950s – not not to become a teacher as had been expected, but to follow a bent that had haunted me in every sense, including the spiritual, since youth: to cultivate an organic smallholding and live off it as far as possible. My hunger was powered in large part as an antidote to a council estate upbringing. *There must be a better way to live,* I believed – one directly connected to nature and to the countryside be-yond where I lived.

At art college I banged on to teachers and to fellow students, wearisomely as I now recognise, about living within the cycles of nature; about compost-ing, mixed farming and the other crucial necessities of this philosophy. These were subjects that few talked about, and no one at all did so in connection with art. Real life, they seemed to think, had little or nothing to do with art.

Everyone I spoke to about my love of nature in that city environment told me I was 'escapist', that our society was essentially urban, that science and technology would cover our failings, provide for all our needs. I regarded this technology as the problem. However, the faith in modern urban life and its technology grew through later decades, seeping even into literary reviewing, where it entered into criticism of the ghetto called 'nature writing'.

Today, in 2010, I read of the Government's 'new vision' for agriculture, the substance of which – the need to become less rapacious – was obvious to this art student fifty years ago. The destruction of the countryside and its crea-tures by farming seemed cataclysmic even then. I did not regard myself as a prophet (well, not too much of one – it was indeed my time of youthful arro-gance). I did not even think of myself as original, for I had culled my stance from a whole genre of long-published books, dating from the 1930s and 40s mostly, and re-issued by Faber in aid of self-sufficiency during the U-boat crises of the Second World War. The war had encouraged this attitude, (among its other unexpected revolutionary achievements such as opportunities for women, general health care and education), yet how quickly we came to forget it.

My 'environmentalism' (as it was not called back then) had much to do with sensibility. Not a specific artistic sensibility: you do not need to be an artist or a poet to appreciate birdsong, a hedgerow wilderness, or the taste of fresh, organic vegetables. It was the unity of simplicity that lit my life. It also informed the art I had been practising and the poetry I had been writing from well before I went to art college. This sensibility, this crucial element of how and what we actually see and feel, is most meagerly treated by both modern government and modern environmentalism, invariably reduced to footnotes or brief, sentimental clichés. To me though, it was the guiding voice. It concurred with my organic-farming and gardening books, but did not spring from them. Rather was I led to that way of thinking by art.

In that sense Van Gogh, more even than say Thoereau's *Walden*, or Richard Jefferies' precise observations, was for me the earliest environmentalist. Look at his paintings, read his letters, and one discovers the illuminating beauty, the *presence*, that he found in a rush-seated peasant chair or a brick floor. Simplicity, locality and the organic – these were delights beyond those provided by sophisticated, industrial products. Others also discovered these pleasures eventually. Soon there was a follow-up in the High Street, where those who appreciated Van Gogh prints could buy simulacrums of his loved subjects imported from an exploited far-away, in stores such as Habitat. A cycle of – shall we call it, of perception – was seized upon by commercial interest. Thus a whole sensibility became muddled and muddied again. Commerce intervened and corrupted, as I feel, it is doing again today, when the necessary purity of environmentalism is muddied once more with commercial and exploitative interests.

*

But for some of us, the direction pointed out by our sensibilities bolstered by art was clear.

My holding consisted of less than half an acre. This may not seem very large – unless one digs it over with a garden spade. It was set on the lower slopes of the Pennines, among East Lancashire's still-working cotton mills. No fertile West Country land this! It was poisoned by a century of soot, apart from being held back by the hostile climate of the unsheltered Pennines. Few people locally made much attempt at gardening, while farming consisted of sheep and cattle – no crops. Yet I am proud to claim that, after a year, my piece of unsheltered field brought neighbouring farmers to stare with some wonder at what this foolish and inexperienced ex-art student had brought forth out of the semi-poisoned East Lancashire earth.

The crucial part of my garden was its compost heap. This was literally its heart; the power centre of the whole philosophy. For symbolic and practical reasons it was built centrally. Almost all waste went into it and all the food of the earth eventually came from it. It was in itself a cycle, and a demonstration of a cycle. I learned that everything organic could be composted, provided one built the compost heap correctly. The material hardest to break down (paper, cardboard, hedge clippings) was put at the base and then the layers were piled to a height of five feet or so – layers of kitchen and garden waste, human and animal waste, and fresh green material (usually scythings). As we had no mains drainage and I rejected the idea of a chemical toilet, manure was provided by our own 'night-soil', as well as poultry manure from our hens and ducks.

After a week, the heap would begin to emit a warm steam. Following an almost precise four to five weeks, it sank to half of its original height and became a mass of dark, crumbly, even-textured compost. It was a precious material – too precious to bury in the sub-soil. I learned to scatter it on the surface, just as humus naturally falls and forms upon the earth, and not to disturb the earth's biology, nor expose my precious garden to erosion. 'No weeding' was my philosophy, just as it pertained in nature where even in the worst droughts, hedgerows and banks flourish with plants, insects, bird and animals.

This, remember, was in the late fifties. Meanwhile my landlord/neighbour – a small-scale farmer with two horses who was not even at that date in possession of a tractor, used to relax by poring over the pages of *The Farmers' Weekly*. There he dreamed of concrete floors, asbestos sheds, hen-battery cages, intensive rearing and quick turnovers. Dreams that were, in many cases, part of the regulations being forced upon him by the Ministry. Dreams foisted onto farmers, large-scale and small, all over England. It was the destruction of the English countryside in a sudden, governmental rush.

I used to borrow *The Farmers' Weekly,* from him. Or rather, he almost forced it upon me, refusing to believe the contrary evidence he clearly saw and appreciated in his tenant's garden. I read the excuses for a ghastly apocalypse. I read of the coming animal and bird concentration camps (to be hidden from the consumers' sights) and of an appallingly wrecked and

poisoned England. At this same period, a new and highly popular radio pro-
gramme, *The Archers,* offered blatant propaganda for this same government
and commercially driven desecration.

It seemed that post-1950s, a whole sensibility to nature, and to our true
dependence,was vanquished and vanishing. Throughout the English counties,
one despaired at the sheer insensitivity, the recklessness, at root, the avarice
with which it was carried out – the massively enlarged fields, the wrecked old
trackways, ancient woodlands and hedgerows, the poisoned villages (with the
effects of chemicals on the land still largely not investigated), and also the
smaller-scale philistinism; the gravelled parking lots carved out of old gar-
dens and orchards, for example.

Meanwhile, people ranging from urban artists to farmers continued to tell
me that I was romantic and 'escapist'. My view remained that it was society
that was 'escapist'. And not merely recently; it had been so, cumulatively, for
many centuries. We had been trying to escape the inescapable laws of nature,
in the belief or delusion that technology could supply the panacea. With all
this, and the strain of a dissatisfied family, I gave in, against all the evidence
of my sensibility. Got a teaching job. Lost a garden. Bought a motor car –
which I had always believed separated rather than joined one with nature. I
compromised.

*

Nearly half a century later, my ideas of that time don't seem escapist and fool-
ishly romantic anymore. Most of us recognise now that we temporarily (but
how temporarily?) dwell upon a beautiful planet that is crumbling under the
weight of humans and their appetites. It is hard to believe or to accept that
humankind is driven towards its own extinction, as other monstrous crea-
tures have been, from lack of adjustment to the conditions. Humans, unlike
dinosaurs, are distinguished by self-awareness and by knowledge. We *know*
what we are doing. Yet instinct is evidently more powerful. And we have next
to no knowledge of instinct; of why the butterfly, the salmon and the wild
goose cross oceans and continents, self-destructively, so it seems. And human
life is certainly showing an instinct for self-destruction.

There are many – though still a minority – who deny that such a winding-
down of our Heavenly existence (which is to say, our Heaven on Earth) is
taking place. This is a minority that usually represents, or is influenced by,
the commercial and financial interests that have, or would have, everything

to lose, even before the final apocalypse. I think we can ignore those 'flat-earthers'. More significant are those who, while accepting that the scares are realistic, still believe science and technology will provide the solutions.

Government, for example, realises it must act, but its own necessities compel it to evade the essential issue (which we will come to in a moment). It seizes upon technology to provide a range of non-fundamental solutions – which means more commercial, or more cosmetic ones. This question has been debated very fully elsewhere. What is the value of 'wind farms', for example, relative to the cost and environmental damage of installation? (Personally I am convinced by James Lovelock's assertion that only nuclear technology is a possible answer to climate change – though even he believes it is too late for that). Technology provides solutions by adding to the causes, creating new problems.

It would be graceless of me personally to decry technology. This past year I have suffered with cancer, and it would not have been cured were it not for, especially, computer technology, and for the interface and complex network of drugs and other supplies on which a hospital depends. I love music on CDs, love browsing the Internet, and even (blush) air travel, as few do. I stare out of the window at a compulsively beautiful planet – Europe, Asia, the Pacific, the Americas.

Despite this modernity I, like almost anyone else, recognise that we must greatly restrict our wants and even our needs. Earlier this year, the US Worldwatch Institute issued its annual report pointing out that, 'the cult of consumption and greed could wipe out any gains from government action on climate change or a shift to a clean energy economy'. Worldwatch called for 'a wholesale transformation of values and attitudes.' Yet who 'transforms', if not compelled to do so? Even the most admired and admirable World Leaders – Obama, say – require several large aeroplanes and a motorcade so as to spend a day or two giving a fatuous address to another climate change conference.

In all of this, through this approach, we continue to evade the delight – now become a *duty* – of a more rooted and simpler sensibility. Of – in a worn-out cliché – 'going back to nature'. Why do we act thus? Why does government not encourage anything different; why does it set up a smokescreen of cosmetics?

Here is an anecdote that may help by way of explanation. My childhood took place during the Second World War, when we were encouraged to eat carrots. We were told over the wireless that carrots helped us to see in the dark – in the blackout, that was an urgent need. At the age of five and six I believed sincerely what I was told so passionately in school. After the war, it turned out that there had been a glut of carrots when there was little else, and we were being told a worthy lie that helped the war effort.

Something of the same kind, though less worthily, is occurring right now with regard to global warming and environmental exploitation. Our Government, so as to delude us that 'something is being done', foists on us schemes that are of marginal benefit or which serve another purpose entirely. The recent car scrappage scheme is one example. An article by George Monbiot recently explained in detail why, if the aim was truly environmental, it would on the whole be more effective to take measures to keep old cars on the road – considering the complex factory structures, supply chains and employment required to maintain the motor industry. But that, of course, would not boost economic growth.

And there is the nub of the matter. The huge dilemma, the one not faced, is that there is very probably no solution to planetary destruction without massive unemployment in rich countries. Less industry, less stock in supermarkets, fewer unseasonable and luxury, imported goods, less trucking and travelling. Less cultivated worship of celebrities, too, whose ways of life that we are taught to imitate (for commercial reasons), should make them not heroes but pariahs. And a real solution demands not merely workers' unemployment. It requires more unemployment of the most conspicuous spenders: the exploitative, the banking Elect, the celebrities and the fraudulent members of Parliament, for example.

No one faces up to the employment question, other than some relatively minor extensions into 'green' jobs. That's about it. It is all minor, relative to the scale of the dilemma. But no politician anywhere, least of all in the now-ascending economies, would consider such vote-losing moves; such weakening of commercial and thereby military power. With an unanswerable dilemma and a recognised, great crisis, we receive spates of hypocritical rhetoric from politicians.

So what is to be done?

*

We require – and it is an old message – people to look through a different window; to see into another world. Not merely to content themselves with minor feelgood activities, to separate their rubbish, say, or feel a bit guilty about their 4×4s. (That does not seem to work very well where I live, incidentally; there seem to be more, not fewer of them.)

We need to look with altered sensibility into a different world; a spiritual one, curiously parallel and visible enough, but curiously unseen. Only such a change of sensibility, such an illumination, would give the strength and energy to adopt a simpler, less commercial mode of existence. This change of sensibility needs to come – from where else? – through art.

Some hope!

'Art' today comes 99% through television. This is what people gravitate to talking about, and all the above is not ever television's concern. Television is a vast commercial enterprise dedicated exclusively to what we must free ourselves *from*. It is not surprising then that nature and country programmes are entirely devoted to escapism, and to a fantasy. What I am talking about is reality.

In our rational, disillusioned age, one has to be careful when speaking of spiritual answers. These, in the name of love and hope, have not earned themselves a good press over several thousand years. As we know too well, their history from Catholicism to communism (essentially another dream-dogma) to militant Islam does not encourage much faith in them. They manufacture and then torture heretics, and freeze much intelligent development. Next, they give birth to extreme and violent reaction to themselves. Then, under a different name, comes more of the same.

Yet, if deprived of spiritual substance, people become insensate fodder to the vicissitudes and deceptions of materialistic society (as we have witnessed so desperately in recent years) or to the unadmirable wings of religious isms. The spirituality we need to cultivate is not an attachment to any human dogma, but our relationship to nature. Not merely nature's practical offerings, but what it offers as a parallel spiritual world – the one that philosophers have pondered for as long as they have considered the stars and contemplated its scientific wonders. Its significance to us, as maybe symbols or directions to another world – as maybe even our post-life destinies. This mystery.

This enlarged awareness is what I believe we are most in need of. Against it, our conferences, our political jugglings, are merely dipping our feet in an ocean – or worse still, peeping through the slits of an ultimately useless bunker.

GLYN HUGHES

To the morning sun

At this time of year the morning sun
rides horizontally at the window
and moon too, smiling along the hills
brightening our residues and trivia.
Oh God oh Sun oh trumpeting Moon
how small we are among our ruins.
Stride forth to tell us what we did wrong
we guess it is quite simple;
enough for even us to understand.
Beach-comb among the stars of your great loneliness
(for it seems you have not noticed us).
Oh God, despite our vanity
maybe you will spot this grain of sand
pick it up and sift and wonder
at last, at last.

DAN GRACE

An Sgurr

One day the whole world will look like this,
he whispered in her ear as they stood
on the calloused tip of a giant pitchstone thumb
pushed through a thin skin of moss and lichen,
their view of Rum and the Cuillins of Skye,
the sun on their arms and legs, and below,
the red tin roof of a farmhouse,
a windmill whirring softly in the breeze.

The flood will come and we will retreat to our island,
our green-grey lung above the waves,
to bathe in the cold water of rock-cupped pools,
to lay flat against these organs,
these body parts of the earth disassembled,
to look for a pattern, search for our face, to finally know
that we are the ashes of long-dead suns.

SIMON FAIRLIE

Myths of civilisation #1

The tragedy of the
Tragedy of the Commons

*The first in a series examining propagandist narratives innocently posing as Facts,
which help underpin our civilisation's view of the world and itself*

In December 1968, *Science* magazine published a paper by Garrett Hardin entitled 'The Tragedy of the Commons'.[1] How it came to be published in a serious academic journal is a mystery, since its central thesis, in the author's own words, is what 'some would say is a platitude', while most of the paper consists of the sort of socio-babble that today can be found on the average blog. The conclusion, that 'the alternative of the commons is too horrifying to contemplate,' is about as far removed from a sober scientific judgment as one could imagine.

Yet 'The Tragedy of the Commons' became one of the most cited academic papers ever published and its title a catchphrase. It has framed the debate about common property for the last 30 years, and has exerted a baleful influence upon international development and environmental policy, even after Hardin himself admitted that he had got it wrong and reworked his entire theory.

But Hardin did get one thing right, and that is the reason for the lasting influence of his paper. He recognised that the common ownership of land and the history of its enclosure provides a template for understanding the enclosure of other common resources, ranging from the atmosphere and the oceans, to pollution sinks and intellectual property. The physical fences and hedges that staked out the private ownership of the fields of England are shadowed by the metaphorical fences that now delineate more sophisticated forms of private property.

Hardin's basic argument (or 'platitude') was that common property systems allow individuals to benefit at a cost to the community, and therefore are inherently prone to decay, ecological exhaustion and collapse. Hardin got the idea for his theory from the Oxford economist, the Rev William Forster Lloyd who asked in 1833:

> Why are the cattle on a common so puny and stunted? Why is the common itself so bareworn and cropped so differently from the adjoining enclosures? If a person puts more cattle into his own field, the amount of the subsistence which they consume is all deducted from that which was at the command of his original stock; and if, before, there was no more than a sufficiency of pasture, he reaps no benefit from the additional cattle, what is gained one way, being lost in another. But if he puts more cattle on a common, the food which they consume forms a deduction which is shared between all the cattle, as well that of others as his own, and only a small part of it is taken from his own cattle.[2]

This is a neat description, and anybody who has lived in a communal situation will recognise that, as an analogy of human behaviour, there is more than a grain of truth in it: individuals often seek to profit from communal largesse if they can get away with it. Or as John Hales put it in 1581, 'that which is possessed of manie in common is neglected by all.'

Hardin, however, takes Lloyd's observation and transforms it by injecting the added ingredient of 'tragic' inevitability:

> The rational herdsman concludes that the only sensible course for him to pursue is to add another animal to his herd. And another; and another … But this is the conclusion reached by each and every rational herdsman sharing a commons. Therein is the tragedy. Each man is locked into a system that compels him to increase his herd without limit – in a world that is limited. Ruin is the destination toward which all men rush, each pursuing his own best interest in a society that believes in the freedom of the commons. Freedom in a commons brings ruin to all.

Having established that 'the inherent logic of the commons remorselessly generates tragedy', Hardin then proceeds to apply this tragedy to every kind of common property that he can think of. From fish populations to national parks, and polluted streams to parking lots – wherever resources are held in common, there lies the path to over-exploitation and ruin, from which, he

suggests, there is one preferred route of escape: 'the Tragedy of the Commons, as a food basket, is averted by private property, or something formally like it.'
Hardin continues:

> An alternative to the commons need not be perfectly just to be preferable. With real estate and other material goods, the alternative we have chosen is the institution of private property coupled with legal inheritance. Is this system perfectly just? ...We must admit that our legal system of private property plus inheritance is unjust – but we put up with it because we are not convinced, at the moment, that anyone has invented a better system. The alternative of the commons is too horrifying to contemplate. Injustice is preferable to total ruin.

To be fair to Hardin, most of the above was incidental to his main point, which was the need for population control. But it was music to the ears of free market economists who were convinced that private property rights were the solution to every social ill. A scientific, peer-reviewed, mathematical formula proving that common property led inexorably to ruin, and postulating that privatisation, even unjust privatisation, was the solution – and all encapsulated under the neat title of Tragedy of the Commons. What could be better?

From the 1970s to the 1990s, Hardin's Tragedy was picked up by right wing theorists and neo-colonial development agencies, to justify unjust and sometimes ruinous privatisation schemes. In particular, it provided agencies such as the World Bank and marine economists with the rationale for the enclosure and privatisation of fisheries through the creation, sale and trade of quotas.[3]

But as well as being one of the most cited papers, Hardin's was also one of the most heavily criticised, particularly by anthropologists and historians who cited innumerable instances where limited common resources were managed satisfactorily. What Hardin's theory overlooks, said E. P. Thompson, 'is that commoners were not without commonsense.'[4] The anthropologist Arthur McEvoy made the same point, arguing that the Tragedy 'misrepresents the way common lands were used in the archetypal case' (ie England before enclosure):

> English farmers met twice a year at manor court to plan production for the coming months. On those occasions they certainly would have exchanged information about the state of their lands and sanctioned those who took more than their fair share from the common pool ... The short-

coming of the tragic myth of the commons is its strangely unidimensional picture of human nature. The farmers on Hardin's pasture do not seem to talk to one another. As individuals, they are alienated, rational, utility-maximising automatons and little else. The sum total of their social life is the grim, Hobbesian struggle of each against all, and all together against the pasture in which they are trapped.[5]

Faced with a barrage of similar evidence about both historical and existing commons, Hardin in the early 1990s, retracted his original thesis, conceding:

> The title of my 1968 paper should have been 'The Tragedy of the Unmanaged Commons'... Clearly the background of the resources discussed by Lloyd (and later by myself) was one of non-management of the commons under conditions of scarcity.[6]

In fact, this background wasn't clear at all, since it makes a nonsense of the idea of an inexorable tragedy. If degradation results from non-management, and collapse can be averted by sound management, then there can be no 'remorseless logic' leading to inevitable 'ruin'. Nor is there any reason why a private property regime (particularly an unjust one) should necessarily be preferable to the alternative of maintaining sound management of a commonly owned resource.

But even within the confined parameters of Hardin's 'Hobbesian struggle of each against all', one wonders whether he has got it right. Is it really economically rational for a farmer to go on placing more and more stock on the pasture? If he does so, he will indeed obtain a higher return relative to his colleagues, but he will get a lower return relative to his capital investment in livestock; beyond a certain level of degradation he would be wiser to invest his money elsewhere.

In fact, the most rational approach for powerful and unscrupulous actors is not to accrue vast herds of increasingly decrepit animals; it is to persuade everybody else that common ownership is inefficient (or even leads remorselessly to ruin) and should be replaced therefore with a private property system, of which they will be the beneficiaries.

*

Over the course of a few hundred years, much of Britain's land has been privatised – that is to say taken out of some form of collective ownership and management and handed over to individuals. Currently, in our 'property-owning democracy', nearly half the country is owned by 40,000 land million-aires, or 0.06 percent of the population,[7] while most of the rest of us spend half our working lives paying off the debt on a patch of land barely large enough to accommodate a dwelling and a washing line.

There are many factors that have led to such extreme levels of land con-centration, but the most blatant and the most contentious has been enclosure – the subdivision and fencing of common land into individual plots which were allocated to those people deemed to have held rights to the land enclosed. For over 500 years, pamphleteers, politicians and historians have argued about enclosure, those in favour (including the beneficiaries) insisting that it was necessary for economic development or 'improvement', and those against (including the dispossessed) claiming that it deprived the poor of their liveli-hoods and led to rural depopulation.

But over the last three decades, the enclosure debate has been swept up in a broader discourse on the nature of common property of any kind. The over-grazing of English common land has been held up as the archetypal example of Hardin's 'tragedy' – the fatal deficiency that a neoliberal intelligentsia holds to be inherent in all forms of common property. Attitudes towards enclosures in the past were always ideologically charged, but now any stance taken to-wards them betrays a parallel approach to the crucial issues of our time: the management of global commons and the conflict between the global and the local, between development and diversity.

A brief exploration of the history of the enclosure of the English commons, arguably the first in the series of global enclosures which today characterise the global economy, demonstrates both the complexity of land ownership systems and the inaccuracy of any theory of the 'remorseless logic' which leads com-mon management of resources into 'ruin'.

Private ownership of land, and in particular absolute private ownership, is a modern idea, only a few hundred years old. The idea that one man could possess all rights to one stretch of land to the exclusion of everybody else would have been outside the comprehension of most tribespeople, or indeed of medieval peasants. In medieval and pre-medieval England, the king, or the lord of the manor, might have owned an estate in one sense of the word, but the peasant enjoyed all sorts of so-called 'usufructory' rights which enabled him or her to graze stock, cut wood or peat, draw water or grow crops on various plots of land at specified times of year.

The open field system of farming, which dominated the flatter, arable, central counties of England throughout the later medieval and into the modern period, is a classic common property system which can be seen in many parts of the world. The structure of the open field system in Britain was influenced by the introduction of the *caruca*, a large wheeled plough, developed by the Gauls, which was much more capable of dealing with heavy English clay soils than the lightweight Roman ploughs. The *caruca* required a larger team of oxen to pull it – as many as eight on heavy soils – and was awkward to turn around, so very long strips were ideal. Most peasants could not afford a whole team of oxen, just one or two, so maintaining an ox team had to be a joint enterprise. Peasants would work strips of land, possibly proportionate to their investment in the ox team. The lands were farmed in either a two or three course rotation, with one year being fallow, so each peasant needed an equal number of strips in each section to maintain a constant crop year on year.

Furthermore, because the fields were grazed by the village herds when fallow, or after harvest, there was no possibility for the individual to change his style of farming: he had to do what the others were doing, when they did it, otherwise his crops would get grazed by everyone's animals. The livestock were also fed on hay from communal meadows (the distribution of hay was sometimes decided by an annual lottery for different portions of the field) and on communal pastures.

In short, the common field system, rather ingeniously, made economies of scale, including use of a whopping great plough team, potentially accessible to small-scale farmers. The downside was a sacrifice of freedom (or 'choice' as it is now styled), but that is in the nature of economies of scale when they are equitably distributed; and when they are inequitably distributed some people have no choice at all. The open field system probably offered more independence to the peasant than a New World *latifundia*, or a collectivised communist farm. One irony of these economies of scale is that when large-scale machinery arrived, farmers who had enclosed open fields had to start ripping out their hedges again.

It is hard to see how Hardin's Tragedy of the Commons has any bearing upon the rise and fall of this open field system. Far from collapsing as a result of increased population, the development of open field systems often occurred quite late in the Middle Ages, and may even have been a response to increasing population pressure.[8] When there was plenty of uncultivated land left to clear, people were able to stake out private plots of land without impinging too much upon others; when there was less land to go round, or when a single holding was divided amongst two or three heirs, there was pressure to divide arable land into strips and manage it semi-collectively.

The open fields were not restricted to any one kind of social structure or land tenure system. In England they evolved under Saxon rule and continued through the era of Norman serfdom. After the Black Death, serfdom gave way to customary land tenure known as copyhold, and as the money economy advanced, this in turn gave way to leasehold. But none of these changes appeared to diminish the effectiveness of the open field system. On the other hand, in Celtic areas, and in other peripheral regions that were hilly or wooded, open fields were much less widespread, and enclosure of private fields occurred earlier (and probably more equitably) than it did in the central arable counties.

But open fields were by no means restricted to England. Being a natural and reasonably equitable expression of a certain level of technology, the system was, and still is, found in many regions around the world. According to one French historian, 'in France, open fields were the agricultural system of the most modernised regions.'[9] There are reports of similar systems of open field farming all over the world, for example in Anatolia, Turkey in the 1950s, and Tigray, Ethiopia where the system is still widespread. In one area, in Tigray, Irob, 'to avoid profiteering by ox owners of oxenless landowners, ox owners are obliged to first prepare the oxenless landowners' land and then his own. The oxenless landowners in return assist by supplying feed for the animals they use to plough the land.'[10]

However, as medieval England progressed to modernity, the open field system and the communal pastures came under attack from wealthy landowners. The first onslaught, during the fourteenth to seventeenth centuries, came from landowners who converted arable land over to sheep pasture, with legal support from the Statute of Merton of 1235. Villages were depopulated and several hundred seem to have disappeared entirely. The peasantry responded with a series of ill-fated revolts. In the 1381 Peasants' Revolt, enclosure was an issue, albeit not the main one. In Jack Cade's rebellion of 1450, land rights were a prominent demand.[11] By the time of Kett's rebellion of 1549, enclosure was a main issue, as it was in the Captain Pouch revolts of 1604–1607 when the terms 'leveller' and 'digger' appeared, referring to those who levelled the ditches and fences erected by enclosers.[12]

CHRISTIAN DE SOUSA

When did it start going wrong?

LANCE FENNELL

Two Paintings

The first recorded written complaint against enclosure was made by a Warwickshire priest, John Rous, in his *History of the Kings of England*, published around 1459–86.[13] The first complaint by a celebrity (and 500 years later it remains the most celebrated denunciation of enclosure) was by Thomas More in *Utopia*:

> Your shepe that were wont to be so meke and tame, and so smal eaters, now, as I heare saye, be become so great devowerers and so wylde, that they eate up and swallow down the very men them selfes. They consume, destroye, and devoure whole fields, howses and cities ... Noble man and gentleman, yea and certeyn Abbottes leave no ground for tillage, thei inclose all into pastures; they throw down houses; they pluck down townes, and leave nothing standynge but only the churche to be made a shepehowse.[14]

Other big names of the time weighed in with similar views: Thomas Wolsey, Hugh Latimer, William Tyndale, Lord Somerset and Francis Bacon all agreed, and even though all of these were later executed, as were Cade, Kett and Pouch (they did Celebrity Big Brother properly in those days), the Tudor and Stuart monarchs took note and introduced a number of laws and commissions which managed to keep a check on the process of enclosure.

A different approach emerged during the English Revolution when Gerrard Winstanley and fellow diggers, in 1649, started cultivating land on St George's Hill, Surrey, and proclaimed a free Commonwealth. 'The earth (which was made to be a Common Treasury of relief for all, both Beasts and Men)' state the Diggers in their first manifesto 'was hedged into Inclosures by the teachers and rulers, and the others were made Servants and Slaves.' The same pamphlet warned: 'Take note that England is not a Free people, till the Poor that have no Land, have a free allowance to dig and labour the Commons, and so live as Comfortably as the Landlords that live in their Inclosures.'[15]

The Diggers appear to be not so much a resistance movement of peasants in the course of being squeezed off the land, as an inspired attempt to reclaim the land by people whose historical ties may well have already been dissolved some generations previously. Like many radicals, Winstanley was a tradesman in the textile industry. William Everard, his most prominent colleague, was a cashiered army officer. It is tempting to see the Diggers as the original 'back to the land' movement; a bunch of idealistic drop-outs.[16] Winstanley wrote so many pamphlets in such a short time that one wonders whether he had time to wield anything heavier than a pen. Nevertheless, during 1649 he was earning his money as a hired cowherd; and no doubt at least some of the diggers were from peasant backgrounds.

More to the point, the Diggers weren't trying to stop 'inclosures'; they didn't go round tearing down fences and levelling ditches, like both earlier and later rebels. In a letter to the head of the army, Fairfax, Winstanley stated that if some wished to 'call the Inclosures [their] own land ... we are not against it', though this may have been just a diplomatic gesture. Instead they wanted to create their own alternative Inclosure which would be a 'Common Treasury of All' and where commoners would have 'the freedom of the land for their livelihood ... as the Gentry hathe the benefit of their Inclosures.' Winstanley sometimes speaks the same language of 'improvement' as the enclosers, but wishes to see its benefits extended to the poor rather than reserved for wealthy: 'If the wasteland of England were manured by her children it would become in a few years the richest, the strongest and the most flourishing land in the world.'[17]

It is slightly surprising that the matter of fifty or so idealists planting carrots on a bit of wasteland and proclaiming that the earth was a 'Common Treasury' should have attracted so much attention, both from the authorities at the time, and from subsequent historians and campaigners. Two hundred years before, at the head of his following of Kentish peasants (described by Shakespeare as 'the filth and scum of Kent') Jack Cade persuaded the first army dispatched by the king to pack up and go home, skilfully evaded a second army of 15,000 men led by Henry VI himself, and then defeated a third army, killing two of the king's generals, before being finally apprehended and beheaded. Although pictured by the sycophantic author of *Henry VI Part II* as a brutal and blustering fool with pretensions above his station, Cade was reported by contemporaries to be 'a young man of goodlie stature and right pregnant of wit.'[18] He is potentially good material for a romantic Hollywood blockbuster starring Johnny Depp, whereas Winstanley (who has had a film made about him) apparently settled into middle age after the Digger episode as a Quaker, a church warden and finally a chief constable.[19]

Winstanley and associates were lucky not to die on the scaffold. The habit of executing celebrities was suspended during the Interregnum – after the beheading of Charles I, anyone else would have been an anticlimax. Executions were resumed (but mainly for plebs, not celebs) initially by Judge Jeffries in his Bloody Assizes in 1686 and subsequently some 70 years later with the introduction of the Black Acts.

The Black Acts were the vicious response of Prime Minister Walpole and his cronies to increasing resistance to the enclosure of woodlands. The rights of commoners to take firewood, timber and game from woodlands, and to graze pigs in them, had been progressively eroded for centuries: free use of forests and abolition of game laws was one of the demands that Richard II agreed to with his fingers crossed when he confronted Wat Tyler during the 1381 Peasants' Revolt.[20] But in the early-eighteenth century, the process accelerated as wealthy landowners enclosed forests for parks and hunting lodges, dammed rivers for fishponds and allowed their deer to trash local farmer's crops.

Commoners responded by organising vigilante bands which committed ever more brazen acts of resistance. One masked gang, whose leader proclaimed himself King John, killed 11 deer from the Bishop's Park at Farnham on one morning in 1721, and rode through Farnham market with them at 7am in triumph. On another occasion, when a certain Mr Wingfield started charging poor people for offcuts of felled timber which they had customarily had for free, King John and his merry men ring-barked a plantation belonging to Wingfield, leaving a note saying that if he didn't return the money to the peasants, more trees would be destroyed. Wingfield paid up. King John could come and go as he pleased because he had local support – on one occasion, to refute a charge of Jacobinism, he called the 18th century equivalent of a press-conference near an inn on Waltham Chase. He turned up with 15 of his followers, and with 300 of the public assembled, the authorities made no attempt to apprehend him. He was never caught and for all we know also eventually became a chief constable.[21]

Gangs such as these, who sooted their faces, both as a disguise and so as not to be spotted at night, were known as 'the blacks', and so the legislation introduced two years later in 1723 was known as the Black Act. Without doubt the most viciously repressive legislation enacted in Britain in the last 400 years, this act authorised the death penalty for more than 50 offences connected with poaching. The act stayed on the statute books for nearly a century, hundreds were hanged for the crime of feeding themselves with wild meat, and when the act was finally repealed, poachers were instead transported to the Antipodes for even minor offences.

Another area which harboured remnants of a hunter gatherer economy was the fenland of Holland in south Lincolnshire and the Isle of Axholme in the north of the county. The main earner was the summer grazing of rich common pastures with dairy cattle, horses and geese; but in winter, when large tracts of the commons were inundated, fishing and fowling became an important source of income, and for those with no land to keep beasts on over winter, it may have been the primary one. In the early 1600s, the Stuart kings James I and Charles I, hard up for cash, embarked on a policy of draining the fenland commons to provide valuable arable land that would yield the crown a higher revenue. Dutch engineers, notably Cornelius Vermuyden, were employed to undertake comprehensive drainage schemes which cost the crown not a penny, because the developers were paid by being allocated a third of the land enclosed and drained.

The commoners' resistance to the drainage schemes was vigorous. A 1646 pamphlet with the title 'The Anti-Projector' must be one of the earlier grass-roots denunciations of a capitalist development project, and makes exactly the same points that indigenous tribes today make when fighting corporate land grabs:

> The Undertakers have alwaies vilified the fens, and have misinformed many Parliament men, that all the fens is a meer quagmire, and that it is a level hurtfully surrounded and of little or no value: but those who live in the fens and are neighbours to it, know the contrary.

The anonymous author goes on to list the benefits of the fens including: the 'serviceable horses', the 'great dayeries which afford great store of butter and cheese', the flocks of sheep, the 'osier, reed and sedge', and the 'many thousand cottagers which live on our fens which must otherwise go a begging.' And he continues by comparing these to the biofuels that the developers proposed to plant on the newly drained land:

> What is coleseed and rape, they are but Dutch commodities, and but trash and trumpery and pills land, in respect of the fore-recited commodities which are the rich oare of the Commonwealth.[22]

The commoners fought back by rioting, by levelling the dikes, and by taking the engineers to court. Their lawsuits were paid for 'out of a common purse to which each villager contributed according to the size of the holding', though

Charles I attempted to prevent them levying money for this purpose, and to prosecute the ringleaders.

However, Charles' days were numbered, and when civil war broke out in the 1640s, the engineering project was shelved and the commoners reclaimed all the fen from the developers. In 1642 Sir Anthony Thomas was driven out of East and West Fens and the Earl of Lyndsey was ejected from Lyndsey Level. In 1645 all the drainers' banks in Axholme were destroyed. Between 1642 and 1649 the Crown's share of fenland in numerous parishes was seized by the inhabitants and returned to common.

Just over a century later, from 1760, the drainers struck again, and this time they were more successful. There was still resistance in the form of pamphlets, riots, rick-burning etc. But the high price of corn worked in favour of those who wanted to turn land over to arable. And there was less solidarity amongst commoners because, it seems, wealthy commoners who could afford to keep more animals over winter (presumably because of agricultural improvements) were beginning to overstock the commons for their own ends.

Between 1760 and 1840 most of the fens were drained and enclosed by Act of Parliament. Since drainage eventually created one of the most productive areas of arable farmland in Britain, it would be hard to argue that it was not an economic improvement; but the social and environmental consequences have been less happy. Much of the newly cultivated land lay at some distance from the villages and was taken over by large landowners; it was not unusual to find a 300 acre holding without a single labourers' cottage on it. Farmers therefore developed the gang-labour system of employment that exists to this day. The 1867 Gangs Act was introduced to prohibit the worst abuses; yet in 2004, when the Gangmasters Licensing Act was passed (in the wake of the Morecambe Bay cockle pickers tragedy), the Government was still legislating against the evils of this system of employment.

By the end of the eighteenth century the incentive to convert tilled land in England over to pasture was dying away. There were a number of reasons for this. Firstly, the population was beginning to rise rapidly as people were displaced from the land and ushered into factory work in towns, and so more land was required for producing food. Secondly, cotton imported from the US and India was beginning to replace English wool. And thirdly, Scotland had been united with England and its extensive pastures lay ready to be 'devowered by shepe'.

The fact that these lands were populated by Highland clansmen presented

no obstacle. In a process that has become known as the Clearances, thousands
of Highlanders were evicted from their holdings and shipped off to Canada,
or carted off to Glasgow to make way for Cheviot sheep. Others were con-
centrated on the west coast to work picking kelp seaweed, then necessary for
the soap and glass industry, and were later to form the nucleus of the crofting
community. Some cottagers were literally burnt out of house and home by
the agents of the Lairds. This is from the account of Betsy Mackay, who was
16 when she was evicted from the Duke of Sutherland's estates:

> Our family was very reluctant to leave and stayed for some time, but the
> burning party came round and set fire to our house at both ends, reduc-
> ing to ashes whatever remained within the walls. The people had to
> escape for their lives, some of them losing all their clothes except what
> they had on their back. The people were told they could go where they
> liked, provided they did not encumber the land that was by rights their
> own. The people were driven away like dogs.'[23]

The clearances were so thorough that few people were even left to remember,
and the entire process was suppressed from collective memory until its history
was retold, first by John Prebble in *The Highland Clearances*, and subsequently
by James Hunter in *The Making of the Crofting Community*. When Prebble's
book appeared, the Historiographer Royal for Scotland Professor Gordon
Donaldson commented:

> I am sixty eight now and until recently had hardly heard of the Highland
> Clearances. The thing has been blown out of proportion.[24]

But how else can one explain the underpopulation of the Highlands? The
region's fate was poignantly described by Canadian Hugh Maclennan in an
essay called 'Scotchman's Return':

> The Highland emptiness only a few hundred miles above the massed
> population of England is a far different thing from the emptiness of our
> North West territories. Above the 60th parallel in Canada, you feel that
> nobody but God had ever been there before you. But in a deserted
> Highland glen, you feel that everyone who ever mattered is dead and
> gone.[25]

The final and most contentious wave of land enclosures in England occurred between about 1750 and 1850. Whereas the purpose of most previous enclosures had been to turn productive arable land into less productive (though more privately lucrative) sheep pasture, the colonisation of Scotland for wool, and India and the Southern US states for cotton now prompted the advocates of enclosure to play a different set of cards: their aim was to turn open fields, pastures and wastelands – everything in fact – into more productive arable and mixed farm land. Their byword was 'improvement'. Their express aim was to increase efficiency and production and so both create and feed an increasingly large proletariat who would work either as wage labourers in the improved fields, or as machine minders in the factories.

The main arguments of those in favour of enclosure were:

That the open field system prevented 'improvement', for example the introduction of clover, turnips and four course rotations, because individuals could not innovate;

That the waste lands and common pastures were 'bare-worn' or full of scrub, and overstocked with half-starved beasts;

That those who survived on the commons were (a) lazy and (b) impoverished (in other words 'not inclined to work for wages'), and that enclosure of the commons would force them into employment.

The main arguments of those against enclosure were:

That the common pastures and waste lands were the mainstay of the independent poor; when they were overgrazed, that was often as a result of overstocking by the wealthiest commoners who were the people agitating for enclosure;

That enclosure would engross already wealthy landowners, force poor people off the land and into urban slums, and result in depopulation.

Between 1760 and 1870, about 7 million acres (about one sixth the area of England) were changed, by some 4,000 Acts of Parliament, from common land to enclosed land.[26] However necessary this process might or might not have been for the improvement of the agricultural economy, it was downright theft. Millions of people had customary and legal access to lands, and the basis of an independent livelihood was snatched away from them through what to them must have resembled a Kafkaesque tribunal carried out by members of the Hellfire Club.

If you think this must be a colourful exaggeration, then read J.L. and Barbara Hammonds' accounts of Viscount 'Bully' Bolingbroke's attempt to enclose Kings'? Sedgmoor in Somerset to pay off his gambling debts. 'Bully', wrote the chairman of the committee assessing the proposal, 'has a scheme of enclosure which if it succeeds, I am told will free him of all his difficulties'. Or read of the Spencer/Churchill proposal, in the face of repeated popular opposition, to enclose the common at Abingdon.[27] And if you suspect that the Hammond's accounts may be extreme examples (right wing historians are rather sniffy about the Hammonds)[28] then look at the map showing the constituency of MPs who turned up to debate enclosure bills for Oxfordshire when they came up in Parliament. Out of 796 instances of MPs turning up for any of the Oxfordshire bills, 514 were Oxfordshire MPs, most of whom would have been landowners.

To use a modern analogy, it was as if Berkeley Homes had put in an application to build housing all over your local park, and when you went along to the planning meeting to object, the committee consisted entirely of directors of Berkeley – and there was no right of appeal.

The commoners lost not only their open space and their natural environment (the poems of John Clare remind us how significant that loss was); they also lost one of their principal means of making a living. The 'democracy' of the late-eighteenth and early-nineteenth century English Parliament, at least on this issue, proved itself to be less answerable to the needs of the common man than the dictatorships of the Tudors and Stuarts. Kings are a bit more detached from local issues than landowners, and, with this in mind, it may not seem so surprising that popular resistance should often appeal to the King for justice. (A similar recourse can be seen in recent protests by Chinese peasants, who appeal to the upper echelons of the Communist Party for protection against the expropriation of collective land by corrupt local officials).

The losers from the process of enclosure were of two kinds. First there were the landless, or nearly so, who had no ownership rights over the commons, but who gained a living from commons that were open access, or where a measure of informal use was tolerated. These people had few rights, appeared on no records, and received nothing in compensation for the livelihood they lost. But there was also a class of smallholders who did have legal rights, and hence were entitled to compensation. However, the amount of land they were allocated 'was often so small, though in strict legal proportion to the amount of their claim, that it was of little use and speedily sold.'[29] Moreover, the considerable legal, surveying, hedging and fencing costs of enclosure were disproportionate for smaller holdings. And on top of that, under the system of poor relief in operation at the time, the taxes of the small landowner who worked his own land went to subsidise the labour costs of the large farmers who employed the landless, adding to the pressure to sell up to aggrandising landowners.[30]

Since it was generally acknowledged that a rural labourer's wages could not support his family, which therefore had to be supported by the poor rates, there were good arguments on all sides for providing the dispossessed with sufficient land to keep a cow and tend a garden. The land was available. It would have made very little impression upon the final settlement of most enclosure acts if areas of wasteland had been sectioned off and distributed as secure decent sized allotments to those who had lost their common rights. In a number of cases where this happened, it was found that cottagers hardly ever needed to apply for poor relief. Moreover, it had been shown (by research conducted by the Society for Bettering the Condition of the Poor and the Labourer's Friends Society) that smallholdings cultivated by spade could be more productive than large farms cultivated by the plough.[31]

In the face of such a strong case for the provision of smallholdings for the people, it took a political economist to come up with reasons for not providing them. Burke, Bentham and a host of lesser names, all of them fresh from reading Adam Smith's *Wealth of Nations,* advised Pitt and subsequent prime ministers that there was no way in which the Government could help the poor, or anybody else, except by increasing the nation's capital (or as we would now say, its GDP). No kind of intervention on behalf of the landless poor should be allowed to disturb the 'invisible hand' of economic self-interest – even though the hand that had made them landless in the first place was very visible, and was more like an iron fist. At the turn of the century, the Reverend Thomas Malthus waded in with his argument that helping the poor was a waste of time since it only served to increase the birth rate – a view which was lapped up by those Christians who had all along secretly believed that the rich should inherit the Earth.

Ricardo's theory of rent was also pulled in to bolster the arguments against providing allotments. A common justification for enclosure, and a key attraction for landowners, had always been that rents rose – doubled very often – after enclosure. This was blithely attributed to improvement of the land, as though there could be no other cause. Few gave much thought to the possibility that an increase in rent would result from getting rid of encumbrances, such as commoners and their common rights (in much the same way that nowadays a property increases in value if sitting tenants can be persuaded to leave, or an agricultural tie is removed).

Rent may show up on the GDP, but is an unreliable indicator of productivity, as contemporary writer Richard Bacon pointed out when he gave this explanation (paraphrased here by Brian Inglis) why landowners and economists were opposed to allotments:

> Suppose for argument's sake, 20 five-acre farms, cultivated by spade husbandry, together were more productive than a single 100-acre farm using machinery. This did not mean that the landowners would get more rent from them – far from it. As each 5-acre farm might support a farmer and his family, the surplus available for tenants to pay in rent would be small. The single tenant farmer, hiring labourers when he needed them, might have a lower yield, from his hundred acres, but he would have a larger net profit – and it was from net profit that rent was derived. That was why landlords preferred consolidation.'[32]

Richard Bacon deserves applause for explaining very clearly why capitalism prefers big farms and forces people off the land. It is also worth noting that the increased rent after enclosure had to be subsidised by the poor rates – the taxes which landowners had to pay to support the poor who were forced into workhouses.

In 1846, after a fierce debate, the tariffs on imported corn which helped maintain the price of British grown wheat were repealed. The widespread refusal to provide land for the dispossessed, and the emergence of an urban proletariat who didn't have the option of growing their own food, made it possible for proponents of the free market to paint their campaign for the repeal of the Corn Laws as a humanitarian gesture. Cheap bread from cheap imported corn was of interest to the economists and industrialists because it made wages cheaper At the same time it was of benefit to the hungry landless poor (provided wages didn't decline correspondingly, which Malthus claimed was what would happen). The combined influence of all these forces was enough to get tariffs removed from imported corn and open up the UK market to the virgin lands of the New World.

Had the labourers of Britain been rural smallholders, rather than city slumdwellers, then a high price for corn, and hence for agricultural products in general, might have been more in their interest, and it is less likely that the corn laws would have been repealed. If England had kept its peasantry (as most other European countries did) there would have been fewer landless labourers and abandoned children, wages for factory workers might have been higher, and the English cotton industry might not have been so well poised to undercut and then destroy thousands of local industries around the world which produced textiles of astonishing craftsmanship and beauty. By 1912, Britain, which couldn't even grow cotton, was exporting nearly 7 billion yards of cotton cloth each year – enough to provide a suit of clothes for every man woman and child alive in the world at the time.[33] What we now call globalisation was a dominant force by the end of the nineteenth century.

Ironically, the same breed of political economists who had previously advocated 'improvement' via enclosure was now arguing for grain imports which would make these improvements utterly pointless. The Corn Law repeal had a delayed effect because it was not until after the construction of the transcontinental American railways, in the 1870s, that cereals grown on low-rent land confiscated from native Americans could successfully undermine UK farming. By the 1880s, the grain was also being imported in the form of thousands of tonnes of refrigerated beef, which undercut home produced meat. There were even, until the late 1990s, cheaper transport rates within the UK for imported food than for home grown food.[34] The lucky farm workers who emigrated to the New World were writing back to their friends and family in words such as these:

> There is no difficulty of a man getting land here. Many will let a man have land with a few acres improvement and a house on it without any deposit.
>
> I am going to work on my own farm of 50 acres, which I bought at £55 and I have 5 years to pay it in. I have bought me a cow and 5 pigs. If I had stayed at Corsley I should ever have had nothing.[35]

Unable to compete with such low rents, England's agricultural economy went into a decline from which it never properly recovered. Conditions of life for the remaining landless agricultural workers deteriorated even further, while demand for factory workers in the cities was not expanding as it had done in the early-nineteenth century. Of the 320,000 acres enclosed between 1845 and 1869, just 2,000 had been allocated for the benefit of labourers and cottagers.[36]

It was in this context that the call for smallholdings and allotments was revived. 'Three Acres and A Cow' was the catchphrase coined by liberal MP Jesse Collings, whose programme is outlined in his book *Land Reform*. In 1913 the parliamentary Land Enquiry Committee issued its report, 'The Land', which included copious first hand evidence of the demand for and the benefits of smallholdings. Both books focused on the enclosure of commons as the prime source of the problem.[37] A series of parliamentary statutes, from the 1887 Allotments Act, the 1892 Smallholding Act, and the 1908 Smallholding and Allotments Act provided local authorities with the power to acquire the land which now still exists in the form of numerous municipal allotments and the County Smallholdings estate.

County Smallholdings, in particular, came under attack when a second wave of free market ideologues came into power in the 1980s and 1990s. The Conservative Party's 1995 Rural White Paper advocated selling off the County Farms, and since then about a third of the estate has been sold, though there are signs that the number of sales is declining.[38]

The enclosure movement was brought to an end when it started to upset the middle classes. By the 1860s, influential city-dwellers noticed that areas for recreation were getting thin on the ground. In the annual enclosure bills for 1869, out of 6,916 acres of land scheduled for enclosure, just three acres were allocated for recreation, and six acres for allotments.[39] A protection society was formed, the Commons Preservation Society, headed by Lord Eversley, which later went on to become the Open Spaces Society, and also spawned the National Trust. The Society was not afraid to support direct action tactics, such as the levelling of fences, and used them successfully, in the case of Epping Forest and Berkhampstead Common, to initiate court cases which drew attention to their cause.[40] Within a few years, the Society had strong support in Parliament, and the 1876 Commons Act ruled that enclosure should only take place if there was some public benefit.

In any case, in the agricultural depression that by 1875 was well established, improvement was no longer a priority, and in the last 25 years of the nineteenth century only a handful of parliamentary enclosures took place. George Bourne describes how in his Surrey village, although the common had been enclosed in 1861, the local landless were able to continue using it informally until the early years of the twentieth century. What eventually kicked them out was not agricultural improvement, but suburban development – but that is another story. But Bourne's comments on the impact of that loss deserve to be heard:

> To the enclosure of the common more than to any other cause may be traced all the changes that have subsequently passed over the village. It was like knocking the keystone out of an arch. The keystone is not the

arch; but once it is gone all sorts of forces previously resisted, begin to operate towards ruin.[41]

*

The standard interpretation of enclosure, at least eighteenth and nineteenth century enclosure, is that it was 'a necessary evil, and there would have been less harm in it if the increased dividend of the agricultural world had been fairly distributed.'[42] Nearly all assessments are some kind of variation on this theme, with weight placed either upon the need for 'agricultural improvement' or upon the social harm according to the ideological disposition of the writer. There is no defender of the commons who argues that enclosure did not provide, or at least hasten, some improvements in agriculture, and there is no supporter of enclosure who does not concede that the process could have been carried out more equitably.

But these disputes miss the bigger picture. The fact is that England and Wales' rural population dived from 65% of the population in 1801 to 23% in 1901; while in France 59% of the population remained rural in 1901, and even in 1982, 31% were country dwellers. Between 1851 and 1901, England and Wales' rural population declined by 1.4 million, while total population rose by 14.5 million and the urban population nearly tripled.[43] By 1935, there was one worker for every 12 hectares in the UK, compared to one worker for every 4.5 hectares in France, and one for every 3.4 hectares across the whole of Europe.[44]

Britain set out, more or less deliberately, to become a highly urbanised economy with a large urban proletariat dispossessed from the countryside, highly concentrated landownership, and farms far larger than any other country in Europe. Enclosure of the commons, more advanced in the UK than anywhere else in Europe, was not the only means of achieving this goal: free trade and the importing of food and fibre from the New World and the colonies played a part, and so did the English preference for primogeniture (bequeathing all your land to your eldest son). But enclosure of common land played a key role in Britain's industrialisation, and was consciously seen to do so by its protagonists at the time.

The above account of the enclosure of the English commons is given for its own sake; but also because the management of English common pasture is the starting point of Garrett Hardin's thesis, so it is against the tapestry of English commons rights and the tortuous process of their enclosure that Hardin's formulaic 'tragedy' may initially be judged.

Hardin's theory springs from the observation that common pastures allowed individuals to benefit from overstocking at the community's expense, and therefore were inherently prone to ecological exhaustion and ultimately 'ruin'. Without doubt there were common pastures which matched the description given by William Lloyd, as amplified by Hardin. But the presence of powerful interest groups, possibly in a position to pervert the management regime, suggests a different scenario from that given by Hardin of 'rational herdsmen' each seeking to maximise their individual gain. Hardin's construct is like the Chinese game of Go where each counter has the same value; real life is more like chess, where a knight or a bishop can outclass a pawn.

Hardin's 'tragedy' bears very little relationship to the management of open fields, to the making of hay from the meadows, or to various other common rights such as gleaning, none of which are vulnerable to the dynamic of competitive overstocking. The only aspect of the entire common land system where the 'tragedy' has any relevance at all is in the management of pasture and wasteland; and here it is acknowledged by almost all historians that commons managers were only too aware of the problem, and had plenty of mechanisms for dealing with it, even if they didn't always put them into force.

The instances in which unstinted access to common pastures led to overstocking no doubt played a role in hastening eventual enclosure. But to attribute the disappearance of the English commons to the 'remorseless workings' of a trite formula is a travesty of historical interpretation, carried out by a theorist with a pet idea who knew little of the subject he was writing about.

The collective impact of that useful theory can be seen all around the world today. In the process of writing this article, I keyed the phrase 'Tragedy of the Commons' into Google. Slots three and four of the results were occupied by an American website containing the following summary:

> Fourteenth century Britain was organised as a loosely aligned collection of villages, each with a common pasture for villagers to graze horses, cattle and sheep. Each household attempted to gain wealth by putting as many animals on the commons as it could afford. As the village grew in size and more and more animals were placed on the commons, overgrazing ruined the pasture. No stock could be supported on the commons thereafter. As a consequence of population growth, greed, and the logic of the commons, village after village collapsed.

Thanks to Google, this tosh is no doubt being copied into sixth form essays across the length and breadth of the English speaking world, and the responsibility for it lies very largely with Garret Hardin.

References

1. Garrett Hardin, 'The Tragedy of the Commons', *Science*, 13 December, 1968, pp1243–1248.
2. William F Lloyd, *Two Lectures in the Checks to Population*, Oxford University Press, 1833.
3. Eg, E.A. Loayza, *A Strategy for Fisheries Development*, World Bank Discussion Paper 135, 1992.
4. E.P. Thompson, *Customs in Common*, Penguin, 1993, p107.
5. Arthur McEvoy, 'Towards an Interactive Theory of Nature and Culture, *Environmental Review*, 11, 1987, p299.
6. Garrett Hardin, 'The Tragedy of the 'Unmanaged' Commons', in R.V. Andelson, *Commons Without Tragedy*, Shepheard Walwyn, 1991.
7. Kevin Cahill, *Who Owns Britain*, Canongate, 2001.
8. Joan Thirsk, 'The Common Fields', *Past and Present*, 29, 1964.
9. J-C Asselain, *Histoire Economique de la France, du 18th Siècle à nos Jours. 1. De l'Ancien Régime à la Première Guerre Mondiale*, Editions du Seuil. 1984.
10. Paul Stirling, 'The Domestic Cycle and the Distribution of Power in Turkish Villages' in Julian Pitt-Rivers (Ed.) *Mediterranean Countrymen,* The Hague, Mouton: 1963; Hans U. Spiess, *Report on Draught Animals under Drought Fonditions in Central, Eastern and Southern zones of Region 1 (Tigray)*, United Nations Development Programme Emergencies Unit for Ethiopia, 1994, www.africa.upenn.edu/eue_web/Oxen94.htm
11. In 1381, the St Albans contingent, led by William Grindcobbe accused the Abbot of St Albans of (among other abuses) enclosing common land. Jesse Collings, *Land Reform: Occupying Ownership, Peasant Proprietary and Rural Education*, Longmans Green and Co, p120; and on Cade p138.
12. W.E. Tate, *The English Village Community and the Enclosure Movements*, Gollancz, 1967, pp122–125; W.H.R. Curteis, op cit 10, p132.
13. W.E. Tate, *The English Village Community and the Enclosure Movements*, Gollancz, 1967, pp122–125; W.H.R. Curteis, op cit 10, p132.
14. Thomas More, *Utopia*, Everyman, 1994.
15. William Everard *et al*, *The True Levellers' Standard Advanced*, 1649.
16. Early hippie organisations in California and the UK called themselves the San Francisco Diggers and the Hyde Park Diggers respectively.
17. Op. cit 15
18. Holinshed's *Chronicles*, Vol 3, p220. Fabyan's *Chronicle* states of Cade 'They faude him right discrete in his answerys'. Cited in Jesse Collings, op cit 15, p139.

19. David Boulton, *Gerrard Winstanley and the Republic of Heaven*, Dales Historical Monographs, 1999, chapter XIII.

20. Barbara Tuchman, *A Distant Mirror*, Macmillan, 1978, pp375–6.

21. E.P. Thompson, *Whigs and Hunters*, Allen Lane, 1985.

22. Anon, *The Anti-Projector; or the History of the Fen Project*, 1646?, cited in Joan Thirsk, op cit 8, p30.

23. John Prebble, *The Highland Clearances*, 1963, p79.

24. Alastair McIntosh, 'Wild Scots and Buffoon History', *The Land* 1, 2006.

25. Quoted in James Hunter, *Skye, the Island*, Mainstream, Edinburgh, 1986, p118.

26. G. Slater, 'Historical Outline of Land Ownership in England', in *The Land, The Report of the Land Enquiry Committee*, Hodder and Stoughton, 1913.

27. J.L. and Barbara Hammond, *The Village Labourer*, Guild, 1948 (1911) p60.

28. Thompson mentions the 'long historiographical reaction against those fine historians, Barbara and J.L. Hammomd.' Thompson, op cit 2, p115.

29. W.H.R. Curtler, *The Enclosure and Redistribution of Our Land*, Elibron Classics, 2005.

30. All the information on the fens in this section is taken from Joan Thirsk, *English Peasant Farming: The Agrarian History of Lincolnshire from Tudor to Recent Times*, Routledge and Kegan Paul, 1957.

31. Brian Inglis, *Poverty and the Industrial Revolution*, 1971, pp89–90, and p385.

32. Ibid, p386.

33. David Landes, *The Unbound Prometheus*, Cambridge, 1969. p452.

34. Thirsk, op cit 8, p311.

35. Letters from America, cited by K.D.M. Snell, *Annals of the Labouring Poor*, Cambridge 1985.

36. Tate op cit 15, p138. These figures are challenged by Curtier, whose *The Enclosure and Redistribution of Our Land,* op cit 10, is an apology for the landowning class. Curtier, an advocate of smallholdings maintained that thanks to landowners' generosity, 'there were a considerable number of small holdings in existence' and that 'the lamentation over the landlessness of the poorer classes has been overdone'. Yet he admits that 'the total number of those having allotments and smallholdings bears a very small proportion to the total of the poorer classes.' Curtier has a useful account of the effects of the various smallholding and allotment acts (pp278–301).

37. Collings, op cit 15; and Slater, op cit 37.

38. S. Fairlie, 'Farm Squat', *The Land* 2, Summer 2006.

39. Tate, op cit 15, p136.

40. Lord Eversley, *English Commons and Forests*, 1894.

41. George Bourne, *Change in the Village*, Penguin 1984 (1912), pp77–78.

42. G.M. Trevelyan, *English Social History*, Longmans, p379.

43. Institut National D'Etudes Demographiques, Total Population (Urban and Rural) of metropolitan France and Population Density – censuses 1846 to 2004, INED website; UK figures: from Lawson 1967, cited at http://web.ukonline.co.uk/thursday.handleigh/demography/population-size/rural.htm#TOP.

44. Doreen Warriner, *Economics of Peasant Farming*, Oxford, 1939, p3.

JAY GRIFFITHS

This England

In the deserts, a woman is staring at the parched landscape of arid plains. Her heart is thirsty, she is downcast and homesick, yearning for the fertile land where she was born, for its moist and tumbling leaves, for the cool mountains and rivers and the meadows of sheer and vivid green.

To allay her nostalgia, her husband builds colonnades and arches, fills a garden with plants and irrigates it all with a filigree of waterlines until it flourishes with myrtles, until almonds bask in the sun, until date palms sweeten and pomegranates swell, until grapevines curl their tendrils to the touch of his beloved queen.

So Nebuchadnezzar created the Hanging Gardens of Babylon for Queen Amytis and so, too, an ancient portrait of homesickness was carved, a love of one's land so specific that its loss can make you sicken, hurt with the 'ache for home' as nostalgia means in the roots of the word. Homesickness is a longing for the place of your belonging, its exact contour and climate, where the land knows you and calls you by some deft especial name, where the heart finds its first hearth. The raw imperative of a first love.

It is as if humans are born with the capacity to love the land on which we first set eyes. It is as if we have an inner template for this home-land-love, which is then adapted to the precise landscape of our childhood. This is a parallel for Chomsky's theory of the template for the grammar of language, by which a child is born with the ability to learn Language, an innate, pre-set template which is then tuned to the specific language which surrounds them. So perhaps we are born with an innate capacity to love our land, though that may be riverlands of wild garlic and bluebells or desertlands of catfish and hot springs; lands which talk with the brogue of heather or the vernacular of oak; lands which speak the argot of snow or the dialect of the savannah. For, despite the diversity of landscapes where humans have dwelled, the one constant is the ready love in the human heart.

In this, more than anything, is a demonstration of the indigenous human being, where the foot is moulded to the land it walks, the language entwined with locale so that the human being knows its dwelling well, somewhere warm for the spirit, snug with the scent of dog-fox and desire.

When I wrote my last book, I was intrigued by many conversations with indigenous people, from shamans of the Amazon to Inuit people of the Arctic, about their love of land, its wildness and its sense of home. Indigenous people said repeatedly, 'We are the land' and exile from their lands – through its destruction, through land theft – ruptures their identity so painfully that it causes a sickness of the heart, mind and body.

This is a birthright, this love of land. This indigenous nativity is a profound aspect of our human identity. But for the English, it is a contorted feeling, knotted with nastiness and silence, complicated by racism, guilt and empire. Yet for many people it is also the source of an almost unfathomable nostalgia, an ache of the heart which all the hanging gardens of the world cannot console.

The English can be either envious of indigenous cultures or poisonously racist towards them. For the racists, contempt suffices. But the envious response invites questions. Where are our old gods and songlines? The genius loci? The spirit of place? Why don't we, or can't we, sing our own folk songs? Why are the English so obsessed with selected pockets of history and simultaneously ignorant of most of it? What are the causes of our exile?

If you are a Palestinian, the cause of your exile is only too knowable, as poet Mahmoud Darwish discovered when he was six years old and the Israeli Army destroyed his village, leaving ruins. He would become an 'internal refugee', a 'present-absent alien'. In 2001, Israeli bulldozers ripped open his village's cemetery for a road, churning up human remains from the ground, bulldozing the past.

For Palestinians, memory is necessary, while for the Israelis it is better to have a sketchy memory for atrocities committed. There was (is) a similar pattern between the English and the Irish, as Eamon de Valera noted, saying that the difficulty was that 'the English never remember, the Irish never forget.' The vanquished are left with nothing but exile and memory while the victors are left with land which does not speak to them. Within Britain, the Irish, Welsh, Scottish and Cornish know a love of land which the English, so often, do not experience. Why so? In part, because the first acts of empire were internal, making Ireland, Scotland, Wales and Cornwall into colonies. But in the long run, it is the English who have become 'internal refugees' in terms of culture and homeland love.

Dispossessing, murdering and enslaving indigenous people, and removing them from their lands, was the story of empire. But if one mentions the reckless cruelties imposed for the sake of empire, the chances are that someone will sneer that one is suffering from a hand-wringing post-imperialist *guilt*, as if guilt is an unhygienic bad habit, a perversion, a personality-disorder. Should the British (and particularly the English) feel guilty for the atrocities of Empire? Of course we bloody should. To abuse people without a flicker of guilt is something only psychopaths would be proud of.

After the empire, though, after a few guilty recollections, what then? We have, collectively, through neoliberalism, through corporations, through consumerism, through extractive industries and the arms trade, continued to crush the peoples of the world who we first impoverished by empire. Should the British feel guilty now? Of course we bloody should. The psychopath insists that one should not dwell on the past. *Onwards, onwards on the road to the future!* But the past is where the deep truths of today were seeded. The past plays cause to today's consequence. Memory has become a political act and it is more radical to remember our history accurately than to don a balaclava and smash up a McDonald's.

But for the English in particular, memory is difficult. We seem to want to remember Robin Hood, King Arthur and Puck perhaps, but Olde England seems to be visible only as some cheesy Avalon seen through the windscreen of a BMW, or some beer mug with the Green Man leering in the handle. For something more profound, deeper in the spirit of the land seems shy of us. The gods won't play. Something in the land will not grant us an authentic dwelling for the soul, as if some shame palls the land for us, as if our English indigeneity is something we want and yet can't find.

You can do a straightforward Google search which gives one answer as to why the indigeneity of the English is a contorted feeling. Type in 'indigenous Britons' and seven out of the first ten websites are BNP related. 'The liberal-left love to applaud Native Americans for their 'soul and soil' approach to life, but we [BNP] reflect such an approach in our own Nationalist mindset,' says one website. Blood and soil. No one in their right mind wants to be seen anywhere near the hateful BNP, so the territory of English indigeneity is stolen by the far right. The human home-land-love is perverted into a hatred of other people's pigmentation and a queasy calculation of blood quota.

The 'Nationalist mindset' and nation states are fake political constructs, used frequently to attack, demean or destroy others. Land, on the other hand, is unarguable and unartificial. By dishonestly merging those two concepts, the far right has poisoned, for all the English, one of the sweetest wellsprings of the human heart. If the white underclass who support the BNP had any education about their own history, they might be able to see that the cause of their feeling of alienation and exile is massive wealth disparity and enclosure; that their true enemies are the odiously wealthy, and a legalised system of land thefts. What the British have done abroad, in the form of imperialism, has also happened within Britain and indeed to most of the English – the corporate colonialism and the colonising of common land by which the wealthy have made serfs of the rest of us.

Start with some contemporary facts of land ownership; some 0.6% of the population owns 69% of the land, so we the commoners are fundamentally homeless in our own land. That is as shocking as any other statistic on the apartheid of land rights. Further, the wealthy landowners have also propelled the factory-farming agribusiness which strips the land of specialness; the hare, the 'stag of the stubble' becomes rare. The land is made dumb and speechless, cannot utter its idiosyncratic thoughts. And if it could, would we the commoners be there to hear it? The enclosures, by which the vast majority of us were made internal exiles, were an outright theft of land from which we English commoners have never recovered. 'Private: Keep Out' signs warn us off our own land, even innocent strollers find that landowners set dogs on them and order the walkers off their own homeland, at gunpoint.

For the English (myself, I'm partly English, partly Welsh), one sublime measure of indigenous English culture is Shakespeare. Native to Warwickshire, his work is steeped in the countryside of Stratford, of remembrance and radish and thyme and rue. All of humanity is there in Shakespeare – lovers and schemers, soldiers and poets, priests, shepherds and fools. Well, almost all of humanity – one is missing, a representative of the tribe of fatuous shoppers, stampeding to get an Elizabethan IKEA sofa at half price. Now, in this age of consumerism, 'Hamlet' is a brand name and the 'Forest of Arden' is an expensive hotel with a golf course.

Shakespeare didn't put the consumer on the stage but in contrast, modernity puts the consumer centre-stage. People on trains are not 'passengers' but 'customers'. People in therapy rooms are not 'patients' but 'clients'. People hanging around on the streets are not 'citizens', 'flâneurs' or 'flirters' but always 'shoppers'. Everywhere, we are not people but 'consumers', the cash aspect of the relationship privileged over every other aspect of travelling, healing, mooching, chattering.

Consumerism causes cultural eviction, dislocating us all with bland shopping arcades, gigantised, off-ground and artificial, always the same, from the sameness of purpose, to the sameness of product, making every place the same as every other, evicting us from the especial nature of locale. Formed in the barrenness of numbness, this is a wasteland for the human spirit. Tourism has been famously referred to as 'cheap holidays in other people's misery.' If only that were all. Consumerism is lifelong holidays in other people's misery; the global exploitation of land and lives for the sake of the pampered consumer. But consumerism, ('because you're worth it and they're not') will also give you the shampoo to wash that guilt right out of your hair, will give you the conditioner to recondition morality to continue the exploitation and extermination, guilt-free. And, yes, extermination is the correct term for the slow mass murders of consumption.

This is Babylon, the corrupt übercapitalism, the tidal waves of corporate takeover, commercial invasion, car parks and shopping malls across the green and singing land, roads on roads, built for commerce and consumerism, blanking out the songlines of this land.

*

For one long moment in my life, I heard the earthsongs of England. For one exquisite time, I saw the old gods honoured with an authenticity that left me in tears.

During the anti-roads protests of the nineties, the motley-wearers (artists, punks, shamans, squaddies, students, the homeless, pagans, and peasants) fought for their land, literally putting their lives on the line when the authorities issued orders so reckless as to risk murdering the protesters. They wore the feathers of birds for the flight of the gods, they lit the fires of the solstices and paid raw tribute to the Earth. They picked up by ear the old songs, gentle as violets, tough as badger's teeth. Crucially, in every aspect of the protests they created a distinction – and an opposition – between the state and the land. They loved their land and hated their state, defied it with all they had, when the bulldozers came, building roads through the homeland of history, ripping apart the beauty which had graced those woodlands for generations. The protesters referred to the world of consumerism, cars and capitalism as the 'Babylon' of today.

To me, the protests were extraordinarily significant, rare as hares, signifying how authentic belonging to the land was something which had to be earned. To belong is to love is to defend with your life if need be. Among the camps – grubby, feral, crusty, sweet-hearted, pissed-up, kind, angry – the gods, who are never for sale, played. I'm no theist, and to me the gods were metaphor and personification and symbol, they were expressions of the land's indigenous psyche. And they were green to the teeth, rampant and gurning.

One day, representatives of an indigenous community from Bolivia, similarly campaigning against a road (the Pan-American highway) visited one of the sites. 'We salute you,' said the indigenous representatives to the protesters, 'as the indigenous people of Britain. Your fight is the same as ours; you are fighting to defend the land.' It was honey to hear the term 'indigenous Britons' used as far from the BNP as it is possible to get.

There is a word so ancient that you can hardly say it in sneering metropolitan circles. It is honour. The protesters honoured the land which came alive in their honour. The drums befriended the trees, the bells woke the woodlands. With their treehouses streaming ribbons, flowers and webs, the protesters created the Hanging Gardens in the Babylon of concrete and tarmac. From Babylon which, both ancient and modern, represents corruption, power and wealth, they wrested a corner for the mead moon, the Green Man of the woods who here was neither toy nor relic but reignited, arising like a phoenix from the ashes of the Beltane fire.

It is as if there is a kind of earth-ethic, an underground morality in this, whereby in order to experience one's home-land-love, in order for the indigenous human heart to belong profoundly to its land, there is a necessary sacrifice. It was exemplified, for me, by the sacrifices made by the protesters; the exposure, ill-health, injuries, stress and burnout, but those are not the only people who know sacrifice to stay true to their lands. The hillfarmers of Wales, the crofters of Scotland and the smallholders of English farms (almost rubbed out by supermarkets and large landowners) also know the high price of fidelity to one's acre.

But for those who steal the fat of other people's lands, who take far more than their fair share, and *then* ask for a taste of mead or the melody of the Ash Grove: those who gobble the resources of others and parade their lives of high consumption and then search for the god Lugh or the spirit of the woods, will find, simply, that they can't have both. You cannot take without giving, and if you refuse to give, then something will be taken from you, probably in the coin of the soul. All religions are wise to this: where there is guilt, the gods flee.

What indigenous cultures seem universally to recognise is that every act has consequence. Where something is taken, something must be given in exchange. Everything is in a state of balance by which there is a price for everything, a measure for every measure in the scales.

You cannot change the laws of physics, but I'd add that you cannot change the laws of metaphysics either. For high-consuming lifestyles (which indirectly but certainly rob other people of their homeland) have a boomerang effect, causing a loss of belonging to the consumer.

I have tried to look at this in moral terms, but our language of morality (so good on person-to-person morality) seems to gloss over collective morality, and wholly omit an ethic of Earth. I am searching, then, to describe some truth of the psyche so profound that it is not only a psychological truth but also an ethic grounded in the mind's land and the land's mind, some irrefutable and intrinsic geometry of Earth-kind.

For the English to have back our deep, lovely Englishness, we need to remember our past soberly, and to stop repeating its iniquities today through the devious reach of corporate colonialism. If we want to experience our home-land-love, we need to honour other people's homelands. We need to educate ourselves about our real history. We need to oppose our nation state for its racism, dishonesty and greed. We need to renounce the political and financial gains made from our nation's exploitations and wars. If we want our English identity back, if we want to belong to our lands, we have to take our hands off other peoples'. And at home, the wealthy, if they want to belong, have to return the lands to the Commoners. They won't, I know, but what they lose, without question, is the true belonging of the human heart.

Indigenous people frequently say that they belong to the land. Landowners claim that the land belongs to them. Ownership is the opposite of belonging and for the large landowners of Britain, the more they own, the less they belong. Some of these large landowners evade tax by calling themselves 'non-domiciled'. Intended simply as a tax category it in fact carries a far greater (and sadder) poetic truth.

Aboriginal Australians often speak of belonging to their land, and when there is any sense of 'owning' land, it is an ownership which involves not money but knowledge. The knowers of the land, the knowers of the song-lines, are the true owners of it. Hedge by hedge, hare by hare, stanza by stanza and grove by grove, the land of England is there to be known, and there are those whose nostalgia for it hurts them. But as it was the very wealth of Babylon which both seduced and exiled Queen Amytis, so it is the wealth of a modern Babylon which seduces and exiles us all who, yearning for a sense of home, find that all the power, wealth and corruption of a consumer Babylon will not console this yearning unless some powerful restitution is made.

the lost gods

the feld is grene it is high sumor the long grass runs ofer to a clere ea and from ofer the waeter rises roccs great and deorc and high they rises high and on them is a great stan torr and in this torr a wifman yonge and with cilde. deop in the frenc lands in this torr this wifman she is to bring forth a grendel a cweller of cyngs a fyr deoful but now she cnaws nuthan but that she has been fuccd by the greatest man in the land though she is not his wif and now is owned by him

and in this torr this blaec torr risan abuf the grene felds now this wifman dreams. from her guttas where this deoful is brewan she sees growan a great treow and this treow it cum up high abuf the felds abuf efen this great torr abuf all the lands of the frenc and it does not stop there it grows higher still. and the sceado of this treow she sees spraedan and mofan out and out until all of this ducdom is deorc and then ofer the sea the sceado mofs and the treow still growan and the sceadow cums upon an other strand and still it spreads until all this other land is in deorcness. and when she wacans this yonge afeart girl all is blaec as the blaec stan what enfolden her

well the fyr has cum now. it has cum and it has beorned high and strong and for sum years and it has eten all angland in it and now angland is a tale from a time what is gan. if thu can thinc on what it is to be losan efery thing thu is thinc on this and if thu belyfs thu wolde do sum thing other than what i done if thu thincs thu wolde be milde or glad to those wolde hew away thy lyf from thu then thu is sum dumb esol who lyfs may be in sum great hus with all warm fyrs and ruggs and sum cymly wif and has nefer suffred naht

but as there is a time after angland so there was a time befor and i thincs of this sum daegs when i am moste wery and i thincs of when my grand fathor toc me to see where the eald gods lifd befor the christ cum. this place was sum way from our hus it toc us one half of a daeg to raecc this place i was still a yonge cilde and until we had cum to it i did not cnaw what we was doan for my grand fathor he wolde not sae he was a man who wolde not sae. he had toc me from my fathors hus early in the daeg it was in the monath of litha when all is bright when blosms is open and buterfleoges is floteran on them. we was in his boat and on to the waeter of the fenn and in litha with all bright and hued wyrmfleoges and all the heofon writhan with lyf and with the risan sunne on the nebb of the waeter the fenn what can be so blaec and deop on this mergen was a thing of beauty

mucc rowan did my grand fathor do through the secg below the reed and down streams deorc and windan and nefer did i thinc we wolde find our way baec efer to our hus so far was we in to the fenn. after many hours we cum to a place where the secg what had bene cuman in ofer us for a long time and macan lic we was in a deop place in the grund it fell baec and there cum up befor us a great mere a great deorcness of still waeter hecged around with yeolo secg and singan with the cry of dabchicc and hraga

my grand fathor then he rowed us slaw to the middel of this mere and he stopped rowan and he tacan the ars wet and dryppan into the boat and we roccd then with the wind and the waeter. and my grand fathor he saes to me loc into the waeter boy loc dune

and i locd then into the deorc waeter and at first i colde see nuthan but the blaec and the ael and the writhan caddis and the grene ropes of moss on the waeter still but my grand fathor was specan lic he meant to hear a good answor from me so i cept loccan and then lic sum masc had cum from my nebb sudden i sene the treows

under the boat under the waeter and not so deop was the stocc of a great blaec treow torn to its root lic a tooth in the muth of an eald wif. a great treow it was wid and blaec as the fyrs aesc blaec as the deorcness beyond the hall on a night when the mona slepes and as i was loccan i sene an other and an other and i colde see that under this mere was a great holt a great eald holt of tre- ows bigger than any i had sene efer in holland and ealdor i was sure ealdor efen than my grand fathor. and through the waeters these treows they semed to stir though in triewthe they was still as the graef and blaeccer

then i specs to my grand fathor lic he is sum wicce. what is this grand fathor i saes what is this holt growan under the waeter what world is this. i was thin- can many things that fear me then i was thincan this was the land where aelfs cum from or that entas or dweorgs was here or efen that it was the hall beneath the mere in what grendel was lyfan and that his mothor was cuman for me under my lytel boat. until my grand fathor spac i efen thought he was him self an aelf or an eorca in a mans masc cum to tac me to his world of blaec and yfel and me nowhere to run

and my grand fathor he left the ars still in the boat and we was driftan slaw on a wind that was so lytel we colde not fele it and nothan near but the yeolo secg and nothan hierde but lytel fugols and the wyrmfleoges and driftan then ofer the great blaec treows he telt me of the holt of the lost gods of angland

he telt me that in the time befor the christ angland was ham to a hus of gods what was born of this grund and what lyfed in it among the folc. and these gods he saes was not lic the christ they was not ingenga gods bound about in lyes and words not gods of fear unsene in the heofon what priccd man sore and bound him with laws and feart him with fyr but these was gods of the treows and the waeter lic we is folc of them

ealdor of these he saes was woden also called grim who walced the duns and the high hylls. woden cyng of the gods of angland from who all triewe an-glisc cyngs is cum in blud. and befor the christ saes my grand fathor and i haf hierd from others also that this is triewe though then i wolde not belyf him befor the christ he telt me it was woden was hong fyrst on a treow and woden holed with a spere until clere waeters cum from him and woden who fell lic he was cwelled then cum up again and in risan was giefen the wisdom of the world in the runes. and woden then was called upon by anglisc folc in holt and feld and now the preosts they tells us he is the deoful him self though they has tacan his lyf for the tale of their own god the hwit christ who nefer cums

woden has a wifman my grand fathor saes also and her name is frig and for all wifmen frig is a freond in the birth of cildren and in luf and in all wifly things. and the first son of woden and frig was thunor freond of all wyld places god with a hamor what waepen brought on the lightnan itself. and his brothor was balder whose beauty was greater efen than the beauty of the fenn in win-ter efen than of my wifman edith and his brothor also was ing ealdor of the holt who stered the waggon of lyf through the grene monaths who colde becum a boar for feohtan and for specan to the land and all wihts

and these gods saes my grand fathor these gods was lic our folc lic my edith to me and thy good mothor to thu befor she was tacan. these gods was lifan here in this holt in the daegs befor the waeters cum and drenccd it. this was the holt of the eald gods for they had no hus lic us now they was not weac lic us they was of treow and grund

and ofer all these gods he saes ofer efen great woden was their mothor who is mothor of all who is called erce. erce was this grund itself was angland was the hafoc and the wyrmfleage and the fenn and the wide sea and the fells of the north and efen the ys lands. and great erce it was who brought these waeters to close ofer the holt of the eald gods and to drencc the treows so they is now lytel stoccs for she sene that the folc of angland had turned from them to this christ the lyan god who specs of heofon but cnawan not our own grund.

for erce she is the grund her self and until anglisc folc sene what they haf done the holt of the gods will be for efer under the deorc waeters of this fenn and the gods will be lost to us. and the gods he saes the gods them selfs waits still beneath these waeters for us to cum baec and when angland is in need if we calls them they will cum all of them from the eald holt below this fenn mere and feoht again with anglisc men against any and hew them down

the treows in the mere was beorned in to me that daeg and until i am in my deop graef always i will see them. ah my grand fathor the christ he said wolde nefer cum all the strength of preost and biscop he wolde sae all their hold ofer men is in this one lye that the christ will cum to recen with them all but he nefer cums. and my grand fathor he had sene this for when he was a yonge man mucc of the world was in high thryll for it was a thousand years ago the christ cum saed all the preosts and biscops and for many years it had bene saed this was the year he wolde cum again

for one full year folcs was wepan and biddan and sean signs in the heofon and all preosts and biscops was saen it will be tomergen and then again tomergen. and then when the year was gan at last with a thousand fyrs on a thousand hylls ofer angland and folcs callan up to heofon on all and when it was done and the christ was still not cum then the preosts and the biscops they saed nuthan mor and it was nefer spoc of again. and then saed my grand fathor then their lyes was clere and yet dumb men still belyf them and triewely he saed most men is hunds or esols and not to be locd up to

well my grand fathor was a wise man in many things and of the hunds and esols he spac triewe and of the christ also. but of the lost gods under the mere the eald gods who wolde cum again when angland called well i was callan them i was callan them from fenn and holt and lic the christ they did not cum. not woden not thunor not ing neither they cum not for harald cyng they cum not for dunstan or eadberht or odelyn they cum not for hereweard nor for us in the holt. they cum not to feoht the bastard and send him baec to the sea with the frenc hunds he bring to et our land lic goats

    but i sholde spec with care for i did call and sum thing

    sum thing cum

    sum one cum

    sum one cum and is still here

---

the lost gods *is an extract from a novel-in-progress, set in occupied England in the aftermath of the 1066 invasion, narrated by a man of the Lincolnshire fens bearing witness to the end of his world. It is written in a hybrid of Old and modern English.*

MARK WATERS

On the neck of the bull

Finisterre

Catharsis comes from the Cathars, he said on the coach.
They ran into the sea over the wide white beach of pilgrims
And the shells lay still at the sound of their footsteps.
Some rolled swiftly over to hide their attractive ridged shoulders,
Not out of fear or defence, just hide and seek playfulness.

He chanted songs of native Americans, making up the words, the sounds,
As best he could remember, and skipped outdated silver pesetas
West across the water in a gesture, an offering.
After four, his shell found him.

They drank fire water together in a field of purple
Thistles and gorse at this world's end.
She said the elves and sprites had marched by in hordes
To attend the party, even the queen of the Fairies
Riding with her bees, in a kind of *who me?* pose and expression
Which she demonstrated to him.

They remembered their dead under the halo of a hot sun,
Its aurora visible all afternoon around his raised eclipsing palm,
And he knelt down to the little people
With gifts of hard round biscuit and fire water,
For having, even mistakenly, suggested our crumbs would be enough.

Perhaps the pylons were shocked.
They stood around us like pilgrims
On their singular way to the power station.
Their concrete nakedness confirmed
    They had burnt their clothes

On the rocks behind the lighthouse.
Their thin outstretched arms
Must have swung a long walk to end up
Open palmed and humming
So near this hilltop generator.
Perhaps they were beyond caring
Or didn't sense the resentment of their presence
In our temple of Apollo. They didn't say.
And then he said thanks to the sun, to the light
That shines through everything and everything
Was light and looked around at everything else
And laughed, the pylons too.

Ghosts of the *Discovery*, and other ships,
All decked with hopefuls looking their last at Europe –
As their Captain Smiths turned to the West
And threw up their sails to catch the Atlantic trade winds –
Dotted the ocean.
Full stops
Waiting for Europa's sentence to end,
But it didn't.
We sent, with our ideals, disease
And the sentence without the syntax and grammar of compassion
Collapsed into over-packed slave-ship holds of dying words
Black black black red murder and shame
Still unresolved, ongoing, unwept
Period.

Still.
They sang of new hope, and as he had been told
Seven days before, yellow fell
Like water through and over boulders
On the side of a mountain. Yellow gorse.
Dense and impenetrable shrub of the bull's shoulder.
Perhaps something left of the frightened souls,
Those panicked Roman soldiers, prickly yellow bellies,
Flowering there in the trade winds and the burning sun
Of Finisterre.

MELANIE CHALLENGER

Paradise

'I'm going to leave a heart in the earth
So it may grow and flower.'
Rosario Murillo

Leave your heart in the earth –
Its gracious mandrake-like nature
Cries out against our reign. Slender shoots stir the mire,
From whose overcast materials comes the rebirth
Of all we've adored, all we've brushed aside,
A generation's obsessions – the clay of the goylem,
The beautiful imprimis, our lifeblood in the bud.
Plant your heart in the earth that it'll bloom
Against the body's thwarted openness,
Gospels unspoken in life left in the fraught
Whispers of leaves at the close
Of their affiliations. Plant it in the night
Soil that the sods of its stock
Be rampant and bless it (*or, dress it,*
As I could say) while the kindlier fruit
Of our arrested affections swells in the muck.
The End of the World
Falcons suspend the earth from under them,
Fettering the ground to their sights. What will become
Of it all when they're gone? Their hungers done, each bond
Riveted on their flight bites the dust.

                              The downturned

Edges of the world debunk the skyline's authority.
Some stinted impulse to break from shame
Cannons a hobbled tramp into the tower – heroism and pity
Spent by the infidel blackness of space. And now atom
From atom turns loose from each private kiss to die alone.
And we lovers lie, fresh to the approaching end, the one
Thrust up inside the other as if to counterweigh
Some weakness. We'll not come undone.
Eternal, perfectly falling, held fast to by the falcon.

CHARLES DAVIES

four poems from the sequence

The Way Home

(a work in progress*)

one

no one can show you the way
only the way they know.
they can give you steps to take,
but then you have their steps
and not your way.
because your journey started before you
took your first step
and your first step laid out a path for you
alone.
now whenever you stand still
you're back there
where your journey started.
and whenever you move
there you are
on your way.
standing still or moving
it's all the same.
i know that and i know my way.

* this is based on the tao te ching
  it's not translated from the Chinese
  (it's just hacked together from English translations)

two

look for beauty and you'll find ugliness
look for goodness and you'll find evil
look for high points and you'll find
depths
look for shortcuts and feel your journey
get longer.

what if you don't look for anything?
what if you don't try to get anywhere
and don't show anyone the way?

things will come and go
don't reach out for them
don't hold on to them.

if you claim nothing as yours
then no one can take it from you.

nine

if you fill a bowl that's full
you'll only make a mess.
if you sharpen a knife that's already sharp
you'll only wear it out.
if you think some savings
will make you safe
if you think some recognition
will prove your worth
that's still more than you need.
if you depend on something you can lose
you'll spend your whole life trying to
hold on.
just do the work
then walk away.

fifteen

once upon a time
everyone knew the way
but that was a very long time ago
how could you describe them now?
imagine someone crossing a frozen river
taking care over every step
or someone constantly alert
sensing possible danger everywhere
or a careful guest
on their very best behaviour.
they would give way like melting ice
they were as plain and simple as a stick
of green wood
as open as a valley
and as hard to fathom as muddy water.
who has time for that now?
waiting for a natural path to open up
only acting when the moment arrives?
when making your way
if you don't hunt for enlightenment
you'll find your footsteps becoming
lighter.

nineteen

i gave up on wisdom and abandoned
learning
now everyone benefits from my stupidity
i gave up on humanity and abandoned my
duty
everyone benefits from my acceptance
i gave up on skills and abandoned profit
i exploit nothing and no one.
but giving up these things doesn't help
me find my way.
i also have to see what i see
do what i do
and have what i've got.

TOM SCOTT

Stain

Mist hangs in the lower valley, like a burnt
offering that's failed to reach heaven.
From the far side we'd be hard to tell apart,
my brother and I, two tall men in dark coats
and the wrong shoes for a January walk,
climbing the path at the wood's ragged edge.
Not so the dogs, no mistaking them –
a rangy lurcher, skittish as a colt,
and a staffy, rolling on bowed legs,
a brindled barrel with gin-trap jaws.
The lurcher frisks around the older dog,
twanging with pent-up speed, but the other
won't rise to it, keeps its sawn-off muzzle
close to the damp earth, the scents that trail
into the undergrowth. We talk of children,
houses, work, money gone up in smoke,
our minds barely engaged with the terrain
that our feet know by rote. Halfway up we pause
for breath and the familiar view. And then
we hear it, between a grunt and a scream,
or maybe the two overlaid, and see
a brambled thicket move. A crackle of twigs
and a fallow deer breaks out, cream spots on tan,
lovely as only wild things can be. Five yards more
and she'll be away, but before she clears them
the lurcher has her by a leg. She pulls free
but veers back to the bushes and the older dog
that lunges at her soft, white underside.
The other grips her throat. Adrenalin

pricks my fingers as we run, shouting
for them to stop. With desperate strength
the deer drags the dogs uphill towards us
before her legs give way. My brother
loosens the lurcher's grip but the other
has tasted blood and won't let go. And now
we see the damage can't be undone.
I want it over, cast around for something
to make it so — a rock, a heavy stick —
but the ground is soft and all I find
are saplings and green twigs. I clench my fist
and hit hard behind her head with its edge
five, six times. Where I expect soft tissue
is hard, ridged muscle. My hand bruises, the deer
still twists and jerks. My brother aims a kick
at her head. I do the same, and twice again.
The staffy has backed off and with the other dog
Is watching us finish the kill, pleased
we've got the point. At last it's done, the open
eyes empty, the legs still. We leave her
on the hillside and walk home. The dogs
are quiet, savouring the blood. We talk
of butchers and venison, trying to find
some sense in what we've done. Looking down,
I see on my right shoe a wet, black stain,
and know at once that it will not come out.

RUPERT CATHLES

In the Wasteland

When no one could imagine a scarcity of wild and uncultivated land, the word 'wasteland' was given to what we now call wilderness.

Today, there is a new wasteland, a wasteland in our cities and in our urbanised, industrialised countryside. As was once the case with wilderness, it is rarely appreciated for its natural beauty, for being of value in itself.

Look around your neighbourhood or anyone else's and you'll see many 'vacant lots', voids within the urban universe. Some come and go within a matter of months, others have remained vacant for as long as anyone can remember. They are vacant because they are not 'developed', built on or utilised. They lie empty, lands of waste, filling up with garbage, the detritus of hyper-consumption. It may be where buildings have been demolished, or could be a neglected graveyard, or a forgotten corner of a park, or excess land where some businessman has been unable to fulfil his ambitions, or land whose ownership has been mislaid in pre-computer archives, given up for lost. It would be apt to call it 'forgotten land'. It is a kind of no man's land, like the marches of an ancient kingdom or neutral zones on disputed borders.

These wastelands are often found in the most unlikely places; they need not be large. If you move to a new house, your garden may be a wasteland. Perhaps you have stumbled into such places and experienced a sense of unbelonging, of being a wanderer in the wasteland, although you may have shrugged it off and forgotten all about it. Forgotten land; forgotten feelings.

Remember being a kid, with long holidays, when you've just reached the age of freedom, having slipped away from the mothering home, off alone or with the other kids. You wandered off, without direction, looking into all the places which adults don't frequent, on an adventure of discovery.

Kids of that age are wanderers in the wasteland. They know what it is to be in no man's land, that place between worlds, between the worlds of dependent childhood and independent adulthood. You may have forgotten, but you discovered the wasteland, metaphorically and literally, in those long holidays. Even kids kept on the tightest reins at some time experience wandering off with other kids or alone, discovering the world and its wastelands.

They say that we lack the rituals to mark the passage from childhood into adulthood, as practised by the tribes of our ancient ancestors. Instead of an acknowledged cross-over point, we have a painfully long initiation, unacknowledged by the tribe, called adolescence. Many people would agree that this adolescence is a wasteland, wildly chaotic. It can also be seen that most of childhood is a wasteland. From the first time we wander off on our own until we leave home, we are wandering through a land which must be crossed. In a culture without initiations we still experience rites through the many stages of growing up; they just aren't often recognised as such.

Remember the time when you first went off without adults, alone or with other kids, learning the non-adult ways of your little tribe of children. Remember going beyond the bounds, out of bounds, with the thrills of not being caught. Remember when you all went haring off and when you fell behind. They ran on, leaving you alone. You stand in the middle of nowhere, some nameless wasteland, wondering which way to go. Remember the feeling then, the feeling of being alone, vulnerable in a desolate place. You feel panic, but something stops you running away. Something makes you stop, a sense perhaps of the open sky, making you feel small and insignificant. You see a bird on the ground, perfectly at home, and realise that you too feel at home there, under the open sky. The wasteland has become something new to you, something beautifully wild of which you are a part. Children don't talk about such things, don't even form them as thoughts, but the feeling is there.

Walk out into the middle of an abandoned space, be kid-like and feel the sense of being in an unclaimed world, with broken fences and discarded refuse, where you have as much right to be as the birds and insects. Unknowingly you have entered a new world, stepping through a magic door.

The first and the last rites of childhood are always in the wasteland. As adults we can return to remember where we started.

Wasteland may look desolate from a distance, from the road, but you will always find life if you look for it. Weeds break through the hardest surfaces. Lichens, mosses, ivies cover every kind of material, moulds and fungi in dark damp corners, grasses taking a hold in the shallowest soils, tree seedlings lodging in cracks, roots breaking up tarmac and concrete. Nature does what nature has always done, which it is in the Spirit of Life to always do, invading, colonising, transforming dead matter into living things. Nature covers everything, very slowly, in layers of biota, always creating and mending the biological film which clings to the surface of this living planet.

Go in spring or summer to any abandoned land, to what seemed so forsaken in winter, and you will find life flourishing in surprising places, in unexpected ways. Given time, left to itself, even the most lifeless polluted land will become full of life.

On even the most desolate land you can usually see nature performing the miracle of soil creation. A green carpet creeps over thick concrete, lichens and mosses hugging the artificial rock, making a mat into which grass seeds fall and spread out their long-ranging roots. Annually the grass dies, giving its substance back as humus, rotted leaves of grass. Mixed with weathered rock particles and the dust of the air, this humus-compost of the grass becomes that precious resource called *soil*.

In wasteland children pick up a lot of dirt – smudged over their faces, ground into their clothes, under their nails. Wastelands are dirty places; dirty means bad in our squeaky clean society. The dirty child is assumed to have been up to no good.

Dirt and water equals mud – even messier than plain old dirt. Mud, however, is saturated soil. If the mud dries out but is kept damp, and not compacted, then old seeds in it or new ones floating in on breezes, or falling in birds' fertile droppings, will germinate and sprout, growing up, up – turning the dirt into living green earth.

Children need the randomness of childhood freedoms for their minds to become fertile, need to be wanderers in the wasteland, not kept clean and safe all the time. For that, we need to remember why it matters, remember and rediscover the importance of wasteland. Having grown up we forget how much it mattered that we had the freedom to take risks and get dirty.

The end of childhood is not a once and for all event. There's always a wasteland to cross. Perhaps the end of the childhood of humanity will be when we have come to appreciate the beauty of wasteland as well as of wilderness.

NICK HUNT

To the bone

We didn't stop clubbing the afanc with our paddles until we were sure its back was broken. On this point Reverend Williams had been most specific. 'Don't stop clubbing the afanc, boys, until you are sure its back is broken,' he'd said. 'Merely battering the bugger will not suffice. You must cleave its spine'.

He was sitting on a pony at the top of the first slope, where the track wound up into the mountain. He was wearing a black hat stiff with frost; his spectacles were steamed. His left hand held a small black book, in which his right hand diligently recorded which men were on their way up to the lake, and which men were on their way down.

We quickly climbed the rocky slope that ran upwards to the first great peak, beyond which the black lake lay. The land below was black and white, with no smudge of colour in between. The rock of the mountain stuck here and there through the drifted snow in a way that resembled porpoises breaking through a wave.

'Don't forget the head!' the Reverend called, his voice unsteady in the wind. Already we were high enough above him to make him appear just a black spot in the snow.

There were eleven men from my village altogether. Most of us had played together as children. The anticipation made us children again, tripping each other on the narrow track, flinging echoes off the mountain walls. We teased fat Rhys, who had a face like a trout, that he might be mistaken for the afanc himself and get clubbed in its place. Our spirits were high with the Reverend's whiskey and the sense of being part of something bigger than ourselves.

But it was a steep, tricky climb to the lake, and soon enough the quietness overtook us. Before we were halfway to the top, a light snow began to fall. We started to ache in our fingers and thumbs. The cold made us shrink inside our bodies; turned us to men once again.

Word of the afanc's capture had spread far. It had reached our village the previous night, and everyone knew that Reverend Williams of Beddgelert was requesting the help of every able-bodied man in the land. Bells had clanged between villages; summonses had gone out. They had even lit the old beacon on the cliff-top at Aberdaren, and now men from as far away as Ynys Enlli had come to lend a hand in the clubbing.

I'd have liked to have been there when the afanc was caught. I think I'd have preferred the beginning to the end. It must have been a powerful sight to see it bellowing on the shore, water spurting from its nose, lashing out with its fearsome tail. Chains had been fastened around its body, attached to teams of oxen. It was said that these oxen strained so hard in dragging the afanc from the lake that one of them popped an eye. It was also said that a chain had snapped, the creature had lurched and maliciously rolled over, and a father and son had had the lives crushed out of them.

I'd also have liked to have seen the maiden: the beautiful virgin they'd stationed there to lure the afanc to shore. If I closed my eyes I could picture her, all alone at the water's edge. Her dark eyes nervously watching the lake, pretty face flushed with cold. Icicles sparkling in her hair, frost on her perfect lips. It was said that the beast couldn't help itself: it had dragged its foul body from the murky depths, and laid its hideous head in the maiden's lap.

It was also said that the maiden had offered to kiss the man who finished it off, the one who delivered that last decisive blow. This was in all of our minds as we climbed; even fat Rhys, with the face like a trout. We gripped the wooden paddles the Reverend had provided, swung them to feel their weight. The paddles felt serious and smooth in our hands. Anything was possible that morning.

Ascending the final uphill stretch, we came upon a party of fifteen men coming in the opposite direction. They had purple faces and small, resentful eyes, squinting like sulky children. They appeared exhausted from their work; their hands were clawed with cold. They demanded cigarettes, which we gave. Few of them looked at us directly.

'Have you come from the lake?' asked Aled excitedly. None of them spoke, but one man nodded.

'And how does it go?' Aled asked again.

'A hard job,' said this man.

'But it's not finished yet?'

'It's not finished yet'.

'And what's the creature doing? Fighting back?'

'Taking it,' the man replied. There was a pause in which no one else spoke. And then they spat their cigarette butts into the snow, and resumed their path down the mountain.

We heard the noise before we saw. At first we didn't know what it was. Echoing from somewhere just over the last rise – beyond which, we knew, the black lake lay in the shadow of the mountain's peak – a steady whap-whap, whap-whap, whap-whap that sounded like slush dripping off a roof, or an audience clapping along to music.

'That must be the sound of the beast's great tail, slapping on the water,' I heard Aled say. But it wasn't, as we soon found out. It was the sound of the paddles.

There must have been twenty or thirty men actively clubbing away down there, with many more gathered round, awaiting their turn. The afanc lay in the middle of them all, tethered to the rock by heavy chains. The paddles were going up and down, rebounding off the afanc's flesh, rising and falling mechanically and without passion. The oxen huddled off to one side, dolefully swinging their horns.

The way I heard it related later, the afanc was the length of a barn and as high as an elephant. This wasn't quite true, but it was still big; longer than a cottage or small orchard. At first it just looked like an enormous seal, but then we saw the fur around the chops, the sullen, doggy features. It had a fish's tail and fins, while its front appendages appeared to be something between paws and flippers. Its wrinkled muzzle was fastened with rope, and a few blunt teeth protruded grimly. We got up close to look into its eyes; they were open, with an oily sheen. There was no expression in them.

We also passed the two bodies nearby: the father and son who'd been crushed when they first hauled it out. The bodies were laid on wooden boards with their feet pointing towards the lake and their heads towards the mountain. I could see the father's likeness in the smooth face of the boy, and already a little snow had settled on it.

'Where are you boys from?' A short, stubbled man with a brown bowler hat had approached us.

'Near Llanystumdwy,' I told him. He noted this down, and the number in our group, in a small black book like the one the Reverend had been keeping.

'You see what to do. It's still not dead. We've been keeping this up since yesterday evening. We take it in shifts, two dozen at a time. Some of these boys could do with a rest. Go ahead'.

So we hefted our paddles and set to work. The clubbers wordlessly shifted aside to let us into the circle. I glanced at Aled, Ellis and Rhys and then raised my paddle high in the air, bringing it down hard on the gleaming flank. It bounced straight back, almost leaping out of my hand.

'You got to watch for the bounce,' said the man next to me without breaking his rhythm. 'One fellow smashed his nose'. Whap-whap, whap-whap, whap-whap, whap-whap. He let out a hiss with each impact, like steam escaping from a kettle.

I got the hang of his technique, following his fluid swings. It was easy enough to fall into the rhythm, to learn which part of the handle to grip, how high to raise the paddle before bringing it down.

At first, I found it enjoyable. It was like slapping a jelly. The afanc's body was thick blubber, like the whale I saw once washed up on Black Rock Sands. The paddles rebounded off the rubbery hide, sending wobbles up my arms and into my shoulders. The regular smacks made the monster's flesh shimmer like the skin of a rice pudding.

'Where's the maiden?' I asked the man beside me, glancing at the crowd. They were watching dully, mostly standing, eating scones and drinking beer. Not a beautiful virgin in sight. All I could see was men.

'The maiden went home some time ago,' the man beside me replied. He swung and hissed, swung and hissed. 'She didn't want to see'.

And so we settled into it. First the men on the left side swung, then the men on the right. Whap-whap, whap-whap, whap-whap, whap-whap. The rhythm helped us keep it together. I learned to anticipate the bounce, letting the paddle rise and fall like a pendulum, following its own momentum. The snow fell faster, then slackened off. Shadows moved across the empty lake. The wet slaps echoed off jagged rock walls that had been hacked for slate a hundred years before.

I was disappointed about the maiden, but focused on the job at hand. I was determined to keep pace with the others, to ensure my blows landed clean and hard, that my movements were as regular as a machine. I had never taken part before in a great work such as this. I was proud to be here with the boys from my village, with Aled, Ellis, Owain, Dai – even fat Rhys, with the face like a trout – the best men I had ever known.

We clubbed steadily for the best part of an hour, and then took a break to rest our arms. My muscles ached initially, but little by little the ache burned away to leave a pleasant warmth, a numbness. The feeling was like after chopping up logs for a fire. We had each brought a bag packed by our mother, with bread, ham and apples. I shared my food with a couple of men who were standing a little way back from the lake, at a spot where we could see right down the mountain to the fields and even – if it had been a clear day – to the sea.

'Reverend Williams thinks the afanc came from there,' I said to the man beside me. 'It got stranded up here when the waters went down. That was thousands of years ago, he says'.

'Well it shouldn't be here now'. The man took another slice of ham, folded it into his mouth.

We returned to work, and clubbed all the way through the morning and early afternoon. The steady whap-whap, whap-whap went on. The afanc's thick flesh began to soften and bruise. The paddles gave us splinters. I saw that the ground around our feet was covered in a layer of tiny black spines that must have once bristled from the hide; now all these spines had been snapped off, and the body was as smooth as a slug's.

The next time I took my rest, I walked around to the front of the afanc to examine its quivering face. I could see no change in its expression. Its eyes were spotted with oily blotches; it was hard to tell if it could still see. I held the palm of my hand near one nostril but could feel no breath. Fur hung off its muzzle like wet moss, half torn away. A rope of saliva, or slime of some kind, attached its bottom lip to the ground.

'Keep it up, boys,' called the stubbled man in the bowler hat through a cloud of pipe smoke. 'Eventually we'll soften the muscle, loosen it down to the bone'. He was still standing there with his black book, though new arrivals were fewer now. There were still about forty men gathered round; always twenty active paddles.

'We must break that back by nightfall, boys,' he shouted again a little later, when the sun was lower in the sky. The afanc's skin had turned a different colour, become blotched and darkened in places. My arms were swinging mindlessly, pounding a soft, shining dent in the flank. The motion had become so familiar to me that it felt strange when I stopped.

We kept it up through the long afternoon and into the first shades of evening. The land grew dim; shadows gathered and spread from the folds of the mountain. Snow began to fall again. Despite the warmth of exercise, we had to pull on extra layers, scarves and thick woollen jumpers that had been donated from the nearest village. The bitter wind whistled through the holes anyway. There weren't enough gloves to go round.

Sometimes the rhythm of the paddles would change. I could almost close my eyes. It went from whap-whap, whap-whap, whap-whap into triples like a steam train picking up speed: whap-whap-whap, whap-whap-whap, whap-whap-whap, whap-whap-whap and then whappity-whappity-whappity-whappity until we lost the rhythm entirely and the sound became a cacophony, like stones clattering together, like applause. Sometimes it seemed I heard the impact before my paddle actually struck – the way soldiers say it is when you get hit by a bullet – and sometimes it seemed the sound was delayed, an echo in a well. But it didn't matter now whose impacts were whose, whose swings connected with which blows. We were working as one paddle now, a machine that didn't know how to stop. I couldn't feel my arms anymore. My hands felt a long way from my body, moving up and own of their own accord. They barely corresponded with any other part of me.

I could feel by the way the paddle connected that the pounded blubber in front of me had changed in consistency; I was making headway now. All the bounce had gone out of the flesh, its tightness had been broken. The paddle no longer jumped back when it hit, but splatted wetly into soft mush, even sinking in a little. The light brown pulp reminded me of rotten pears; of the orchard at home, last summer's pear jam. I had spoilt the skin and was breaking through fat, smashing the muscle to slop. I wanted to work further changes, batter and batter and batter this flesh until it became something else. There was bone down there. I could feel it knocking. My efforts redoubled, the paddle swung faster, pain stabbed into my shoulders and neck but somehow didn't reach my brain; everything seemed small and far away. The snowflakes spiralled so fast they made me dizzy.

It took me some time to realise that someone was trying to get my attention, and more for my paddle to slow down enough to stop. A voice was addressing me from behind; a hand was on my shoulder. I glanced round from the mess of pulp to see my friends Owain, Ellis, Rhys and Dai, their features as screwed and purple-looking as the men we'd met descending the mountain all those hours ago. Rhys had his trout face turned to the ground, and one of his arms was cradled in a sling.

'Dafydd, stop, just stop a second. Dafydd. Dafydd. Hold'.

'Rhys can't use his hand anymore. He can't carry on. We're going back'.

Rhys lifted his right hand apologetically, supporting it with his left. It was grossly swollen from the wrist to the thumb, luridly purple and shining. His arm was trembling.

'I can't move my fingers,' he mumbled at me, staring at his feet. There were tears welling in his small eyes. He moaned a little, and I couldn't help thinking that if the beautiful maiden was here she'd have probably never have laid eyes on a man who looked quite so pathetic.

'We're going back, Dafydd. Are you coming or staying?'

'I'm down to the bone,' I said. 'I can feel it. We can finish it now'.

'We're going back. There's been enough of this'.

'We're there, we're almost at the end'.

'No, Dafydd. There's been enough'.

'All of you are going back?' I asked, feeling the anger in me.

'Aled says he'll stay, if you won't come'.

I looked at my own hands, torn and blistered, rubbed raw in patches. There were splinters worked deeply under the skin that I wouldn't get rid of for weeks. My hands were crabbed in the shape of the handle; it hurt when I straightened my fingers.

'I'll stay,' I said. 'I'm not leaving now'.

'As you like. You keep going'.

They left their paddles in the growing pile beside the two dead bodies. I watched them retreating down the track, growing smaller in the darkness. Fat Rhys shambled in the middle with Owain's hand on his arm. I waited until they were out of sight, motioned Aled to step up beside me, and fell back into rhythm.

There were only a dozen of us left. Darkness moved up the mountain, seeping into the blackness of the lake. Before the night fully fell and the land around us was swallowed completely, the man in the brown bowler hat organised the lighting of torches, which encircled the afanc to cast sliding shadows across its ruined body. The flames lit the snowflakes from beneath and turned them into nests of sparks. The faces of the remaining men looked like flickering masks. The wide world shrunk to this bubble of light, outside which nothing else mattered.

I concentrated on the bone. After these hours of working soft flesh it felt good to connect with a solid thing, though the impacts jarred my arms. My elbows and wrists absorbed the shocks. The blood in my veins seemed to ache. The sounds of the neighbouring paddles told me that others had also hit bone; they had changed from whap-whap, whap-whap to a hollow thock-thock, thock-thock, thock-thock like axes against a tree. The clubbers were huffing with exertion now, urging each other on. We could feel that we were near the end, and all of us wanted to be the one there first.

'This is the buried treasure, boys! This is what we've been digging for!' The man in the brown bowler hat was holding his paddle like a flag. He had hopped up on top of the afanc's back, slipping around in the skinless mush, thudding time with the heel of his boot.

'Here's the last nut to crack! Come on, come on!' he shouted later when the beat was a frenzy, thock-thock, thock-thock, thock-thock, thock-thock,

like one of those drums the Irish use, and the afanc's body was bouncing from
the blows. But we had stopped listening to him long ago. Our ears were tuned
for one sound, one sound only.

And then it came: the unmistakable craaack. We felt it in our bones as well.
And at once the paddles stopped.

It was Aled who'd swung the breaking blow. He had been working next
to me. His paddle had stuck right there in the spine, wedged between two
vertebrae. One by one, we went over to look. The vertebrae were as big as
fists. The paddle had been jammed so hard he had trouble pulling it out.

While Aled tugged back and forth, trying to get his paddle back, I walked
round to see the afanc's face. It looked bloated in the light of the flames; its eyes
were the texture of poached eggs. I bent close to its muzzle and heard a noise
like air escaping through a pipe, a bubbling moan that continued as Aled
grunted and shoved at the spine, and then the body shivered and was silent.

'That's it, boys,' concluded the man in the brown bowler hat in the quiet-
ness that came next. 'The job is done. Like the Reverend said'.

Later, I knew I would be disappointed. I knew I would feel it so keenly
that I'd clench my fists and bite my tongue and still it wouldn't help. I had
been so close, it had nearly been me; perhaps just a few more blows. But Aled,
Aled had got there first. Even without the maiden here, offering herself freely
to him, my stomach would turn with resentment. My oldest friend. Back in
the village I'd have to endure him relating this story again and again, while
women crowded around, admiring him. It would make me tug the hair from
my scalp; the afanc was wasted now.

But I didn't feel that yet. I didn't feel a thing. A wall of exhaustion hemmed
me on all sides. We stood quietly. Aled sighed. One man coughed, wiped his
hands on his trousers. Another let fall his paddle. The man in the brown
bowler hat looked as if he was about to speak again, but then he turned away
to fill his pipe.

Some remained standing, some sat down. The only thing to sit on was the
afanc. The tenderised flesh sunk downwards with my weight. I wedged my
feet at an angle with the ground and leaned back with my arms folded across
my chest, allowing my eyes to close. There was pain in my forearms; my
wrists; my neck; but the pain was so distant I felt it might almost belong to
someone else. The fat supported the back of my head like the cushions in a
chapel support the knees. It sounded strange to hear no blows, like when a
clock has stopped.

It was warm and it was numb at the same time. Snowflakes settled on my face and didn't melt, and I thought of the two bodies lying on planks who cared even less than I did. It was the most comfortable bed I'd ever known. Like a mattress I imagined rich people slept on. One day, I thought, I would sleep on a mattress such as this.

I thought of the beautiful maiden beside me, how her arms would feel. I imagined taking her cold hand in mine, our fingers sticky with the afanc's mush. I wiped a fleck of gore from her hair. My muscles hurt because she'd fallen asleep and was lying on my body. Our skin was stuck together in certain places.

And then, beneath our backs, the mattress moved. All of us felt it: it passed the length of the afanc's body from head to tail. The slow bulging-out of something deep inside, like a trapped air bubble or a thought. As undeniable as that crack. Like something trying to shift itself from one place to another.

None of us spoke. None cursed or even sighed. But one by one we got back to our feet, kicked the snow from our boots, stretched our arms, picked up our paddles where we'd let them drop – and continued clubbing.

LOUIS JENKINS

Violence on television

It is best to turn on the set only after all the stations have gone off the air and just watch the snowfall. This is the other life you have been promising yourself; somewhere back in the woods, ten miles from the nearest town, and that just a wide place in the road with a tavern and a gas station. When you drive home, after midnight, half drunk, the roads are treacherous. And your wife is home alone, worried, looking anxiously out at the snow. This snow has been falling steadily for days, so steadily the snowplows can't keep up. So you drive slowly, peering down the road. And there! Did you see it? Just at the edge of your headlight beams, something, a large animal, or a man, crossed the road. Stop. There he is among the birches, a tall man wearing a white suit. No, it isn't a man. Whatever it is motions to you, an almost human gesture, then retreats farther into the woods. He stops and motions again. The snow is piling up all around the car. Are you coming?

Mountaineers

Lewis Bassett is an aspiring writer (and many other things). He presently works as a builder's apprentice in France and is thinking about what 'the communes' are and how to build them. His blog is tendercalves.wordpress.com

Christine Bousfield returned to writing poetry in her forties when she became a lecturer in literature and psychoanalysis. She developed creative writing workshops on masters' courses and beyond university. She has always been interested in the connections between poetry and music and founded a poetry jazz quartet, *Nightdiver*. She is now retired and concentrating on her creative work. For more information, visit www.christine-bousfield.com and www.nightdiver.org. 'White Out' was first published in *Pennine Platform*, Winter 2009.

Seamus Brady lives in Ireland and works in the IT industry.

Rupert Cathles lives in County Durham. Current works in progress are *Simplicity: Global Philosophy* and *Worgate: A Celebration of Obscurity*. He cultivates an allotment, a wild backyard and a sense of humour.

Melanie Challenger's first collection of poems, *Galatea* (Salt: 2006), won an Eric Gregory Award and was shortlisted for the Forward Prize for Best First Collection. She is Creative Fellow at UCL's Centre for the Evolution of Cultural Diversity and is completing her non-fiction work on extinction, which is forthcoming from Granta.

Charles Davies was Features Editor at *The Face* and the founder of *Pick Me Up*, an online magazine described as 'Why Don't You? for grown-ups'. These days he lives in the south of France and helps people think about money and stories.

Christian de Sousa is an artist using mainly photography, movement and words. His work attempts to trace the febrile threads that run between the state of the world and the state of our souls. A book, *Postcards from Babylon*, is nearing completion. www.dancingeye.net

Mark Dickson lives and works in Nottingham as an artist, illustrator and educator. His work defies easy classification and his art often involves close attention to the human form and expression.

In the early-twentieth century, **Simon Fairlie**'s grandfather left the farm where he was born in eastern Scotland to make his living in London. Since 1966, Simon, born in London, has worked as an agricultural labourer, dustman, plongeur, builder, stonemason, journalist, planning consultant and scythe importer in a vain effort to save enough money to get back to the land. A longer version of 'The tragedy of The Tragedy of the Commons' first appeared in Issue 7 of *The Land*.

Lance Fennell is a graduate of the Bath Academy of Art. His work explores landscape and the 'nostalgia of now'.

Daniel Ford has worked as a removal man, magazine editor and educator. He is currently writing *Between Dog and Wolf* – an investigation into the demise of the art school tradition. *The Lesson* is his first graphic narrative.

Born in Leytonstone, east London, **Dan Grace** has been migrating slowly northward ever since. Currently settled in Sheffield, when not writing he works in his local library. This is his first published poem.

John Michael Greer, a prolific writer on peak oil and environmental issues, is also a leading figure in contemporary Druid spirituality and serves as Grand Archdruid of the Ancient Order of Druids in America. The author of more than twenty books, including *The Long Descent: A User's Guide to the End of the Industrial Age* and *The Ecotechnic Future: Envisioning a Post-Peak World*, he also writes a weekly blog, *The Archdruid Report*. He lives in the Allegheny Mountains of western Maryland with his spouse Sara.

Jay Griffiths is the author of *Wild: An Elemental Journey* which was shortlisted for the Orwell prize and was winner of the Orion book award. She is also the author of *Pip Pip: A Sideways Look at Time,* which won the Barnes and Noble Discover award for the best first-time writer in the USA. She lives in Wales.

William Haas eats, bikes and breathes in Portland, Oregon, USA. His work has appeared in *River Teeth, Bull, Underground Voices, Appalachian Heritage* and elsewhere.

Dougald Hine is co-founder of the Dark Mountain Project. He has worked as a busker, a door-to-door salesman and a BBC journalist. In order to avoid writing, he starts organisations; so far, these have included School of Everything, Space Makers Agency and the Institute for Collapsonomics. He writes a blog called *Changing the World (and other excuses for not getting a proper job)*.

Kim Holleman is an artist living and working in New York. She attended The Cooper Union in New York and The Rietveld Academie in Amsterdam, Holland. She shows a wide variety of work including public art, utopian architecture, sculpture, installation, large-scale murals, drawings, and photography. Much of her work and exhibitions can be viewed at kimholleman.com

Glyn Hughes has published an autobiography, novels, poetry, and broadcast radio plays and features. He was awarded the Guardian Fiction Prize and the David Higham Prize for his first novel, *Where I Used To Play On The Green*, has been shortlisted for the Whitbread Prize, considered for The Booker, and has won national prizes for his poetry collections. A national poll of Guardian readers picked two of his books as 'Great classics of English nature writing'. His most recent books are *Dancing Out Of The Dark Side* (poems, 2005) and *Life Class*, an autobiography in verse, both published by Shoestring Press. www.glynhughes.co.uk

Nick Hunt writes fiction in an attempt to grasp the cultural and psychological implications of climate change and the mass extinction of species and languages. He is also a freelance journalist. Read more of his work at nickhuntscrutiny.wordpress.com

Louis Jenkins has published poems in *Magma* in the UK and in numerous magazines in the US. He has worked with Mark Rylance on a play titled *Nice Fish: The Amazing Adventures of Ice Fishermen*. Mr. Jenkins most recent book is *Before You Know It: Prose Poems 1970–2005*

Paul Kingsnorth is co-founder of the Dark Mountain Project. He has worked in an orangutan rehabilitation centre in Borneo, as a peace observer in the Zapatista villages of Mexico, as a floor-sweeper in McDonalds and as an assistant lock keeper on the river Thames. He is the author of two non-fiction books: *One No, Many Yeses* (2003) and *Real England* (2008). His first collection of poetry, *Kidland*, is forthcoming from Salmon.

Rob Lewis is a natural materials painter and plasterer living in the northern Puget Sound city of Bellingham, Washington, USA. His poems and essays respond to the earth, in both its beauty and its pain, as well as its humans enmeshed in their stories and illusions.

Simon Lys lives in Sussex with his partner and their son. His work has mainly been for the theatre and for television. He has written his first novel Black Dog Running and is a co-founder of the gaia theatre collective. His website is www.simonlys.org

Anthony McCann is a writer and academic who specialises in analysis of personal, political, and social enclosures. He is the founder of Crafting Gentleness (www. craftinggentleness.org), and a lecturer at the University of Ulster, Northern Ireland.

Alastair McIntosh is the author of *Soil and Soul* (Aurum Press), *Rekindling Community* (Schumacher Briefings) and *Hell and High Water: Climate Change, Hope and the Human Condition* (Birlinn). He is a Fellow of the Centre for Human Ecology and Visiting Professor at the Department of Geography and Sociology, University of Strathclyde.

Adrienne J. Odasso has just completed her PhD in English at the University of York. Her poetry and fiction have appeared in a number of magazines on both sides of the Atlantic, including *Aesthetica*, *Sybil's Garage*, *The Liberal, Farrago's Wainscot, Mythic Delirium, Jabberwocky, Not One of Us, Goblin Fruit, Dreams & Nightmares*, and *Expanded Horizons*. Her first print chapbook of poems, *Devil's Road Down*, is currently available from Maverick Duck Press, and her first full poetry collection, *Lost Books*, is forthcoming from Flipped Eye Publishing in April 2010.

Dr Jeff Ollerton teaches and researches ecology and biodiversity at the University of Northampton. The main focus of his research has been to study how communities of plants and pollinators interact and the importance of these interactions for the continued ecological functioning of natural ecosystems. His research papers, commentaries and reviews have been published widely in the professional literature, including journals such as *Nature, Science, Ecology* and *Oecologia*. He has also written poetry privately for some 30 years.

Mat Osmond lives and works in Falmouth, Cornwall. After a number of years in which his practice was focussed purely on drawing, since 2006 he has combined words and images within small edition works of authorial illustration. This work is rooted in his repeated walking of the Falmouth and surrounding coastline, the accrued memories of that tidal landscape providing a reservoir of imagery around which the stories coalesce.

Chris Pak is a PhD student exploring how science fiction uses the theme of terraforming to explore global politics and climate change. He has a broad interest in the fantastic in many mediums, including film, television and games. More details can be found at www.chrispak.webs.com

Mario Petrucci, a natural sciences graduate with a PhD in optoelectronics, is an award-winning poet, writer, educator and broadcaster. www.mariopetrucci.com. 'Three hot drops of salmon oil' is an edited transcript of his address to the international conference 'Remembering Chernobyl: 1986–2006' held on the 11th March 2006 in Marostica, Italy, organised by The Institute for Research into Social and Religious History. He is indebted to *Interdisciplinary Science Reviews*, and to *The London Magazine*, in which versions of this piece appeared in 2006 and 2009 respectively.

Ran Prieur has lived most of his life in Washington state. Since 2004 he has been dabbling in homesteading near Spokane and writing about a variety of subjects at www.ranprieur.com

Tom Scott is a freelance writer based in Cornwall, where he teaches on University College Falmouth's MA Professional Writing course and is involved in locally focused environmental campaigns. He recently started writing poetry again after a long break and is a member of the Falmouth Poetry Group.

Reinhardt Søbye was self-taught as an artist. His first exhibition took place in 1987. Twenty years later, he is the only contemporary Norwegian artist to be part of the official art history curriculum in Japan and Australia.

Maria Theresa Stadtmueller draws on experience as an environmental writer and a New York-based stand-up comic in YouTurnRadio.com, her podcast about changing to an authentic cultural story. She received an MFA in Nonfiction Writing from The University of Iowa, and has published essays and features in *Utne Reader*, *Seattle Magazine*, *The Iowa Review*, etc. An active kayaker and Nordic skier, she shares a yurt homestead with other rescued animals in the foothills of Vermont's Green Mountains.

Tony Walton was born in London in 1950 and lives in north Herefordshire. Under his own imprint, Tigerfish Books, he has published three volumes of his poems: *Rough Notations* (2006), *On Yatton Hill* (2008), and *Such Sweet Music* (2009), with the series title *Seasons of the Heart*. This poem – which was sparked by Christopher Hitchens' *The Portable Atheist* (Da Capo Press, 2007) – comes from Volume 4. *Particular Realities*, scheduled for publication towards the end of this year.

Mark Waters is a writer. You can find him stuck in the mud on the green slopes of the dark mountain marked amateur dramatics and open heart surgeons remove your skis and jump. He tries to cross the road whenever he sees a McDonalds up ahead. He believes it's worth it. Keeps the smell out of your hair. Don't need so much shampoo.

J.D. Whitney teaches environmental literature, creative writing, and Native American literature and mythology at a campus of the University of Wisconsin Colleges, in Wausau, and (now & again) at College of Menominee Nation, in Keshena, Wisconsin. He lives with his wife Lisa Seale and their dog Animosh on the east bank of the Wisconsin River. His most recent book of poems is *Grandmother Says* (Arctos Press, 2005), and his forthcoming book is *All My Relations* (Many Voices Press). He is guided in his work by the words of Simon Ortiz: 'There are no truths, only stories.'

Uncivilisation:
a primer

'So we find ourselves, our ways of telling unbalanced, trapped inside a runaway narrative, headed for the worst kind of encounter with reality. In such a moment, writers, artists, poets and storytellers of all kinds have a critical role to play... Words and images can change minds, hearts, even the course of history...'

– Uncivilisation: The Dark Mountain Manifesto

What does Uncivilised art and writing look like in practice? This journal has showcased how some of today's best writers and creative artists begin to answer this question. But is there a tradition in which they stand? Who are the forerunners? Can we trace a counter-canon of existing work which embodies the spirit of the Dark Mountain? These are questions which we have been asked, in one form or another, since the publication of the manifesto. Here is an attempt to begin to answer them.

A work of literature or art is not a means to an end, nor a place for retrospective politicking. Many of the writers we highlight here are or were healthily allergic to the very idea of movements or clubs. We have no desire to impose Mormon-style retrospective baptism, to enclose them within the fold of Uncivilisation. Our intention is simply to point to those who have inspired us, and who write in a way which chimes with what we are about. When we issue a call for certain type of writing, we hold these up as inspirations; examples of what is possible; of creators facing the reality of our place in the world, our past and our future, and conveying that reality clearly and uncompromisingly, whatever the costs to themselves and their reputation.

This is not, needless to say, a comprehensive list. It focuses, for one, only on writers: there are whole areas of imaginative work left unaddressed, from cinema to theatre to visual art. But this is a place to start. Scribble your own additions in the margins, cross things out, add things in. Think of it as the beginnings of a conversation.

POETRY

Ted Hughes Widely known as a 'nature poet', Hughes was more accurately a poet of the other-than-human world, a writer to whom 'nature' was not simply a backdrop to human existence or a screen on which to project human fantasies, but a world in itself, carrying on with no reference to Man and no interest in his morality or judgement. This combines in his work with a deep feel for the power of myth, and the ability of stories to lead us through the darkness which lies outside the city walls.

Robinson Jeffers A crucial writer to come to terms with, Jeffers was a rising star in the twenties and thirties, but saw himself cast into literary exile as he developed the poetic philosophy he called 'inhumanism' – 'a shifting of emphasis and significance from man to notman; the rejection of human solipsism and recognition of the transhuman magnificence.' Jeffers attempted to transmute what we might now call 'deep ecology' into poetry, and from his lonely home on the Californian cliffs he produced poems quite unlike anything else being written then or now. 'Carmel Point', 'Rearmament', 'Shine, Perishing Republic', 'The Purse-Seine' and 'Original Sin' are good points of entry.

W.S. Merwin To read W.S. Merwin is to be confronted by a poet of great calm and generosity of spirit, which makes the picture he paints of humanity's cannibalisation of the Earth somehow more shocking. In poems like 'To a coming extinction', 'The Last One' and 'The Asians Dying', Merwin's focused anger and deep sadness at the fate of the world and of humanity itself has a shocking power.

Mary Oliver After reading several of Mary Oliver's poems you realise what they have in common: there are very few humans in them. Oliver writes of 'nature' in close-up, of its impact on the human soul and of the human impact on the wider world, and does so in a way which makes the reader feel not like an observer but a participant in the great dance of life.

R.S. Thomas A stiff-backed Anglican clergyman, Thomas might not on the surface seem an obvious candidate for Uncivilised status, but his poems, especially his later work, take the reader to the brink of what it means to be human and force him or her to look over. Seamus Heaney called him 'a loner taking on the universe', and it is telling that, like Merwin and Hughes, Thomas claimed Jeffers as one of his inspirations. The most uncompromising of Thomas's work paints a picture of a world of wild, fierce beauty, inhabited by atomised people in thrall to 'the machine', overseen by an apparently malevolent god.

FICTION

John Berger Throughout his career, Berger's writing has been characterised by a movement between the intimate and the cosmic. In the space of a few lines, he will move between the time of mountains and the time of a camera shutter; the irreplaceable uniqueness of a particular place or a particular friendship, and the grand historical and evolutionary narratives in which they find themselves. This radical sense of perspective is grounded in his deep feel for the visual arts, his political commitment and his direct experience of other ways of living. To dwell with the great distances of geological time and retain a sense of tenderness, to not be hardened by it; this is the challenge of writing – and living – through times in which our certainties and comforts begin to unravel.

Joseph Conrad One of the key excavators of the darkness at the heart of the civilising project. From *Heart of Darkness* to *Lord Jim* via *Nostromo*, his novels shine a light on the hubris at the heart of the white man's attempted colonisation of those people and places he considered beneath him, and what it did to both them and his soul. They are now historical documents from a key phase in the development of the project we have come to call 'civilisation'.

Alan Garner Pegged misleadingly as a 'children's author' and a writer of 'fantasy', Garner's work is grounded in a deep sense of place and time. Recent novels such as *Strandloper* and *Thursbitch* evoke the strangeness – the autonomy, even – of the past, in a prose whose tautness and precision has few equals in English today. Such writing can rescue us from the illusion of history as a prototype of the present, returning it to us as a source of alternative possibilities, other ways of being in the world. In Garner's description of the writer as *mearcstapa*, boundary-walker, we find a model for our idea of writing which goes beyond the city limits, which meets the non-human world in all its mysteriousness and negotiates with it on our behalf.

Russell Hoban *Riddley Walker*, Hoban's classic novel, is set in a primitive, post-apocalyptic Kent, some centuries after what appears to have been a nuclear war. Riddley's world of warlords, rituals and an almost religious quest by the authorities to rediscover the secret of gunpowder is rendered in a broken, corrupted English which creates a world unlike any other.

D.H. Lawrence The fiery, paganistic writing of this proudly working-class writer stood openly outside the 'civilised world' he blamed for neutering modern society both literally and figuratively. His novel *The Plumed Serpent* entwines pre-Christian religion, passion and landscape in nineteenth century Mexico and offers up a strange clash between 'civilised' and 'primitive'. His poems often do the same, in flowing and idiosyncratic verse. Unafraid to be wrong, to be foolish, to exaggerate, his writing takes the kind of gambles we are looking for, and eschews the safety of civilisation.

Ursula Le Guin Quite apart from having written a (considerably better) series of novels about young wizards while J K Rowling was still in nappies, Le Guin's fiction, set in fantastic worlds, paints a better portrait of our own world and values than much 'literary' fiction. By using other planets or other worlds to address essentially human themes, and to explore ecological and anthropological avenues, Le Guin is able to look at the human journey from a distance and give it a perspective it lacks in most mainstream writing.

H. P. Lovecraft Unknown in his lifetime, Lovecraft was an obscure pulp fiction writer from a small town in New England who produced some of the weirdest science fiction ever seen. Over several decades, his short stories built up his own personal mythology – the 'Cthulhu mythos' – which imagines humanity at the mercy of malevolent and amoral beings vaster and more powerful than it is even able to conceive. Lovecraft's horror stories were woven around the scientific discoveries of his day, and revelled in cutting humanity down to size in a disturbing and sometimes worryingly convincing fashion.

Cormac McCarthy *The Road*, McCarthy's latest novel, has attracted huge attention, and is as eerie a portrait of a post-apocalyptic Earth as has ever been painted, executed in masterful prose. Perhaps more interesting, though, are McCarthy's portraits of people in their landscapes in books like *No Country for Old Men* and his Border Trilogy. Here we see decent, compromised people confronted by evil in landscapes they belong to and understand, but cannot overcome or escape. McCarthy's feel for the culture of the contemporary American West has few parallels, and his unflinching gaze turns up snakes under the stones.

Mary Shelley Daughter of the pioneering feminist Mary Wollstonecraft and husband of poet Percy Shelly, Mary Shelley can too often be defined by her connections rather than her writing. But she was also a genuine radical, associated with the Romantic movement but also critical of its failings, and her writing, most famously in *Frankenstein*, takes a dark look at myths of human perfectibility and the infallibility of Enlightenment science. In *The Last Man*, Shelley produced a pioneering apocalyptic novel at a time when such things were shocking rather than clichéd, and in doing so laid bare her age's humanistic arrogance.

NON-FICTION

No other kind of writing offers so many starting points for Uncivilisation as non-fiction. Some classic 'nature writing', such as Thoreau's *Walden*, or the works of Barry Lopez, would clearly qualify, while a whole literature of 'collapse' has emerged in recent years. Here, for now, is a short selection of key writers.

David Abram An academic philosopher and anthropologist, Abram also happens to be a sleight-of-hand magician. *The Spell of the Sensuous* is his attempt to understand how language and writing shape our relationship to the world, starting from his personal experiences among indigenous magicians in Southeast Asia. 'The task of the magician,' he says, 'is to startle our senses and free us from outmoded ways of thinking.' His argument about the origins of the skills of literacy in the skills our ancestors used to 'read' their surroundings is appropriately startling. This is a book which examines the nature of anthropocentrism and contain some brilliant insights.

Hugh Brody An anthropologist who abandoned his allegiance to the academy in favour of the peoples among whom he found himself, Brody's experiences are charted in books such as *Maps and Dreams* and *The Other Side of Eden*. His writing reminds us that tribal peoples are not 'living in the past'. They are our contemporaries, and in his accounts of his experiences he describes people making deliberate choices about which technologies they do and don't wish to adopt: what is and isn't compatible with the way they want to live. Through observations such as those of Anaviapik – an Inuit friend of Brody's, visiting London for the first time – we get a sense of the strangeness of things which we take for granted. At the same time, Brody offers a larger historical argument about the deep roots of our ways of thinking in the relationship between hunters and farmers, stretching over thousands of years.

John Michael Greer *The Long Descent: A User's Guide to the End of the Industrial Age* is one of the most thoughtful direct accounts of our present situation and the changes which may lie ahead. Greer ranges from a presentation of the case for Peak Oil, to a speculative survey of the prospects for different religious traditions in a world of global economic contraction. He insists on the inevitability of such a contraction, and is equally scathing about those who believe it can be avoided, and those who anticipate a sudden, dramatic collapse. Each group, he claims, is deluded by a classic Western myth: the myth of progress and the myth of apocalypse.

Ivan Illich Best known for books like *Deschooling Society* and *Energy and Equity*, which were widely read in the 1970s, Illichs' later writings are deepening historical investigations into the assumptions which make possible the way of living which he saw the West exporting to the rest of the world. His understanding of history is summed up by the Latin motto *corruptio optimi pessima,* 'the corruption of the best is the worst.' How is it that institutions and structures born out of good intentions can come to produce the opposite of their intended effects? His work is a quest for the origins of those institutions which – as he writes in his final book, *In the Vineyard of the Text* – 'create needs faster than they can create satisfaction, and in the process of trying to meet the needs they generate ... consume the earth.' What comes out of this is the importance of distinguishing ground-level human needs from the systems by which we happen to meet them at this point in time.

Subcomandante Marcos The masked, pipe-smoking Mexican guerrilla leader known pseudonymously as Marcos is celebrated by anti-capitalists for his military and political leadership of the Zapatista rebels who since 1994 have held out against the government in the Mexican state of Chiapas. Marcos's journey from orthodox Maoism to a politics based on justice, indigeneity and the needs of local communities is remarkable enough, and points to a potentially useful path through the clotted thickets of conventional left/right politics. But Marcos is also a writer - of short stories, of poetry, and most of all of his famous 'communiques', issued from his jungle fastness, in which he employs comedy, paradox, poetry and invective to attack purveyors of self-serving falsehoods on all sides of the fence. *Our Word is our Weapon* is a perfect introduction to his writing. His dialogues with John Berger and with close collaborators of Ivan Illich are evidence of the threads which connect the writers, thinkers and activists who have inspired this project.

Dmitry Orlov Stands out from the (mostly American) 'collapse' genre of writers for his personal experience of the economic and social breakdown of a society. Drawing on his experiences before, during and after the fall of the Soviet Union, he calls his work 'a comparative theory of superpower collapse', and his writing is laced with a dark Russian humour. In Orlov's account, collapse is ultimately personal: however large-scale its causes, the experience varies from individual to individual, and plays out differently according to how we and those around us respond. *Reinventing Collapse* is a reminder that the circumstances envisaged with horror by much of the collapse literature are the lived experience of people in many places today.

Roll of honour

The publication of Dark Mountain #1 has been made possible by financial and non-financial support from a large community of supporters around the world. The following Dark Mountaineers provided financial support above and beyond the call of duty; we are very grateful for their generosity and commitment, and for that of those others who chose not to have their names printed here.

Josef Davies-Coates, United Diversity
Richard Owen Frost
geekyoto
Ida Hagen
Robin and Ann Hine
Julia Macintosh
Patrick J. Redmond